The Couscous Chronicles

The Couscous Chronicles

STORIES OF FOOD, LOVE,
AND DONKEYS FROM A LIFE
BETWEEN CULTURES

Azzedine T. Downes

DISRUPTION
BOOKS

Austin New York

Published by Disruption Books
New York, New York
www.disruptionbooks.com

Distributed by Disruption Books

For information about special discounts for bulk purchases, please contact
Disruption Books at info@disruptionbooks.com.

Cover design by David Gee
Book design by Brian Phillips Design

Library of Congress Cataloging-in-Publication Data is available
Printed in the United States of America

Print ISBN: 978-1-63331-075-9
eBook ISBN: 978-1-63331-076-6

First Edition

TO THE GIRL FROM TANGIERS

Contents

Foreword

"My son Charif hears that you can speak 'chimpanzee language,'" said the kind-looking man with piercing blue eyes who approached me, holding the hand of a little boy. "He hopes he might learn from you." With these words, my friendship began with Azzedine Downes—father of Charif, president of the International Fund for Animal Welfare (IFAW), and author of this book.

The little boy gazing up at me, wide eyed, was perhaps the youngest and most earnest attendee at a 2000 conference in Ireland sponsored by IFAW. So I taught him how to make a "pant-hoot" greeting, how to laugh like a chimp, how to swagger and to look big and fierce when trying to prove his dominance. And I soon began to learn how his father, too, is fascinated with the language and behavior of others—and how Azzedine has studied countless ways of communicating throughout his courageous search for human connection in some of the world's most fascinating (and dangerous!) places.

The Couscous Chronicles is one of the most extraordinary books I have ever read. It is, as Azzedine says, a journey through time and place. But the real magic is in the way he takes you with him on that journey, takes you to some places you have probably never heard of, let alone visited. Because quite apart from the story of an incredible life, what makes this book so spellbinding is his skill as a writer and storyteller. Though he writes the book in English, we sense that he is fluent also in French, various Arabic dialects, and the ways of humans in general. And so compelling are his descriptions of the places he has been, the experiences he has lived through, that we, the readers, find we are accompanying him on his adventures, sharing moments of joy, amazement, sadness, and fear, and above all, a sense of fun.

Azzedine and I have often discussed the importance of cultivating a good sense of humor, without which I'm certain he could not have survived to become the person he is today. As you read this book, you will discover what he has discovered: why you must never walk with your hands clasped behind your back, why you might decide to put knives under your baby's mattress, and how to pretend to drink fresh camel's milk straight from the bowl despite the flies clustered along its rim. And of course, you will discover the importance of couscous!

For many years, Azzedine lived in Morocco—particularly in Fez— where couscous is fundamental to the national cuisine. He learned to find his way around the medina, the old town, where none of the maze of narrow alleyways are wider than six feet. He learned to recognize just where he is by closing his eyes and using his sense of smell: Burning wood and warm dough—here is the district where they bake bread. A strong odor of glue, of course, means this is where they finish off the babouche: traditional yellow shoes with pointed toes made of hardened leather. And the sickening smell of tanning leather reminds you to walk through that neighborhood only after sticking sprigs of mint up your nose.

Follow Azzedine through the maze, and all day long in the medina you will meet strings of laboring donkeys—and donkeys appear repeatedly in this exceptional book. One donkey lives on the ground floor of the building which, for years, is Azzedine's home. The donkey's owner is kind to his four-legged colleague (which is not always the case among donkey owners in Morocco), but amazingly, this donkey hasn't got a name.

Why not? Azzedine asks.

Well, he's a donkey! comes the reply.

Follow Azzedine and you will learn, too, how his quest for a new pair of babouche led him to a tiny room halfway up his building, where he befriended two glue-sniffing cobblers. What's more, you will learn the story of beautiful woven carpets brought down to the medina from the mountains where they are made, and how those carpets are priced depending on just who the customer is and where they come from.

But what about couscous? Why is this dish singled out in Azzedine's chronicles? Well, as you will see, the gathering of family and friends to eat couscous plays an essential role in his story. This steaming, love-infused dish is not only a part of everyday life in his adopted culture, but on occasion a startling, unwanted invitation to marriage and other bizarre consequences. All through the book, couscous meals accompany momentous events in his life—especially the moment when he glimpsed Nadia, the woman who would become his wife. You will be delighted to hear the astonishing story of how, with the help of her relatives, their marriage finally came about!

I, for one, was delighted to read so many stories about couscous and babouche and donkeys, too, for I have always had a special fondness for these animals. Yet I encourage you to read between the lines to understand the deeper significance of Azzedine's stories. His skillful use of dialogue—in the book and in real life—will have you smiling, but at the same time will offer you a glimpse into how humans around the world think about things so very differently. For attitudes toward animals and a great many other things differ greatly from country to country, and even within countries and cultures.

When Azzedine describes how a donkey lands upside down and must be rescued from drowning in a water-filled ditch, you will surely laugh out loud. This particular skirmish is part of a larger story, however, about two foolish American tourists who thought they knew best and ended up in a perilous situation that escalated from an unfortunate bottom-pinching incident. As at many other moments recounted in this remarkable book, Azzedine's quick wit and cultural insight may have saved his life and certainly saved him from serious injury. But it is also a commentary on how being truly responsible for our actions means taking into account the environment in which we find ourselves.

Indeed, Azzedine's descriptions and dialogue will take you right into each of the many worlds he has explored, all of which, for most readers, will seem utterly remote from their own lives. His absurd conversations with government officials are just one example, such as when a bureaucrat refuses to believe Azzedine is his real name. Why?

    Because you don't look like an Azzedine, the man insists.

    What should I look like? Azzedine asks.

    You should not have blue eyes.

Don't worry, I've saved the punch line for you to read later.

Azzedine's reactions to such individuals all around the world range from amusement to irritation to anger to ferocity. Although each episode is written with great humor, he does not hesitate to reveal how unnecessary questions and an obsession with government forms can lead to endangering lives. International crises are decidedly not so funny, and Azzedine does not shy from the gravity of such scenarios. On the contrary, he has shown himself to be a most extraordinary and courageous man.

As a member of the Peace Corps, he was assigned to teach English and later to oversee English programs in volatile and hazardous locations—in Yemen, Palestine, and Jerusalem. At various times, he became known as a doctor and, despite his repeated assurances that he was not, was consulted by young men embarrassed by problems . . . well, below the belt, as it were. At other times, he was suspected of being a spy for the CIA. For instance, the Palestinians thought he was spying for Israel, and Israel thought he was spying for Palestinians. He was living in Jerusalem when violence escalated between Palestine and Israel in the 1990s, and you will feel vicariously his terror when car bombs explode, when he is surrounded by an angry, frightened crowd, and is desperate to reach his wife and family.

That's when Azzedine decided to take his family back to the United States—but not for long. Employed by the US government, he accepted several assignments in Eastern Europe after the collapse of the Soviet Union, and further expanded his understanding of an entirely new set of cultures. He travelled to Romania to investigate the orphanages that housed rows of babies lying in cribs without love or even proper care. He went to Bulgaria to promote small-business development and entrepreneurship in a post-communist society and was caught up in a peculiar project involving brassieres designed for women so generously endowed that one might question their ability to walk upright. And in the pages of this book, you will go with him.

All of this happened long before Azzedine became the head of IFAW. Today, he once again finds his job—and his courage—taking him into some of the world's most dangerous countries. And often Nadia accompanies him, for she is as courageous as her husband, and their life together demonstrates how even an unlikely marriage (and even less likely career postings) can sometimes lead to a perfect partnership and great happiness.

A final comment: This book is much more than a well-told, sometimes hilarious, sometimes suspenseful story. For even as you laugh or weep, it enlightens. It delivers insight into the complexities of human nature, a lesson on the importance of getting to understand different cultures with their own priorities, tastes (in food and otherwise), and ways of treating animals, people, and the world around them. Azzedine underscores a life of breaking down the barriers that prevent so many people from finding friendship with those in circumstances dissimilar to their own, and we are blessed to meet his eclectic circle of friends, from imams, princes, kings, and diplomats to carpet sellers, shoemakers, bakers, children, and the owner of a donkey.

I am truly honored to count myself as one of the true friends of such an incredibly gifted person. Azzedine and I talk and laugh a lot when we are together, which is not nearly often enough. But we feel quite comfortable also when we sit in silence, connected in a way that goes deeper than words. For our friendship, like the adventures that inspired *The Couscous Chronicles*, has unfolded slowly and profoundly over time and place.

Jane Goodall, November 2022

Fez

The Labyrinth

Language, Cleanliness, and Yellow Babouche

Bread and the Other Smells of Life

Feet Smell and So Do Yellow Babouche

Sniffing Glue and Lessons Learned

Nassarani

An Endless String of Apologies

Donkeys and Virility

Talking in My Sleep

Couscous, the Foundation of All Life

The Baraka and Sacrificed Sheep

Bargaining with an Accent

Karim, Merchant of Carpets and Bagger of Tourists

The Simple-Minded Mathematician

My Love Affair with French

The Gray-Haired CIA Agent

Donnybrook at the Cinema

Cardboard Keyboards

Arabic Lessons

Undoing the Spell

The Curse of Fatouma

Peep Show at the Café

Alone in My Pain

The Intoxicating Dessert

The Rif Mountains and the Hirsute Body

The Hammam and the Circumcised Foreigner

Salade Niçoise and My Wayward "Wife"

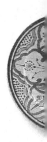

THE LABYRINTH

The year was 1402, and the summer air in the city of Fez was warm and dusty. I walked through the alley that led from the vizier's palace to the market overflowing with the day's offerings. It had been three months since I had wandered through these tight passages at three in the morning, a discarded piece of chalk pinched in my hand as I timidly marked the corners of buildings in hopes of finally being able to find my way home each day. I was still nervous, unsure of myself in this labyrinth city, but it was important not to show it.

Above all, I had to project an air of authority and assuredness. I had to demonstrate that I had mastered the routes only a resident of the *medina*, the ancient city, would know. If I could not master the alleys, I would be forever hounded by the hawkers and illicit guides who preyed upon the unsuspecting, the weak, the lost, the tourists.

The old city of Fez was founded in the ninth century. My first steps into this old world came over a thousand years later, in the Islamic year 1402—the year 1981 in the Gregorian calendar; I was twenty-three years old. My first night in the city had been every bit as overwhelming as the math required for this conversion of ages. From my room I could hear the recitation of the Quran through the night, a salve for the lonely, and later animals waking from sleep, the creaking of carts as the sleepless pushed them toward the markets of morning. I was kept awake not only by the sounds that only an ancient, bowl-shaped city could produce, but by incredulity at the sheer beauty of the palace in which I now made my home.

The vizier's palace was not as grand as it once was. The tiled, mosaic walls were crumbling in places, and my ruthless landlord continued to break the palace into ever-smaller apartments and rooms in order to increase his profits. The central room was adorned with a cedarwood cupola that soared high above the floor, conveying a certain grandeur despite the dust that often floated down from the vaulted ceiling anytime a person walked on the roof above. Living in a crumbling place, one finds it hard not to gain a sense of history. UNESCO has designated the old medina as a world heritage center, and my palace was a welcome escape from the modern world.

The idea of sneaking out of the palace at three in the morning to mark a route through the city with chalk had been born not of mischief but of necessity. In the entire city, no street was wider than six feet. Each was a procession of endless people, horses, and donkeys. For me, getting lost was a daily ritual.

Donkeys from Fez were said to be the smartest in the world. They listened carefully to their drivers' instructions even as they groaned under the weight of their load, somehow maintaining their composure amid the maze of dirt and cobblestoned paths. It was not rare to turn a corner and find myself staring into a procession of donkeys wholly uninterested in my navigational struggle. And such encounters were not without danger.

I once saw a teenaged boy who failed to heed the call of "*Balek!*" ("Watch out!")—and found himself crushed between a donkey's load, fastened to its side in a wicker basket, and an alley wall. The wall itself was an instrument of torture, gravel-filled stucco thrown roughly over a hesitant mud infrastructure. The lad somehow thought he could press himself into it and avoid the impending clash. His body did begin some magical process of flattening itself into the stucco but was suddenly caught in mid transformation. Panic flashed on his face as he realized he had no such magical properties.

When the wicker basket first bit into him, I could see that he was confident in his ability to sustain this brief encounter. But as the load shifted, the boy scraped along the wall at the speed of the lumbering donkey. He began to twist his slim body as if to slither out from under the basket's weight, but this only precipitated a series of crushing, flattening flips against the wall. He faced the wall, he faced the donkey, over and over again until an indentation in the wall released him. After that, he sat crumpled in that alcove as the procession of goods passed him by.

There was no sympathy for the scraped, slightly bleeding victim. A few sniggers even highlighted his stupidity. He had walked straight into traffic. What had he expected?

I kept the scene in mind most days as I quickly, but without panic, maneuvered around the donkey trains. The boy had left a trail of blood on the stucco wall, and I had made a mental note: his bloody donation marked the alley where I should take a left turn.

The city late at night, on the other hand, was devoid of these crushing run-ins with donkeys but full of others. Robbery was a major concern, for instance, but then again, there was no morally acceptable reason to be out so late. The endless mud walls of the old city soared high above my head, yet despite the odd sounds that crept through them, the nocturnal alleys were still, save for the constant running about of cats looking for a meal and a mate—perhaps not for a long-term relationship, but on the hunt, nonetheless. In this deceptive labyrinth, the danger of being robbed seemed remote compared to the real possibility of being lost. Being lost would mean that I would have to ask directions to get home, hence exposing my ignorance, and I was determined to seem as though I belonged in the medina.

The founder of the city, Idriss I (a descendent of the Muslim prophet Mohammed), came from Yemen, where I would one day live, though I didn't yet know enough to see the architectural similarities in the two countries. It wasn't until later—when I made the pilgrimage to Moulay Idriss, the village sitting atop a hill not far from Fez, to reverse the spell of a spurned lover—that I saw the resemblance to the world of Yemen.

Walking down any street, in any age, I often feel as though every person passing by is having the same conversation as perhaps a billion other people, in any number of languages, at the exact same time. It is this evidence of the mundane that drove me to explore—but not in a conscious, planned way—worlds not my own. Seeking the luxurious sense of existing out of time and place is what led me to wander.

Wandering is not the same as being lost, however, and being lost was something that I wanted to avoid in Fez.

LANGUAGE, CLEANLINESS, AND YELLOW BABOUCHE

If you asked a Fassi—a person born in Fes al Bali (as the old city is called in Arabic)—whether there are street names, they would say, "Of course," and then they would point to a nonexistent sign and spit out an unintelligible word in the Fassi accent.

You could tell someone was from Fez when they could not say the letter "Q." Now that I think of it, they can't roll the letter "R" either. You may be wondering what it sounds like, but it's easy to imagine: fill your mouth with hot soup, and then speak without swallowing or allowing the soup to spill out of your mouth. That's what the unaccustomed ear hears when a Fassi speaks. I noticed similarities to the Arabic accent heard in Jerusalem and Damascus, with which I also struggled in my travels. But when learning a language, like a child, you just repeat what you hear and think it's normal.

My fascination with language began many years prior to living in Fez. I learned early on that the way you sound either opens or closes doors in society. Some may think how you speak is unimportant, but I disagree. In Fez, sounding like a native speaker in the market means you get a fair price. Causing confusion became a principle of my bargaining strategies in the old city. With no fixed prices on anything that was being sold, appearing to be knowledgeable about the local ways was simply a way of keeping more money in your pocket. I could pronounce my "Q" and roll my "R," but I chose not to.

Walking alone through the medina at night created a sense of belonging that was shattered only by the reality of the daylight and the stirring of the sweepers, who swept away the evidence of the previous day's hustle using long brooms made of tree twigs. Water magically appeared to sluice where wall met earth, and the brooms danced along, saying farewell to their partners in filth. There were no plastics in Fez in those days, so the mixture of donkey dung, mint leaves, and strewn paper from student copybooks seemed clean somehow.

Years later, I brought my father deep into the medina to meet my adopted Moroccan family, and I mentioned how clean the alleys were, proudly pointing out they were swept each morning. My father paused, looked down at my babouche—the bright yellow slippers we all wore in those early days—and said, "Clean? You are literally standing in a pile of shit. How do you define 'clean'?"

True, it wasn't the Switzerland of my student days, where street sweepers had the same type of broom made of pruned twigs from trees. But at least my Moroccan neighbors did not deny that there was any litter or dirt in the streets. My Swiss neighbors would swear that street sweepers did not exist, because there was no litter in Switzerland. I would point to the street sweepers right in front of our house as evidence, but they would look right through them and comment on the beautiful flowers. The Swiss simply could not accept that their country was anything but immaculate.

In any case, Fez was swept clean every morning, and I thought it was wonderful. I did, however, wash my feet the moment I got home each day, so perhaps it was just the biased vision of someone falling in love with the city that blinded me to the ever-present *plop, plop, plop!* of donkey dung.

BREAD AND THE OTHER SMELLS OF LIFE

Navigating the medina was aided by the smells. Every part of the city had a particular scent, and if you closed your eyes, you could guess where you were within the city walls. The smell of burning wood and warm bread, for example, meant you were close to a public oven.

When the morning light caressed the alleys, the public ovens would come alive and children would rush from home with a wooden board on their heads. The board held the morning's unbaked bread—flat, round dough covered with a light cloth that kept it warm and the flies frustrated—that rose slightly in anticipation of the public oven's warm embrace. My adoptive Moroccan mother showed me how the baker would know every family's bread just by sight: by a slight indentation made in the dough with a fork or knife. Every family had frequented the same public oven for centuries, and to change bakers was considered a grave insult.

When I told my baker that I knew his secret and that he had no special powers, he screamed insults at me. As he seethed, I told him what I had learned about families marking their dough.

"What do you know?" he bellowed. "You are a foreigner with no known family history. How could you possibly know anything?"

He told me that he knew each family's bread not only by the recipe and the level of kneading every mother inflicted on her dough that morning, but by the mere smell of it. He had never made a mistake.

I looked over at the burnt bread tossed in the corner but decided it was better to leave well enough alone.

The word "neighborhood" does not really capture the way the medina is laid out. If you were to look at a map, you would see that the various areas of the old city have names. *Derb* is a word used to describe the series of alleys that a person calls home. One derb flows into another, defining and shaping you as most neighborhoods do. Knowing the borders of where one derb begins and ends, however, is a lifelong endeavor best left to someone born there—or to one of the many scholars sitting in Al-Quaraouiyine, the oldest (my neighbors told me) university in the world.

But back to the smells.

When I smelled a freshly carved table, I knew I was in the carpenters' area. When I smelled acrid smoke, I knew I was near the kiln of a potter. The smell of brass being polished meant I was sitting with my friend Abdullah sipping tea whilst he tapped a new design into a brass tray, before I continued on down the alleyway to the fresh vegetable market to do the daily shopping.

And the smell of leather was an indication that I had decided it was time to buy another pair of babouche slippers.

FEET SMELL AND SO DO YELLOW BABOUCHE

Babouche smell is necessarily mixed with the smell of glue. Ah, the smell of glue in the morning, the afternoon, the evening . . . you get the picture. The babouche sellers I visited would stare out from the mountain of yellow, pointy-toed slippers piled floor to ceiling in the tiny four-by-four-foot shop. There was no public entry to the shop. The babouche men would simply sit motionless in that sea of yellow, waiting for customers. When I approached, they would happily come to attention, grab the most expensive of the lot, bend it, slap it, and smell it. Their antics were all to prove to me that their babouche were of the best quality—the supplest, the softest—and the latest fashion.

The "latest fashion" assertion fascinated me. In reality, the fashion never changed. For centuries, the babouche were always yellow and the exact same shape. It wasn't until much later that the city of Marrakech began to change the color and shape of them, most likely because the hippies—beginning with The Beatles and The Rolling Stones—started travelling to Morocco. With them came the opinion that yellow was out that year.

Most babouche sellers were not in good physical shape. Sitting on a stool for ten hours a day, surrounded by glue-soaked slippers, did not inspire exercise. There was usually a secret door under the counter through which they crawled into and out of their shop. When their backsides got too big to fit through that crawlspace, they conscripted young boys to scamper over the counter to fetch things. The more athletic-minded men had a rope hanging from the beam, holding in place the shutters that served as the door. The boys would reach up and swing like little chimpanzees over the counter, and somehow land in the perfect spot where they would find what the master wanted to sell me.

In the evening, boys would come walking through the alleys with stacks of yellow babouche six feet high. They somehow balanced them all, and to my amazement, I never saw a stack fall. The pointed toes of the slippers fit nicely into one another; the tighter you stuffed them, the higher you could go.

Despite its common English translation, the babouche is not actually a slipper. It's a shoe, and we wore them just as you would wear a shoe today. Living across the centuries poses challenges in choosing the right language that you, dear reader, will understand. If I keep calling them "slippers," you will think they are some giant, puffy things that you wear at home, and then you get drunk and wear them to the market by mistake—but then decide that you can get away with it, so you keep wearing slippers when you should be wearing shoes. No, babouche are shoes, not fuzzy slippers, and they form to your feet as your sweat moistens them. The shoe leather then dries and remains shaped when you take them off at home—a perfectly formed shoe that fits your foot exactly.

Where were these acrobatic babouche boys going, and from where were they coming? Where was the babouche factory? One evening I decided to follow a teetering yellow tower of babouche, and to my amazement, they led me home: to a small room perched halfway up the wall of the vizier's palace. I had never noticed the room—a literal external hole in the palace wall—before and was fascinated to discover the smell of glue I'd always encountered was coming from the two "cobblers" sitting on the floor, making babouche right under my nose.

Sniffing glue is wrong. I deny that I lingered too long at the mini-factory to sniff glue with the cobblers. I was there to learn, however, and sniffing glue in 1402 was not illegal, so I feel comfortable telling you about it now.

I struck up a friendship with the two cobblers and learned that they would not sell me babouche directly, because they were members of the babouche guild and would be arrested if caught selling to me at the much-reduced price on which we eventually agreed. I also learned that they never left that small room, from early in the morning to late in the evening. Their lives centered on carefully cutting the yellow leather into the shape of a babouche. Hundreds of pieces of triangular-shaped leather were stacked around them.

The sole of the shoe, meanwhile, was cut from a hardened brown leather. The cheaper models had paper stuffed between two layers of inferior leather and did not have the bounce of the higher-priced models. The cobblers would sew the soles of the shoe to the yellow triangle. The glue was to hold down the heel of the babouche.

Think of what your old shoes look like when you have to take the garbage out in a hurry because you forgot it was garbage day, and the truck is next door, so you just jam your foot into the shoe and crush the heel down, and it stays that way so you can never wear that shoe to the office again. That is what the back of a babouche looks like.

To the untrained eye, there didn't seem to be any system of sizes. I wanted a pair in size forty-two and asked my new friends to explain how they could possibly find my size from the depths of the pile. It could have been the glue that gave them such a faraway stare, but it was clear to me that they were not going to tell me how they managed to find a size forty-two. The guild forbade the sharing of such secret information.

SNIFFING GLUE AND LESSONS LEARNED

I learned Moroccan Arabic by sitting with these cobblers. I also learned the effects of sniffing glue over long periods of time. When I say "long periods of time," I mean one's entire life.

It was sad to see the cobblers deteriorate over time. I knew that in contrast, my life's path would take me to distant lands, and I would escape the glue-sniffing room that was their world. Still, I learned much from them. I learned that it costs nothing to treat people in all stations of society with dignity and respect. I also learned what it means to have a fatalistic sense of humor.

One day, coming home from teaching my young students, I stopped to say hello to my cobbler friends and sip some mint tea. They were particularly effusive and wanted to tell me a joke; they had been repeating it to themselves all day and now needed an audience: The electric bill had arrived that day. The bill was double their monthly salary.

At this, the two men burst out laughing. I looked up at the ceiling and saw one naked bulb hanging on an exposed wire. "There must be some mistake," I said. "How could one light bulb cost more than a month's salary?"

They repeated the story and fell over laughing, spilling the glue and then laughing all the more. I said that I didn't find the story at all funny and that I was upset to hear they were being robbed. That made them laugh all the harder.

It was hilarious, they explained, that they had worked all day, every day, for a month, and would owe an electric bill that was more than their monthly income. They would have no money for food and would not be able to pay the rent, never mind the electric bill.

I stood in the alley, staring into their workshop hole, waiting for the punch line, but it never arrived.

The mood turned sour. The cobblers said that they had thought my Arabic was much more sophisticated, that I was one of them. But if I wasn't laughing, then I wasn't really one of them, and they would never break the law of the guild and sell me the size forty-two babouche I coveted. It looked as though my days of sipping mint tea and sniffing glue with my cobbler mates were over.

I was stumped. They somehow found humor in their belief that their own actions and decisions did not affect their lives. For them, it did not seem to matter if they worked more or less, used more or less electricity, or sniffed more or less glue. They would remain there in that tiny room because their future was *maktub*: written by Allah and not subject to change. In most languages, there is an expression that mirrors this fatalism—"What can you do but laugh?" is an example—but I found no humor in their condition.

At the same time, I suffered from an element of fatalism in my own belief that there was nothing I could do to change their fate. To me, the understanding that they expressed no desire to change their lives was the saddest thing. To them, however, it was my unwillingness to laugh at their predicament that brought sadness.

In the end, I agreed that the electric bill was funny, just so we could remain civil to one another as I passed their workshop going out and coming home.

NASSARANI

Eventually I didn't need to wander at night to find my way around the labyrinth of Fez. In any case, my scheme to mark the accurate way home with chalk arrows had failed. A small, satanic child had spied my marks and delighted in rubbing them off and changing their direction so that I would wind up walking down a dead-end alley.

He would gather his group of friends whenever he saw me coming. They pealed with laughter as they screamed, "*Nassarani!*" ("Christian!") and then ran for their lives, believing I would force them to convert if I ever caught them. They did not know my true identity as a Muslim, but it mattered not. They would learn over time that I knew the medina better than they did. The little urchins knew their own derb, but not much more. Their world was small, and for some, it would not grow wider even as they grew taller. But to them, I was the one at a disadvantage. Their taunting ended only when they bored of the game.

"The medina is closed," one particular boy insisted on telling me. I would always respond that I actually lived in the medina and that I was simply going home. He challenged me and wanted to know exactly where in the medina I lived.

"But I tell you the same thing every time," I shot back.

He spat in disgust and claimed he had never seen me before. I had entered into his alternative reality, where whatever he said was what was actually happening. It wasn't until years later that I learned to navigate this bent-reality world.

For the time being, I told the boy (again!) that I lived in the old palace of Dar Mokri, vizier for the Sultan Youssef. Then I asked him to please stop following me—and to please put some pants on so we could have a polite conversation.

Pantsless or not, he won every argument. Nothing I could say would convince him that I was anything other than a lost tourist.

AN ENDLESS STRING OF APOLOGIES

Steering a course through the medina during the day became easier once I recognized that the sounds and smells of it were alive. Noisy donkeys were everywhere and knew their way through the labyrinth. I figured I was at least as smart as an ass, so why not follow them?

The porters had their own donkey language, so I learned the two most important words: "Errrah" meant "get moving," and "shaaaa" meant "stop." I also learned that I would find a size forty-two babouche thrown at me if I uttered the word "donkey" and did not follow it immediately with "*hashek*," which meant "excuse me for talking about an ass in public."

I also learned that I could not say "shoes" without also saying "hashek." I was saying "hashek" a lot in the early days, but eventually got so tired of it that I avoided talking about asses and shoes altogether.

Even so, shoes and donkeys became a constant concern in my early life in the medina. The shoe situation was of prime importance. It had so many important connections to status, perceived insults, and political expression. You may remember the famous incident that occurred in 2008, when someone in Iraq threw a shoe at US President George W. Bush. Likewise, years earlier, when the statue of Saddam Hussein was pulled down, his metal face was drubbed with as many shoes as people could get their hands on.

A shoe can be both a sign of great disrespect and an indicator of social status. It is a great insult to show someone the soles of your shoe. For example, the habit some people have of putting their feet up on their desk has always struck me as a subtle way of insulting a guest.

In Morocco, one's shoes must be kept fastidiously clean at all times. If you are a person with any social status, there can be no dust on your shoes. When I lived in Fez, the number of shoeshine boys lying in wait at every corner attested to the importance of keeping one's shoes clean.

These boys had little wooden boxes with their revenue-generating brushes and polish safely tucked inside. They would clack the box top to signal that they were available to provide a shine. I mostly took them up on it because I thought it was a good way to help them out financially. I was also concerned that many of these kids were sniffing shoe polish like others sniffed glue. But along the way, I subconsciously became obsessed with keeping my shoes shined.

Many years later, in my married life, I found my Moroccan wife had the same obsession. She kept a secret shoeshine box hidden in the closet and would sneak out of bed in the middle of the night to check on the status of my shoes. No matter how many times I told her I would get them shined in the city, she continued her nightly shoe inspections. The shoeshine boys were simply not up to her standards.

DONKEYS AND VIRILITY

All goods moved in and out of the medina by donkey. For the more serious loads, mules were the method of transport. I am still not sure if mules are more intelligent than donkeys, but it was the donkeys that taught me the most about commerce.

There are many jokes in Arabic about donkeys, not all of them kind, and I won't bother to tell you any of them because you wouldn't get them unless you speak Arabic. Even then, you may not get the joke. So in order to drive home the punch line, I would just keep repeating the same line over and over until you either laughed or passed out from boredom. That sums up the donkey jokes.

Donkeys carried almost anything and would wait patiently while the porters loaded their baskets. Imagine the strangest thing you can think of, and chances are you would see a donkey carrying it through the medina. Sometimes it was not just one beast of burden but a train of them lumbering by, up to twenty in a line. The lead donkey knew where he was going, of course, but the porter shouted out from the tail of the train, "Turn left! Turn right!" just the same. The donkey train would chug along, winding its way through the labyrinth, seemingly uninterested in the porter's directions.

My cobbler friends and I were not the only ones living within the walls of Dar Mokri. From the outside, the walls were a drab brown with no redeeming qualities, but on the inside, my home was an ancient palace with many hidden rooms and gardens. There were many entrances to the palace, but the one I used most often was a towering hole in the wall. The door itself was a massive wooden wall, a structure that (despite its primary function) was never opened.

Built into the larger door was a door within a door that opened to a darkened vestibule, where hay was scattered on the floor. The outside and inside worlds rarely met. Because of my blue eyes, I could float between the two worlds—sometimes. Blue eyes in the Middle East are a gift left over from the Crusades, a key to opening some doors but to having other doors shut in your face.

On the way to my apartment, I would find children sitting on the steps that led to their one small room positioned halfway up the stairs. In the tiny room, no bigger than the one outside the wall where the cobblers sat making their babouche, sat a young woman with five children who all looked exactly the same age. The woman once told me proudly that the king of Morocco had given all women the gift of having many children. The gift was realized by using the broom-and-condom method of birth control.

To demonstrate this method, the king had sent a phalanx of men throughout the country with an endless supply of condoms. The king's men got tired of being beaten by angry husbands when they tried to personally demonstrate the use of a condom, so instead they showed the men what to do by putting the condom on the broomstick and rolling it carefully down, explaining that there was no need to cover the entire length of the broomstick.

In fact, sheathing the entire broomstick would require a condom three feet long, and the king had determined that no Moroccan man (despite personal fantasy) would require a condom of that length. Among the bevy of king's advisors, however, there was much argument regarding the length needed to be effective. They settled on half a broomstick, which would ensure bragging rights for the men and efficacy for the women. Of course, there were no women on the advisory committee.

In the room on the stairs, the young woman's husband carefully placed the foot-and-a-half-long condom on the broomstick every night and then slept with his wife. He was eighty years old and she was eighteen. They had many children.

The elderly husband was a porter, and he had a donkey. The donkey came home with him every night and slept, along with the family, inside the walls of the palace. I don't think the donkey was ever involved in the broomstick demonstration, but he definitely was a male and served as a biology lesson for the young children. The husband was a man of few words, but he clearly loved his little children, and he cared for his donkey with kindness.

His wife, on the other hand, was very talkative and often came to my door asking to borrow a bucket and a squeegee. Her small, unadorned walls, and the stairs that led to them, were made of beautiful tile work that she washed with water every day. A squeegee was a luxury her husband thought little of and so had never bought for her. Soon, she was celebrating the birth of her sixth child. She had asked for the squeegee so many times, I thought it would be a nice baby shower gift.

Being a young, unmarried man, and not a member of the family, I didn't want to give her anything that could be construed as romantic, but I still wanted to give a small gold bracelet for the baby to wear and a cash gift for the exhausted mother. Being a guy, I also thought it would be funny to stick the cash in the squeegee and present them all together. She clearly wanted a squeegee, so what could go wrong?

Well, if you have ever given your wife a vacuum cleaner for an anniversary present, you know the answer to that question.

In an attempt to engage the husband in conversation, in my still halting Moroccan Arabic, I asked about his donkey. "What is your donkey's name?"

"It's a donkey" came the confused response.

"I know it's a donkey, but what's his name?" I was still adjusting to the fact that I would run into the donkey in the hallway, so perhaps I wasn't picking up on his exasperation.

"How do you know it's a 'he'?" the man asked.

My awkward silence hung, like the donkey's maleness, in the air for a moment as I struggled to remember the polite Arabic word for "testicles." Was there one? Since even saying the word "donkey" added extra time to the conversation (because of having to add the word "hashek"), what level of vocabulary would be required to talk about a dangling appendage?

I tried again. "Anyway, what's his name?"

"Why does he have to have a name? It's a donkey."

"Don't you spend all day with him, every day of your life?"

"Of course I do. You see him with me every day."

"That's what I mean. You must have given him a name."

"Do you think he has a name because he is a male and I am a male?"

"No! Your wife told me the kids ask if he is a boy or a girl but . . ."

"Are you insulting my wife?"

"What? No, of course not! I'm just asking what the donkey's name is."

"So you *are* insulting me. You don't think I am a real man capable of producing another child? I go to the hammam, the public baths, every single day!"

Somehow the conversation had turned to virility, and I never got the name of the donkey or, in fact, the porter. All the years I lived with the donkey in my hallway, I never knew either of their names. Some time would pass, too, before I came to understand why, when I was asking about a donkey's name, he was telling me he takes a daily bath.

In many countries where I have lived, thinking and conversation are linear. A story has a beginning, a middle, and an end: A leads to B, which leads to C. But my life, like many conversations in Morocco, was more circular, and it was never really clear at the beginning of an adventure where it would end.

I learned early on that patience in all things is a requirement and that concepts of time are fluid. If time is endless, why rush to the point of a story? Conversely, if time only exists in that moment, why rush to the next moment? The best strategy was to drink tea, smile, and enjoy the frustration of not knowing where the story leads.

TALKING IN MY SLEEP

For Moroccan families at that time, the story often began with sheep, and not just in the journey of a new babouche. A dinner of mutton, for example, was standard fare for families that could afford to buy meat. And not buying meat when one could afford to was socially unacceptable.

A travelling Buddhist monk from Bhutan found me in the medina one day, and we struck up a friendship. I invited him to break bread with my adoptive family, yet when the massive couscous was presented, with heaps of lamb rising high into the clouds of steam, the monk announced that he was a vegetarian and did not eat meat. The family was incredulous, and I found myself in the role of a translator.

Normally, I took ten minutes to translate a few sentences, and everyone would smile as I circumnavigated the linguistic globe. This time, I didn't know the word for "vegetarian," so I stuck with a simple statement: "He doesn't eat meat."

"Because he doesn't like meat?" said my Moroccan mother.

"No, he doesn't eat meat because . . . he doesn't eat meat."

"Did you just repeat the same thing? As usual, you tell us nothing. But you are my child now, so not making sense is endearing to us all. The entire medina talks about how you speak Arabic. It is so wonderful, even though we have never met your father or mother, and no one even knows why you left your country—or if you have some sort of a secret."

"But Mama, I was just trying to tell you that he doesn't eat meat."

"You don't eat enough. And if he doesn't eat meat, he will be insulting us, and you will be insulting us by bringing this Buta man into our home."

"He is from Bhutan, not Buta." I did not believe there was even a place called Buta.

"I don't care if he is from Bhutan or is a butane gas bottle. By the way, we are out of butane gas, so you need to go to the shop and get a new bottle before this Buta man finds out there is no mint tea because you did not give me the money to replace the butane gas bottle as you have promised to do so many times since you first came to our house. Why are you not rich like the other Nassarani, except for the Spanish Nassarani who are cheaper than the Berbers? Does this Buta man know about the Berbers? Do they have any in Butaland?"

"I'll get the butane gas when we finish the couscous, Mama."

"I know why he doesn't eat meat. It's because Allah has made him insane. His new name is 'Allah's little insane man.' How do you say that in your funny tongue?"

"I can't tell him that," I replied. "He will be insulted. He doesn't eat meat because that is his religion."

"What!? He is not a Buta Muslim? Why did you bring him here?"

"I thought you would be interested to meet him and learn about Bhutan."

"Why? We know you."

"But I am not from Bhutan."

"What's that you say? Did you only dream about it one night when you were mumbling something in your sleep?"

"Talking in my sleep?"

"Yes, that is how we find out so much about you. You live in many worlds at the same time, and there is a light around you sometimes."

"Oh."

In the end, the lamb was eaten by the rest of the carnivorous family. All agreed that having the vegetarian man from Bhutan at the table meant that there was more for us.

COUSCOUS, THE FOUNDATION OF ALL LIFE

Couscous, once you truly experience it, is the meal that lives with you for the rest of your life. When you think of couscous, you think of your mother and the love she expresses through food. Couscous was a mountain that had to be attacked with a strategy in mind. It was not something to be trifled with or simply eaten.

My Moroccan family ate from one staggeringly huge dish placed in the middle of the low, round table. If there were spoons, you ate with a spoon, and if there were no spoons, you made little round couscous balls with your hands and popped them into your mouth. Early attempts at eating couscous with my hands often resulted in couscous cannon balls exploding on my face when I missed my mouth. But I was always disappointed when a spoon magically appeared in front of me. It meant that I was making a mess of things and was not up to the task.

Wheat semolina, the foundation of couscous, could be bought in a packet at the local shop. In those days, going to the shop meant that you stood in front of yet another literal hole in the wall, usually looking into a small room with one light bulb hanging from a wire, where a man (the shop owner) sat in a darkened corner, waiting to get whatever you needed from a wall of shelves. The desired items could be reached only with a long pole that had a grasping claw at the end of it.

That was the easy way to buy your couscous, and Mama always frowned upon it. To have real, homemade couscous, you had to go to the roof—the forbidden world reserved for women.

The outside world and the inside world had invisible barriers. The rooftops held the allure of freedom for women, who spent much of their lives inside a house or inside billowing clothing. Young boys and girls held the key to all the invisible barriers, but puberty changed more than a boy's voice. It changed where he could go. One of the places a young man could not go was up on the roof.

The roofs were flat, and one led to the next without interruption except for an easily jumped alley that signaled the world below. The winters could be cold, and the palace (like most of the houses in Fez) had no heat. It was often warmer on the roof than inside, so going up to the flat roof sometimes seemed like a sensible thing to do.

My first trip to the roof led to the discovery of a sea of couscous drying in the sun. Women made the couscous by hand, and it needed to dry and harden so it could be stored for later use. Seeing the couscous lying in the sun was fascinating, but also, I hoped the roof was really clean so we would not be eating pigeon droppings along with the chickpeas that always adorned the couscous plate. I was also concerned about the pebbles I might find in the couscous, but that was more of a problem when eating lentils (as my teeth later learned).

The most important lesson that day was that I should not have been on the roof. (Also, I should not have been sunbathing in my underwear, but that is another story.) I thought the mothers on the roof were upset because suntan oil leaves a funny taste in the couscous, but polluting the couscous was the least of their concern. The roof was the domain of women, and I had no business being up there.

The women running for cover on all the neighboring rooftops was my first clue. The second clue was my Moroccan mother hitting me with a shoe.

"Get back downstairs, you son of Satan!"

"What happened?" I asked. "I was cold in my room, and I came up to warm myself."

"You will be warm enough spending an eternity in hell with Satan, your father!"

"I was just looking at the couscous!"

"There is no couscous in Satan's bedroom, where you will be cleaning up after his nightly orgies!"

It wasn't at all clear to me why I would be involved in a satanic orgy deep in the bowels of hell, but I put my clothes back on and descended the stairs into the realm of men, never to return. From then on, if I wanted couscous, I just went to the local shop and stared blankly into the darkness along with the other men.

Semolina was not the only part of the couscous experience. There were regional variations, and the couscous from Fez was "royal couscous," which required at least seven different vegetables to earn the moniker.

Each person at the table was allowed to eat only the triangular section directly in front of them. Straying into the section of the person next to you was akin to mowing your neighbor's lawn by mistake. The intrusion was not acceptable, and it indicated that you were gluttonous and sinful, and would therefore spend eternity cleaning up after Satan.

Whilst eating, your mother would simultaneously tell you that you ate nothing and that you were eating too much. We were not really listening because, like my own kids later in life, we were slowly excavating the couscous, getting closer and closer to the emerging wall that separated my section from those of my Moroccan brothers on either side. We were also carefully moving the squash, cabbage, and carrots to one side so that our couscous wall would not collapse.

Arriving at the hidden meat treasure faster than anyone else at the table was another major concern. My true father back in America, a Boston Irish meat-and-potatoes man, would comment one day that he loved Moroccan food but couldn't understand why we hid the meat. It was complicated. There were protocols to be followed, and if you grew up with them, as my own children did, they did not seem strange.

We couldn't just dive into the lamb, because it was a mother's job to distribute the meat in a way that subconsciously revealed her favoritism, displeasure, or absent-mindedness. These became the lore of family stories for the rest of our lives: that horrible day in a child's mind when Mama gave a bigger chunk of lamb to the favored brother, possibly because he had been caught up on the roof, spying on the girls next door. *How did she always know?* he would wonder.

Of course, I was not a child but a young man at the time I was living in Fez, and I suppose my Moroccan family found it amusing that I spent so much time constructing a whole couscous world at my triangle of the table. My strategy was to reenact the days of a sapper digging under the walls of Jerusalem during the Crusades. From the French word for "trench," a "sapper" was someone who would dig hidden tunnels underground to weaken the fortified walls of a city. My goal was to collapse the towering wall of lamb and have it fall into my excavated section of the couscous mound.

My efforts were thwarted by providence. Only the grace of Allah, Mama told me, would determine how much meat fell to me. It was maktub, written and preordained; no feat of couscous engineering would change the path of the falling lamb.

"But Mama," I countered, "you have been tossing pieces of meat to your favorite son for the last half hour."

"Why did you bring the insane Buta man who does not eat meat to our house?"

"Don't change the subject. You said the meat would fall to me if Allah willed it, but you keep throwing the choice morsels to everyone but me."

"Are you going to send me to Mecca and collect the *baraka* that will come? Maybe then more meat will fall your way."

"What is 'baraka'?" I asked innocently.

A horrified look appeared on her face. "May Allah forgive you for not knowing the special powers of baraka! You already have so much baraka, and you don't even know it. Poor boy, didn't you just see a big chunk of lamb fall into your little couscous world?"

"*Al Hamdulillah!* All thanks belong to Allah! But I saw you push that lamb over to me just now."

"Shush now and eat. You have eaten nothing."

THE BARAKA AND SACRIFICED SHEEP

Everything is written, and nothing is done by chance if one has the baraka, the blessing power of spiritual presence that flows through a person who has it. You don't acquire the baraka; it is given. If you are thought to have it, it will bring many blessings and will also cause the chunks of lamb to fall toward you at lunch.

I was never really sure if I had the baraka or just indigestion from too much lamb. As with the journey of a babouche and the couscous, however, sheep were involved. And the lamb's journey begins not in the couscous, but on the farms outside of Fez.

You may know about kosher foods; the Islamic version is called halal. There is a very specific way to slaughter an animal, and the sacrificing of sheep has a long history in a number of religious stories and rituals. Every year, Muslims slaughter a sheep to celebrate the most important holiday: Eid al-Adha, the feast of the sacrifice. It marks the willingness of the prophet Ibrahim (or Abraham, to Christians) to sacrifice his son. Moroccans would tell me that Abraham was the first Muslim because of that submission to the will of God.

In the days running up to the feast day, I could hear sheep bleating throughout the city, because almost every family had brought one home. Many sheep could be seen on the rooftops (if one was allowed up there) or watching TV with the children of the house. The sheep were more attentive to what was on TV, because everyone else in the room was usually just talking. Shutting off the television, however, would bring howls of displeasure from everyone in the room, who swore they were watching that show. Of course, the show was often in Spanish, which no one understood, but everyone liked the hairdos and the latest fashions from the 1960s.

When a sheep was slaughtered, Satan would be lurking about, and he could only be driven away by salt. Satan apparently doesn't like salt, but neither do the jinn (evil spirits). In the countryside, one could find the local well—where people went to get their daily supply of water—encircled with salt. Any jinn trying to enter the earthly realm through such wells would be thwarted by the circle of salt. (It's critical to remember that Satan can also be lurking in your hands, if you hold them clasped behind you as you walk, so it's very important to keep your hands out in front, where an angel can see them.)

In any case, the Eid holiday produced a huge number of sheepskins that had to be processed. Some families had sheepskin rugs made, and others sold the skins to leather merchants. In one area of the medina stood vats of colorful dye. It was best to visit the area during the winter months, when the weather was cool and the smell was not so overwhelming.

Some neighborhoods of Fez are timeless. It doesn't matter if your travels take you there today or when the leather tannery was first built centuries ago—daily life in the tannery remains the same. Half-naked men stand in the vats and stomp on the leather as it absorbs the dye. The men themselves are forever dyed as well and, as a result, forever branded—unable to ascend to any other profession.

Travellers are often brought to the tannery to witness the spectacle. They also become part of the spectacle, with their eyes watering, sweat running in waterfalls from their brows, and their noses stuffed with sprigs of mint.

Mint is an important part of Moroccan culture, and mint tea is the preferred drink after breakfast, lunch, and dinner. I was never quite sure if it was the mint or the sugar that drove the obsession with mint tea. The variations ranged from a fragrant delight to a heavy, syrupy concoction that enticed both human travellers and swarms of bees looking for a quick fix without all that buzzing about in the fields of flowers outside the city.

For a visit to the tannery, however, the mint was lodged in a traveller's nose, tickling the brain, to repel the odorous assault. For me, it was much more pleasant to sniff glue with my cobbler friends as they prepared the sheepskin for the end of its journey: my feet.

BARGAINING WITH AN ACCENT

Following the trail of the babouche revealed as much about Morocco as eating couscous with my Moroccan family. Unlike most commerce, moving through the medina on the backs of donkeys, babouche traversed the city upon human boys instead. Perhaps the irony of a donkey and a shoe travelling together would be too much for any linguist to explain in polite company. How could one juggle the two "hasheks!" required at every mention of the words "donkey" and "shoe"?

Babouche arriving at shops on the back of a donkey would mean no one would ever be able to sell anything, because they would be too busy apologizing to prospective customers. The babouche merchants' wares were therefore carried by young men, and the staggering heights of their yellow stalks were to be admired and respected—an integral part of the sales pitch.

Shopping in the medina is not an outing that can be completed quickly. Bargaining is a way of life and a way to pass the time. For me, it was also a way to learn the Moroccan dialect, which was so different from the Arabic spoken in Yemen, Jerusalem, Mauritania, Egypt, or Dubai, where my travels would later take me.

At the time, I did not know just how different the dialect was—in many ways, it was another language entirely. I found additional incentive to master it when I discovered that I would be treated differently based on the language I spoke. Even my word choice and the accent of my Arabic would drive the price of an article up or down. Only by placing you correctly can a merchant extract the maximum price from you. Bargaining is a game, but it must be a profitable game all the same.

Walking through the markets of the medina is like living in a store where the shelves speak and items shout. As a neophyte, you are not in control. Carpets allure, bending your sense of time. The mint tea seduces you and leaves you in a euphoric sugar high, capable of spending far beyond your means.

To enter a shop and leave without a purchase is a failure. The promise to return later to complete a purchase is an empty one and leaves the merchant disgruntled. You and the merchant exist only in that moment. Upon completion of a sale, if both parties are happy, someone was robbed.

My vegetarian Buddhist monk friend, for example, was not a good shopper. He would tell the merchant that he did not truly exist and that he only appeared to be real through the existential hope of a good sale to be made that day. The word had already spread throughout the medina that he would not eat meat, and it was therefore well known that he was insane.

The Lebanese poet Khalil Gibran perhaps best captured how I approached my merchant friends and bargaining: "They deem me mad because I will not sell my days for gold; and I deem them mad because they think my days have a price." How does one bargain for something that holds no value for you?

"Just for the pleasure of the eyes" was a common phrase heard as I passed by a merchant hawking goods.

"My eyes are tired," I replied most of the time. After hours of walking in my babouche, though, my feet were more tired than my eyes, and often I succumbed to the lure of mint tea and a sales pitch.

Once a merchant tired of telling me to come inside, buy nothing, and just delight the eyes, I would enter the carpet shop. His desire to place me correctly would soon fade, however, as the possibility of a sale evaporated. There were other sales to be made and customers to lure inside, so I sat quietly sipping my tea, becoming invisible.

As my eyes adjusted to the darkness, the world of carpets awoke. The colors, the musty smell, and another smell—one that I have never to this day truly identified—seemed magical. I was transported in a caravan that never moved from this one place.

The linguistically challenged tourist is always at a disadvantage. The merchants of the medina seem to speak every language under the sun. The only travellers they never seemed to put much effort toward were those arriving from Andalusia. Perhaps it was because the Spanish tourists bargained too much, never bought anything of import, and were blamed for the expulsion of Muslims from Spain in 1492.

That date became part of a children's rhyme centuries later, but for those of us living in Fez, it had a very different significance. Idle banter among merchants focused on that tragic year not as the year Columbus sailed the ocean blue, but as the year the Islamic world in Europe ended. If it had been an Arab explorer sailing to the New World, carpet merchants in the medina believe they would be speaking American Arabic as a mother tongue. Drooling over a sale in dollars, they dream of selling their wares in an Islamic America, while still lamenting their families' departure from Andalusia and relocation to Fez.

Asking the price of a carpet was no simple affair. The first sign that you were going to pay too much was that the sprig of mint in your nose was removed gracefully and replaced with a bull's nose ring. The tourist, therefore, could be led down the road to slaughter with great ease.

To bargain effectively, I discovered, one had to understand how money worked. In many places around the world, the country's money has a name and people use that name and the story pretty much ends there. Not so in Morocco. Moroccan merchants not only had different names for the various denominations, but assigned different values to their goods according to your chosen currency.

If the merchant answered the first query about price with "What currency will you pay with?" and you, the tourist, answered with a currency from faraway lands, you never felt the slice of the knife and the seeping away of your hard-earned life's blood from your wallet. Answering that you would pay in dirhams, Morocco's official currency, provided you with some protection but indicated that you were intellectually lazy and not good at math.

If you answered that you would pay in francs, it meant you had travelled from Casablanca and might have money, but you also might have a Fassi cousin lurking somewhere in the medina who could thwart the sale.

If you answered that you would pay in riyals, you had a better chance to survive the sale, but you could fall into the trap of quoting a riyal price from the north of Morocco when you meant to quote a riyal from the south.

There were no price tags on any carpet. You were alone.

KARIM, MERCHANT OF CARPETS AND BAGGER OF TOURISTS

Rumi, an influential Persian poet from the fourteenth century, was fond of saying, "The quieter you become, the more you are able to hear." Hearing is not the same as listening, however. Likewise, eavesdropping is not the same as spying.

My education about the medina came not from any formal study but from its cacophony of sounds. After all the hours I sat quietly hearing, listening, and watching, I thought I had figured out the inventory system of the carpets, at least in one store. As in the babouche shop, carpets were piled high, from floor to ceiling, and I sat on the floor sipping tea for hours at a time. Eventually, the carpet merchant became my friend. Karim knew every single carpet in the shop and could pull out the right one at exactly the right moment.

I learned that people of different nationalities had different preferences regarding color, and Karim would pull carpets down from the piles depending on what language the traveller was speaking. He seemed to sense what would excite a customer.

When a couple entered the shop, he knew exactly who was the weaker of the two. He also knew that most people were uncomfortable with silence and so the unsuspecting would divulge too much in the first foray. The traveller would sally forth with gusto, saying they knew all about carpets, had bought many before, and could not be hoodwinked.

Karim would smile and say, "Tell me more, my friend."

It was like watching a vizier gazing through a crystal ball, encouraging the traveller to divulge all they desired. And they did. They would vomit up all the details of where they were staying, how much cash they had on them, why they couldn't buy such a large carpet. Their excuses for not buying the carpet exposed their fears.

They feared that they couldn't carry it back to the hotel where they were staying or that they wouldn't have any money to eat that night if they bought the desired carpet. Food, porters, and more mint tea would magically appear until the traveller was sent off with a boy carrying their carpet back to their hotel, where Karim had already sent word to provide a cheese sandwich for his guests that evening and charge him for it—but not to use today's expensive bread if they had any left over from yesterday.

When it became clear to Karim that I truly lived in the medina, had already bought as many carpets as my purse would allow, and would not disrupt his bargaining, I became a fixture on the wall, sitting in the near darkness, listening and learning as an unseen apprentice.

To his brother, Moulay Walu, I was somewhat of an unwanted ornament in the shop. Moulay Walu's mind was in a constant whirl as to why I was there. To him, I was a spy from the sultan's palace. His tales of my exploits were legendary, but his sphere of influence extended only to the four stools, three askew, outside the door of the carpet emporium.

The sadness of his worldview was that I could not truly be a friend to his brother because his brother was not worthy of such a friendship. There was no pleasure in his repeating to passersby, "Come in just for the pleasure of the eyes." There was jealousy in the drippings from his tongue. He never trusted our friendship and continuously cautioned Karim not to let me hear them speak of business. But listen I did.

The first time I saw a Berber merchant arrive at the front door of Karim's shop, there was a donkey with him. The donkey carried a load of carpets from the mountains. I vowed that I would follow the journey of the carpet as I had done with the babouche. As I told you, the donkey and the shoe shaped many events in my story. For now, however, it's best to focus on the carpets.

I wanted to know how the carpet weavers from the countryside were paid by the merchants of Fez, but the pricing of a carpet was secret information and closely guarded. Moulay Walu always did his best to prevent me from learning the true prices. Karim was less concerned and found it amusing that I had figured out his pricing system.

Each carpet had a woolen fringe, and tied to one of the yarns of the fringe was a small piece of tightly rolled paper with numbers on it. Early in our friendship, I asked Karim what the numbers meant. He told me it was his way of remembering where to put the carpets back in the pile. Travellers were never allowed to browse. Karim was fully in control of what was seen and what was not seen.

After pulling a carpet from a pile, Karim would throw it open in dramatic fashion. Travellers would protest that they were just looking and didn't want him to open all the carpets, yet all the while the carpets on the floor piled higher and higher. I never saw a traveller look at one of the small pieces of paper. I also noticed that Karim never put the carpets back in the same order in which he pulled them out.

Karim was almost never the one who put the carpets back anyway. A young boy would appear from nowhere—people were always appearing from nowhere magically, it seemed, like mint tea—and put all the carpets back in a way that did not seem to follow any system, despite what Karim had said. In the shop, I spent a great deal of time looking at those secret numbered messages. But I never saw Karim write a number and attach it to a carpet.

THE SIMPLE-MINDED MATHEMATICIAN

People who smile a lot are always suspect. I happen to be a smiler. I smile naturally, and some consider me simple-minded as a result. On the day the Berber merchant arrived from the mountains with his carpets on the back of a donkey, I sat quietly sipping my tea. I smiled when the Berber glanced at me, confirming his assessment that I was a simple-minded wall ornament. Then he gave Karim the asking price for his first carpet and proceeded to win the bargaining game with ease.

My world changed that day.

Karim's brother, Moulay Walu, had been defeated. His hold on the mystery was broken because his mastery of numeracy had been ill-constructed. Unlike Karim, he could not hold the prices of hundreds of carpets in his tiny, jealousy-infected mind. On the tightly rolled papers were prices written in riyals. To parry Karim's bargaining thrust, therefore, all one had to do was to cut the number in half and drop the last zero, and you had the original price of the carpet.

If someone told you that the price of a cheese sandwich was 100 riyals, you would cut the number in half and drop a zero, and voilà! You paid 5 dirhams for the sandwich. When the numbers got larger, you would revert to your school days, when you had to calculate fast enough to avoid being smacked with a ruler (and hoping it was not one of those fancy ones with the little metal strip along the edge). So, a carpet offered in the shop for 20,000 riyals actually cost only 1,000 dirhams to purchase from the carpet seller.

Mystery solved.

Over the years, I would see Moulay Walu sitting on the stool with a coterie of underwhelming entrepreneurs who listened to the stories of how he sold *his* carpets, never mentioning it was his brother's shop and his brother's inventory of carpets. Meanwhile, at some point, I realized Karim was no longer seen in the market. I did suspect foul play, but after the third time asking, I was afraid to know where Karim was. And I wanted to remember him the way I first saw him.

To me, he was an older teacher from whom I learned much. When you are young, however, often you think everyone is much older than they are. I have always suffered from the inability to determine someone's age. So Karim could have been my own age, and perhaps he lives to this day. He also could have been rolled up in one of his carpets all the while Moulay Walu reaped the fruits of his brother's labors.

The layers of the medina reveal themselves slowly, and peeling them back requires time and patience. The young move through life at a different pace, and I never learned Karim's fate.

MY LOVE AFFAIR WITH FRENCH

Language was the framework of my life in those early North African days. In the medina, for me the fog of fatigue from speaking a new language was often thick. There was also the lure of lapsing into speaking French, which seemed, to me, a surrender. Moroccan Arabic is peppered with French to such a degree that, even as a French speaker, I found it hard to recognize the bastardized words so ingrained in everyday Moroccan Arabic. To reveal that I spoke French would end my discovery of Arabic. I was not willing to surrender to the ease of speaking French in the medina.

Speaking both Arabic and French allowed me to live in two worlds, two centuries, at the same time. I was determined to keep the two worlds separate.

To walk out of the medina was to emerge from one world and enter another. The contrast was immediate and jarring. Morocco had been a French colony, and the vestiges of colonization were there in architecture, traffic, and cafés. The bending of time shimmered as you left the cool darkness of the medina and entered the glaring sun of La Ville Nouvelle, the New City. The light was not the only thing that shifted. In La Ville Nouvelle, the French language that came more easily to me flowed, and the fog of linguistic fatigue slowly lifted. I had experienced the same sensation during my time as a student in Switzerland.

Language has always fascinated me. My Irish grandmother was a Gaelic speaker who pronounced words in English with a delightful brogue—an accent that sometimes was more pleasant than what she had to say. The various sounds that people make are part of my lifelong fascination with languages.

French is not my mother tongue. It first came to me not in an academic sense, but by enveloping me, because I lived close to the Canadian border. Montreal was not too far a drive, and we visited with some regularity.

In grammar school, I was selected to take part in the first attempt by the administration to teach a foreign language to children before they reached high school. I think it had been reported that I often blurted out, "*Merde alors!*"—"Oh, shit!"—which I had learned on the Metro in Montreal.

My mother spoke no French but insisted that she did. When we took the Metro, she was equally insistent that we should get off the train at the stop named "*Sortie.*" No matter how many times I met her insistence with my own, explaining that "sortie" just means "exit" in French and thus every Metro stop had that sign, I was ignored. I recall one frustrated French-speaking passenger who could no longer take listening to our conversation. He, too, blurted out, "Merde, alors!" and then left the train.

After hours of riding the endless loop around the city, searching in vain for the station named "Sortie," we left the train, saw nothing of Montreal, and began the long, sullen ride home. Why everyone in the car, including the driver (my father), continued to believe that my mother should take the linguistic lead was another mystery. As we passed the highway sign for "Les États-Unis" for the tenth time, my mother continued to scream out the window at every passing car: "Where is America?"

I decided to fall asleep, and we completed the four-hour drive in a lumbering ten hours while I had my first dream in French, which consisted of me saying, over and over again, "Les États-Unis, merde alors!"

Many years later, the dream of speaking French was still with me as I headed to Fribourg, Switzerland, to study linguistics. The city of Fribourg sits on the linguistic border between Swiss German speakers and Swiss French speakers. I lived first in a twelfth-century home high on the cliff overlooking the entire city, and then in an abandoned brothel in the Bas Ville, the Old City at the bottom of the cliffs. The French speakers on the cliff looked down, figuratively and literally, on the German speakers below.

While living in the Old City, I walked daily up 632 granite steps from my brothel cell to the university where I studied. Every day I walked by my former stately home on top of the cliff and thought of the fall from grace that had resulted in my eviction: having snuck a forbidden girlfriend into my bedroom. The matron of the house told me I had to leave because her sister had a fire in her house and needed my bedroom, but I knew it was the girlfriend who was my downfall.

Many of my university friends in Switzerland would go to Morocco on our spring break vacation. Travelling across Europe by train was the only affordable way students could get to Morocco, which meant I was unlikely to join them. The first problem for me was time. I worked on weekends to support my studies—even during school break. The second problem was Spain, because the train in Spain moves slowly across the plain.

The dictator Francisco Franco had installed a narrower-gauge railroad track throughout the entire country so his realm could not be invaded by train. Spain's train system was pretty awful, and it would have taken more than the week I had for vacation just to arrive at the ferry to take me to the city of Tangiers. So, Morocco evaded my travels until I joined the Peace Corps and was sent to live in Fez.

Part of the reason the Peace Corps sent me to Morocco was that, in Switzerland, I had studied to teach a foreign language. The only catch was that I had studied to teach French. In Morocco, I taught English.

It became increasingly hard to keep the three languages—English, French, and Arabic—from flowing together. In the Fez medina, I spoke only Arabic. It was the Arabic of a child, repeating what I heard in the accent in which I heard it. And sometimes, with my limited vocabulary, I could only revert to childlike responses.

While waiting for a friend one day in his living room, his six-year-old brother stood in front of me, staring at my head. I asked him why.

"Your head is so big," he taunted.

I wanted to say something clever in Arabic like, "Because my brain is so big." But I could only stick out my tongue at him.

We were friends after that—kindred spirits, I suppose.

THE GRAY-HAIRED CIA AGENT

The fact that I insisted on keeping my two worlds separate—the medina and La Ville Nouvelle—is part of the reason I was first suspected of working undercover for the CIA. The school where I taught English was in the New City. On my first day, as I walked into the room reserved for the teaching staff, my reception was frosty. Suspicion saps the energy of some whilst energizing others to concoct conspiracy theories. Although there was certainly no welcome committee for the new teacher, the rumors began almost immediately.

Conspiracy theories are the playground of those suffering from ennui. Seeking to squeeze excitement from the mundane is a special skill that can inspire hours of idle gossip and malicious guesswork. So it was in Fez, among my teaching colleagues from France. My first mistake was telling them my age. In their book, it was my first lie. Had I matched the "truth" they had already established I might have avoided their growing belief that I was not who I said I was.

It may have been the suit I was wearing on my first day of school, or it could have been the color of my hair. To my colleagues, my hair had far too much gray in it for me to be telling the truth. Surely no young man of the age I'd claimed—my true age, I might add—would have gray hair.

I had used the gray to my advantage during my travels, securing status reserved for stately gentlemen, but now it was working against me in ways I had not anticipated. And it was not only my French colleagues who suspected me of hiding my true nature, but my Moroccan colleagues too. They suspected I was not really a teacher but rather a spy.

When all is maktub, one is not supposed to act out of turn, even by allowing one's hair to gray prematurely. It makes people uncomfortable. The beaten path is beaten for a reason. Straying from it often results in being scratched by the briars of life—and mistrusted by the little minds of the bored.

DONNYBROOK AT THE CINEMA

The first time I was forced to break my own rule about speaking only French in the New City was when I went to the local cinema. In the lobby, I did not notice that I was the only foreigner in the queue. I did not anticipate that buying the cheap ticket, instead of the more expensive front-row seat in the balcony, would cause a small donnybrook.

There were no women in the cinema, and there was no one over the age of twenty. I was not far beyond that age, but my gray hair complicated my ability to blend into the crowd of teenage boys. The attack came early.

With ticket in hand, I headed for the cheap seats. A young man was in my face immediately, screaming in Arabic, his own face contorted in anger. He shouted that I did not belong in the cinema, that I was too old to understand the three great films we were about to watch in under an hour. In order to achieve that small cinematic miracle, all the dialogue was cut out of each film, and we were left with explosions, car crashes, and fistfights. Foreigners of my age were not supposed to enjoy the sophistication.

Most fistfights start with posturing. In this case, there was a lot of screaming in my face, while I said nothing more than some version of "What the hell are you talking about? And also, step back."

His first blow landed squarely on my jaw. I was surprised that he had struck me. He was equally surprised that his blow had little effect.

My inner dialogue was focused on why I had left the sanctuary of the medina and come unprepared to this other world. My ability to become invisible in the medina had failed me here in the New City.

I stepped back and widened my stance. Upon turning my body sideways to become less of a target, I saw that a crowd of teenagers had appeared around my young assailant. Most of the boys were egging him on whilst others just stared. His second punch hit me again in the jaw. When my fist began its journey to his nose, I was grabbed by the mob and dragged outside along with the aggressor.

The other boys, suddenly friendly, apologized profusely and explained that the boy was crazy and sniffed glue whenever he could. I told them that I would simply go home, but they insisted that I watch the films from the beginning or I would miss the plot.

One of the boys then recognized me and announced that I was a "professor" at his school. The mob was both horrified that a student had punched me and amazed that a professor was at the cinema. Someone of my position and age should have bought a seat on the balcony, they said, and they insisted I do so immediately, after which they would escort me to the upper reaches of the cinema. This crowd of friendly students morphed again, into a new mob threatening violence if I did not watch the film. So I paid the extra money, sat in the front row with my fists clenched, and watched the rich boys in the balcony spit the shells of their sunflower seeds down onto the heads of the poor boys below.

Even young people can suffer from the shackles of expectation. Somewhere along the line, the open mind of a child becomes the fenced-in mind of a teenager.

CARDBOARD KEYBOARDS

Monday morning presented a new challenge in the staff room. The headmaster came to tell me that I would be teaching a typing class, in English, to the secretarial students. Among the teachers present, there was quite a bit of sniggering at my expense, but I thought I was up to the teaching challenge.

My first class had ten young girls sitting silently whilst staring at me. There was not a typewriter in sight. My objective was clear: in the typing classroom, I was to speak nothing but English to girls who spoke no English and had no typewriters.

I was not exactly a hunt-and-peck typist, but nor did I have any experience with teaching typing. I was not that good at typing myself. My first lesson was to tell the girls my name and ask if anyone knew any English words. The first hand that came up belonged to a girl who proved to be both clever and mischievous.

"Sir, I speak perfect English," she said in French.

"That's wonderful. Let's speak in English so the others can learn."

"Why are your eyes so blue?" came the question in French. Two things were immediately clear: there was neither English language proficiency nor typewriters present in the classroom, so I asked, in French, "Where are your typewriters?"

The students reached into their voluminous handbags, and each girl pulled out a piece of cardboard on which a keyboard was printed. Each girl placed it carefully on her desk and started to "type." At first, I thought it was some sort of practical joke. Then I realized, sadly, that the school had no budget for real typewriters.

The students were just as happy to bang away on cardboard keyboards, shouting out that they all had perfect scores. I had no way to correct their typing, so on their first day I gave them all 20/20. Word got back to the headmaster that the girls were most likely to graduate if the grade inflation continued—a catastrophe for the national education budget. The headmaster sent me a note saying I was already on probation.

On my second day with the girls, I found them all in their finest djellabas, the Moroccan traditional garb. Their faces were slathered with cosmetics, and they were dancing on the top of their desks while a cassette recorder blared the latest heartthrob song. I had become the next Old Blue Eyes after only one class.

When the story got out, enraged fathers stormed the administration building, claiming that I was seducing the entire class. My tenure as the typing professor ended, and I was transferred to a class of boys studying mechanics. Naturally, there were no cars or machines in the entire school.

ARABIC LESSONS

On my way to the staff room one day, I met a young Moroccan woman who was teaching math to students who had a future. The students at the school were divided into sections; the clever students were taught math and science and were deemed to have a bright career ahead of them.

My students, on the other hand, were expected to meet a much dimmer future. In any case, the teachers from France were telling everyone that I was a CIA agent, she said, and was there to sabotage something. As the story went, my first foray into espionage—undermining the future of typing in Morocco—had failed, and thus France would reemerge as the power in Morocco.

Among the faculty, something about me had been lost in translation.

We agreed that the Moroccan math teacher would be my Arabic tutor. It was maktub—it was written, and it was fate.

Our first Arabic lesson took place in the staff room. The janitor documented our movements and listened in on our conversations. There were constant interruptions from one French woman who let slip that she had seen me in Karim's shop in the medina. I already spoke Arabic, she reasoned loudly, so why spend time with the young mathematics teacher?

No excuse I offered for wanting to study Moroccan Arabic in particular would convince the woman that I had no ulterior motives. My tutor, Fatouma, suggested we move our lessons to her home to avoid the prying eyes of the other teachers. Foolishly, I agreed.

The next week, I arrived at her family's home at the appointed time. Fatouma opened the door and beckoned me in. I took off my babouche and saw we were alone save for our Arabic lesson books on the round table in the center of the room, so I asked after her mother. She demurred, saying we should get started on the lesson. Foolishly, I agreed again.

The salon was set up in the traditional Moroccan way, with banquettes—the endless couches that line the walls surrounding the entire room—and small tea tables. One table held a set of colorful glasses and a steaming pot of mint tea. The lesson books went unopened, but we chatted in Arabic while sipping tea. Her mother, father, sisters, or brothers—they never arrived.

The following week, I again arrived at the agreed time to find the round table, devoid of any books at all this time, in the center of the room. On the table instead was a steaming mound of the most glorious couscous I had ever seen. There was no one else in the room—no father or brothers to chaperone us, no bustling in the kitchen, no younger sibling to stare at my enormous head. I asked where everyone was, and Fatouma told me that we would be eating alone that day.

No one eats alone in Morocco.

After we made a small dent in the couscous, Fatouma told me that she would walk me back to school.

I asked if I could thank her mother for making the couscous.

She replied that her mother had died the night before, and she had made the couscous herself.

I apologized profusely for intruding on such a sad occasion, but Fatouma just smiled and said that all was written, and things were going to work out just fine, as long as I agreed to her plan.

She made it sound as though the couscous had been poisoned and she alone held the antidote. But her plan was even more nefarious.

Fatouma explained that she owned the house where we had just abandoned our efforts to finish a couscous large enough for a small army. She had purchased it with a mortgage, something that I must understand because all foreigners like to be in debt for the rest of their lives. Unfortunately, her meager salary as a teacher could not pay the mortgage, but now that we were to be married all her troubles were over.

I had eaten her couscous, she explained, as a sign of our betrothal.

As my stomach gurgled, the couscous settled. My mind, however, did not.

Like in the cinema, I had been in the wrong place at the wrong time.

I headed back into the safety of the medina, where I could reenter my centuries-old life. By chance, I ran into a merchant I knew who brought me into his home, another ancient palace, for more mint tea. As I told my friend of my poisoning, he smiled and said that I had misinterpreted the word "poison." What Fatouma had done was simply a "spell" and the work of the jinn.

A visit to the tomb of Moulay Idriss in the mountains would undo the spell, the merchant revealed, and he would arrange for that journey in the morning. In the meantime, he suggested I avoid Fatouma at all costs, or the spell would intensify.

UNDOING THE SPELL

The next morning, members of my friend's family arrived at the vizier's palace to take me to Moulay Idriss. This sanctuary sits atop a hill, inspired by the Yemeni-fortress mentality of its founder, and is open only to Muslims. There were no other foreigners in sight. This is where I would get my first glimpse of Yemeni architecture, which seemed out of place in Morocco but was something I would become very familiar with years later.

As requested, I wore a clean, white djellaba and my yellow babouche. The mosque is a beautiful, peaceful place, and my friend and I said prayers together and talked quietly about my predicament. My friend calmed me and said it was time to go to the tomb, where the spell Fatouma had put on me would be neutralized. There was no further briefing.

The tomb is covered by a heavy tapestry with Arabic writing, similar to the one you see covering the Kaaba in Mecca. Any frequent visitor to the tomb would know what to do, and I had come to realize that I was often simply expected to know such things too. Everyone else seemed to find the fold in the tapestry—the secret entrance—without trouble. I, on the other hand, fumbled around looking for it, much like the first time you switch from wearing pants with a zipper to one with buttons. I eventually found the opening, slipped through, and stood in utter darkness, not knowing what would come next.

My first thought was just to stand there for five minutes, then exit and announce that the spell had been lifted and we could return to Fez. But a low voice in the darkness startled me and told me to sit down.

If I had to guess, I would say that the space between the tapestry and the tomb was no more than three feet wide. The invisible voice began to recite prayers, and I did my best to say "Amen" at what I thought was the appropriate time. I did not want to appear ignorant, but nor did I want to inadvertently strengthen Fatouma's spell.

My heart pounded in the darkness. I thought, not for the first time, *How do I get myself into these situations?*

The praying suddenly stopped.

After a long silence, during which the all-encompassing darkness never lifted, the voice began another incantation. Then silence again, followed by another prayer.

The sequence repeated for a good five minutes. Finally, the voice suddenly insisted, rather angrily, on being paid.

No one had told me that lifting the spell would set me back all the money I had in my pocket. What was the price of being free of Fatouma? A whopping three dollars.

Once I returned from the pilgrimage to Moulay Idriss, I wondered if the situation with Fatouma was really all that serious. Indeed, it was. I had not yet learned the Arabic word for "delusional," but new vocabulary of this sort would soon come fast and furious.

THE CURSE OF FATOUMA

When I arrived at school the following Monday morning, the teachers' room was crowded and there was an excited buzz of anticipation. The janitor was working to pry open my locker. I asked him what he was doing.

"You'll soon find out," he replied smugly, exclaiming that my true identity was about to be exposed.

When the locker door was sprung, a letter fluttered to my feet. Before I could grab it, though, the janitor picked it up and ran off to the head-master's office.

How did the janitor know there was a letter in my locker, especially when I didn't even know it myself? And why did he feel the need to pry open my locker—and pry into my personal life? Rather than being undone, the spell had intensified and transformed into a curse.

Fatouma, sensing that I would not marry her, had become enraged. She was most upset not by the loss of my love, I realized, but by the loss of her future mortgage payments.

Her letter was full of revelations: how I had promised to marry her, how her reputation as a chaste woman had been destroyed, how I had eaten couscous with her—alone with no chaperone—and how my intentions were, therefore, very clear. It was a scandal that could not be overcome. How could she ever find a suitable husband now that I had soiled her good name?

Of course, my perspective was far different. Perhaps I had soiled her tablecloth, given my foreigner's inability to eat couscous without spilling almost every spoonful, but that was the extent of our dalliance.

This was clearly a clash of cultures that went beyond marriage expectations. Ancient and modern times were clashing as loudly as the dishes Fatouma threw against the wall in anger. Whilst the Peace Corps had given us cross-cultural training, it was based on a view of how males and females *should* interact in a traditional society—not necessarily an accurate instruction on how to navigate between the ancient and modern worlds.

To be a modern woman in Morocco at that time meant to dress in the French fashion, and Fatouma did not strike me as a very traditional person. I never saw her wear the clothes worn by women in the medina: a djellaba or a hijab (the Islamic headscarf). Though the impact of French colonization was far-reaching, I learned that all was not as it seemed. The Western accoutrements of La Ville Nouvelle were but a veneer.

PEEP SHOW AT THE CAFÉ

I assumed that the whole affair would blow over. I was very wrong.

In the habit of arriving at school early so I could enjoy a good morning coffee and croissant, I went the next morning to the local café. Students were rarely customers of the café, but that morning I arrived to see fifty young male students strategically positioned to observe the impending flood of emotion. Sadly, I was unaware of what was to come.

Fatouma made her way through the audience to my table. In those days, a woman would never be in this café, so Fatouma's very presence signaled something amiss. When she sat at my table, the room stared in disbelief.

"You won't marry me?" she asked.

"No, thank you."

"You said you would when you ate my couscous."

"I never said that, and I have no idea what you are talking about."

"You will marry me or suffer the consequences."

"I have already gone to Moulay Idriss and had the spell annulled," I said. "Leave me alone please. Our Arabic lessons have concluded. I am now adequately fluent."

"I am a monster!" was her reply.

I looked around the café and saw a whole room of teenage boys leering at the scene before them, as if they were watching their first porno film. The sexual tension in their pubescent minds was almost unbearable. Here before them was an unmarried woman entering the realm of men to sit with a young foreigner with blue eyes. It could only mean one thing: two teachers were about to have sex right on top of a plate of croissants.

Instead, I agreed with her assessment. "Yes, you are a monster."

"What?" As she reached into her bag of spells to recapture me with an amorous dust, the boys broke out in riotous laughter. She had no option but to flee.

The content of Fatouma's letter lingered in conversation in the teachers' room and in the mind of the headmaster. Teachers from France were now more convinced than ever that I was an agent provocateur who had used Fatouma to sow discontent among the students. Undercover espionage paled in comparison to the challenge I faced in this lover spurned (if only in her own mind). When student riots broke out later that year, all schools were closed and the government declared an "*année blanche*"—a total cancellation of the academic year. I never saw Fatouma again, but the damage had already been done.

My reputation as the cause of school closures became legend, and the student invitations to share Friday couscous with their families flooded in from across the city. I accepted many, but eventually decided I had consumed enough couscous with students from the countryside. When the senior class invited me to slide down an irrigation trough with all the other naked boys, I sensed there was something not right about that and declined.

ALONE IN MY PAIN

With the school year ended in La Ville Nouvelle, I folded myself back into the medina and spent time in the markets. I encountered no further matchmaking or witchcraft that year.

Daily life was calmer but still brought the challenges typical for a young man living in a new world. Things that may have seemed commonsense to most were new to me, and I made the same mistakes over and over again. Some lessons are never learned.

I travelled by bus between the New City and the medina. The bus was almost always filled with students, and I learned a lot about the inner workings of the teenage mind by listening to the banter. Young teenage boys jostling against one another and against the various women on the bus provided, to their minds, adult physical contact of a sexual nature. As they got off the bus, I listened with amusement as they recounted how they had seduced the women on the bus.

When I learned that a peanut seller roasted his product right at the bus terminus, I—like most of the students—bought the warm peanuts he sold wrapped in a paper cone. The peanuts were delicious, and despite my suspicion that they were the cause of my frequent bellyaches, I continued to buy them.

As I walked home through the medina one day, I slowly unwrapped the paper cone only to discover that it was a page torn from the copybooks students had sold to the peanut vendor at the end of the school year. I laughed when I found a homework assignment from one of my students, with my comments still clearly visible through the oil-stained evidence of the peanuts I had just eaten.

I was not laughing later that night as the first pangs of food poisoning began their intestinal assault.

Lying alone in bed in the vast, beautiful, crumbling palace, I knew that

I was truly alone in my pain. There was no one to offer medical assistance or a comforting word. The waves of cramps would slowly grow in intensity, only sometimes offering a few moments of relief post-crescendo. Sleep was not possible, so I began to think of ways to tolerate the pain. Unable to block it out, I imagined that I could float above it and embrace the pain as if nothing else existed. If there was nothing to compare it to, then I would *become* the pain and experience it in its totality.

As bizarre as this strategy may sound, it got me through the night. *Become the pain rather than fight it* was a life lesson that I employed through difficult times in all of my journeys through time and space.

THE INTOXICATING DESSERT

Couscous continued to be an important part of my life, although I never again sat alone with a woman whilst eating it. Friday couscous was always a social family affair. After Friday prayers, the couscous was waiting, hot and steaming, to be served. Students continued to invite me for couscous, but I was careful not to accept too many invitations.

Making a large couscous with meat was an expensive undertaking. I did not want to be a financial burden on my hosts, and I did not want to find myself too often in a situation where the meat would fall, by the grace of Allah, into my section of the plate. Of course, if no meat fell to the boys who had invited me into their home, it was preordained.

At times, I was invited into a wealthy home and Allah graced us all with a generous portion—as much meat as we could imagine falling into our laps. I was encouraged to eat and eat and eat. If I did not, I was insulting the family. So it was strange when at one such dinner, after feasting on an enormous amount of couscous at the insistence of the mother and then moving on to dessert, we were told to stop eating so much.

Couscous is delivered in a *tajine*, a dish with a cover shaped like a giant cone. The cone motif is repeated throughout Morocco. Ornamental dishes made of silver have cone-shaped covers. The gift of hardened sugar that guests bring to a host is cone-shaped. So, too, is the dessert called *sfouf*—a cone-shaped mountain covered with a concoction of roasted almonds, sesame seeds, and powdered sugar that, at first glance, looks like cocoa or chocolate powder. As with most Moroccan dishes, you eat sfouf out of a shared dish by taking a spoonful and then having a sip of your mint tea or espresso. It is delicious and expensive.

The consistency of sfouf is different in every home, depending on the household's recipe and budget. In some homes, it is dry and loose; in others, it has a heavy, wet consistency. In all cases, it is delightful to look at and to eat.

At the wealthy home in question, my hosts presented a massive sfouf that was of a slightly moist variety akin to a fudge brownie. I thought it odd that the parents left the room after finishing the couscous. Only my student, his friends, and three of my colleagues were left to indulge. I thanked the parents for their hospitality and dug into the sfouf.

After two or three spoonfuls, the student protested that I was eating too much. He said it was too expensive. I found that odd given that they had been cajoling me to eat ever since I had entered the house. I sipped more coffee but snuck in a few more heaping spoonfuls before my student jumped up and took the sfouf away.

Then the boys smiled and told a joke that made no sense. Despite the weak punch line, I burst out laughing. The first laugh was more of a giggle, but then the boys laughed and so did my colleagues. I repeated the punch line, and we laughed all the harder. The rhythm of the laughter grew steadily, and next came the clapping and chanting in Arabic, with me leading the way. I was amazed that my Arabic had improved so quickly in the span of an hour, and that I was now on par with the most accomplished Arab poets.

We had arrived for lunch at two in the afternoon. It was now two in the morning, and the father arrived to tell us we had to leave because the entire neighborhood was complaining about the laughing.

That's when I learned the sfouf was laced with *kif*.

In the Rif Mountains, in the north of Morocco, you will find fields of kif—otherwise known as marijuana. The young hippies of the 1960s had made their way to Morocco, especially to the town of Ketama, for that very reason: to float away in clouds of hashish (kif) smoke. I never saw younger people smoking a kif pipe in public, but it was not unusual to find older men sitting in the medina, smoking a long, thin kif pipe.

And now this seemingly sedate family had served us a dessert laced with kif, as easily as adding a bit of powdered sugar to the sfouf.

THE RIF MOUNTAINS AND THE HIRSUTE BODY

I was becoming obsessed with knowing the origin of everything I encountered. Even though I lived in the city, it was not all that difficult to follow the trail from farm to table, or in the case of the babouche, from farm to the foot. So, the morning after my marathon kif-induced laughing jag—with my jaw sore from the hilarity and my hands raw from the clapping—I headed to the *souk* bus station at Bab Bou Jeloud, the Blue Gate of the medina, planning to get on the first bus to Ketama and trace the journey of kif from the fields to the table.

My use of the term "bus station" is not to be taken literally. Bus stations were for the people who had enough money to buy a ticket in the New City. The souk bus was for the common folk, and it meandered its way through the mountains, from market to market—the souks.

"Pandemonium" is a good word to describe the process of arriving, finding the bus that goes in your general direction, and then fighting your way onto the bus. The loading of the luggage was also a sight to behold. Scaling the mountain of luggage piled on the roof rack of the bus required the skill of a Nepalese Sherpa.

In truth, describing the load on top of the bus as "luggage" does not accurately capture the scene. I'm not lying when I tell you that amid the bundles of wool, furniture, and food, there were live animals as well. As you twisted and turned your way along any of the mountain roads to your destination, it was advisable not to think too much about the load shifting. At the base of many a cliff were the shattered, rusting hulks of souk buses, but since all was maktub, written and preordained by Allah, onto the bus you went all the same.

Boarding the bus was an exercise only slightly easier than a camel going through the eye of a needle, but the number of people going through the small doorlike opening was impressive nonetheless. Once aboard, you did not choose a seat so much as you were jostled into one. These "seats" were actually benches built for two people, but it was rare to find a bench loaded with fewer than three.

Once all the passengers were crammed into their benches, the music began. The musician was typically an older, toothless gentleman playing a guitar made out of an old oil can. Songs typically were a combination of a plea for money and a curse to all who did not donate.

As the musician played, a man at the front of the bus would begin to shout, "Who doesn't have a ticket?" Weeding out those who did not have a ticket seemed like an impossible task, but the system seemed to function.

I assumed the ticket taker would think I had a trusting face and simply pass me by. That assumption was wrong. He insisted that I not only buy a ticket but also pay for the sheep tied to the roof rack. Although I assured him that I was not travelling with a sheep, in the end I paid for the sheep, and the bus rolled away at last. There was neither a fixed time to leave nor an estimated time to arrive.

As usual, the day did not go as planned.

In Ketama, the kif capital of Morocco, I was greeted by a group of nefarious-looking men who welcomed me with an ulterior motive.

"Do you have a hairy body?"

"What?" I asked, nearly certain I had misunderstood.

"Lift up your shirt! We want to see your chest."

"Umm, no?"

They tried a different approach. "Take off your clothes now, or you are going to spend the next ten years in jail for smuggling kif."

My quest to learn the provenance of that delicious, hilarious dessert suddenly seemed like a very bad idea.

I lifted up my shirt, and the men seemed disappointed. My chest was hairy enough, but my back did not pass muster. The group of men moved on to an enormous man with very long hair who, by the look of his hairy knuckles, promised to reveal a very hairy body as well.

These mafia types, I later learned, were hashish dealers. They had come up with the idea that they could get the shaggiest travellers to roll around naked in a field of cannabis, thus collecting seeds on their hirsute bodies. Then, back in Fez, the human kif mule would be washed down in the public baths so the seeds could be collected, crushed, and turned into hashish oil to be sold to the hippies.

I got back on the bus immediately and headed back to Fez, content in knowing enough about kif.

THE HAMMAM AND THE CIRCUMCISED FOREIGNER

Like most people living in the medina, I went to the hammam on a regular basis. Many went at least once a week, but one gentleman was there almost daily, just like my neighbor—the donkey porter with the young wife and six children. I still didn't understand why my elderly neighbor had told me in the same breath about siring many children and visiting the hammam every day. But this fellow was elderly too, and whenever he entered the room at the hammam where we got undressed, the men would start to congratulate him.

No one had ever congratulated me when I entered the hammam. Why was he getting such attention? Instead of congratulations, I usually got all sorts of questions—mostly from the guy who was there to scrub you down, removing a great deal of your skin in the process.

"Where do you live?" he would ask.

"Dar Mokri."

"Ah, so you belong in the medina?"

"Yes."

"Are you clean?"

"No. That's why I am at the public bath."

"Are you Muslim?"

"Yes."

"Are you circumcised?"

"What?"

"Are you circumcised? Let me see."

"No, you can't see."

"Do you know how to wash your private bits?"

"Umm, yes, I think so."

"We shall see."

The process at the hammam is fairly straightforward. You undress in the outer vestibule, leaving your underwear on, and then move into one of the three rooms that get increasingly hotter and steamier as you get closer to the source of water. This is a completely normal undertaking if you grew up going with your father or mother or older brother. But the protocols are many, and I knew none of them my first time around.

I also was not too keen to have a stranger throw me around the floor in my underwear, scrubbing every part of my body. I was especially concerned that he had been asking quite a bit about my bits. Then again, looking around, I saw very clean bathers receiving a delicious orange after their scrub-down, so I agreed to the scrubbing.

How best to describe this public cleansing? In short, I was amazed at the anatomical navigational skills of the man with the *kees*, the Moroccan version of a loofah. It's hard not to feel as though you should be a close friend with someone who is so intimately exploring your entire body with soap and a kees.

As he was scrubbing, he asked me how often I came to the hammam. I had the sense that he thought I was not as clean as I should be, but I answered, "Once a week."

"Are you married?"

"No. Why?"

"Because you don't come to the hammam very often."

"What does that have to do with being married?"

"How old are you?"

"I am young."

"You should be married."

"Why does that old man come to the hammam every day, and everyone smiles and congratulates him?"

"Do you sleep with girls when you are not married?"

I knew better than to answer that question.

I eyed him warily. Even the most uninformed travellers in Morocco knew sex before marriage was not something to brag about.

"Everyone congratulates the old man because he has sex with his wife every day, which is why he needs to come to the hammam. He needs to perform ablutions before prayer."

And there was my answer.

"You need to get married," he continued, "and then you would come to the hammam every day too, at least when you are still young."

I wasn't quite ready to be married, but I looked forward to the future, when I would be congratulated every time I went to take a bath.

SALADE NIÇOISE AND MY WAYWARD "WIFE"

The topic of me getting married began to overtake the daily gossip in the medina and supplanted the debate over the espionage theory. It was never clear to me how knowing the price of a carpet or teaching girls to type on a cardboard keyboard could possibly enhance the US intelligence network. I welcomed, for a time, the shift to marriage discussions.

The assumption that I was married, or should be, led to a series of complicated situations, and extracting myself from them became increasingly difficult. When the topic of marriage got too tiresome, I would leave the world of the medina and head to the New City, where one had the impression of being in Europe.

Every Wednesday I would meet up with a friend at a restaurant tucked away under the noisy bar a floor above. The dark room was filled with

Moroccan men, and we were the only foreigners I ever saw in the place. There were never any women, of course.

Drinking alcohol in the open was not legal, so men would gather in a café like this one that also sold beer and wine. It was forbidden to serve these sinful beverages where others could see and could place a curse on the offender. Men drank nonetheless, but always inside—never on the street terrace. In this particular bar-cum-café, a room downstairs served food and copious amounts of alcohol.

Our Wednesday ritual included a salade Niçoise and catching up with each other's news. We never had any problems until one night when we decided to take two American friends with us, who happened to be women.

We ordered the usual, which for me meant a disassembled salade Niçoise: no eggs and certainly no oily anchovies. Basically, I was left with a simple green salad without much on it. My order was tedious, and I'm not really sure why the waiter put up with me, but he didn't protest because I was paying for all the ingredients despite only taking a few. In any case, the night started out as it always did.

Soon enough, though, we started to get dirty looks. Then the comments started—just loud enough so we could hear them. We had clearly made a bad miscalculation in thinking that the presence of our friends would be tolerated because the two women were foreigners.

After glaring at us from across the room, the drunkest of a group of men got up and came staggering to our table. The abuse was immediate, and given the clenched fist and its proximity to my face, the possibility of physical violence was real. I was not eager to oblige, however, and the drunken man's goading failed to lure me into a fistfight.

In his final attempt to engage me, he looked at our female companions and shouted at the top of his lungs, "I made love to your wife in Zurich!"

Now, that is an insult of major proportions in any culture. I'm sure the whole room was expecting me to fly into a rage and throw a few punches. I suppose I would have been angrier if one of the women with us was, in fact, my wife—or if indeed I had been married at all—but neither was true.

By then, quite a few people were standing, waiting for the fight to start. My friend was making his escape with the women, which left me alone to deal with the drunk and his mob. After what seemed like an interminable amount of time, as my mind whirled, struggling to decide how to get out of the situation without fisticuffs, I stood and looked the man straight in the eye.

"That's great," I said. "So did I."

The guy looked as though he was going to explode. But then he burst out laughing, and we both joked about what a trollop my nonexistent wife was. I left without his fists ever landing a punch.

After my experience with Fatouma, one would think I had learned my lesson. What was I thinking, to appear with an unmarried woman in a café? My two worlds, ancient and modern, were colliding. I was failing in my attempt to move seamlessly between them. I was increasingly more comfortable in the ancient world of the medina, but apparently it was maktub that I would not live there much longer.

Casablanca and Beyond

NOT LIKE THE MOVIE

Fatouma had convinced the school administration that a scorned lover and a suspected CIA agent could not work in the same city of Fez. The suspected CIA agent had to go. When I was transferred to Casablanca, I suddenly found myself in a modern city with little comfort of the medina.

Casablanca was a city of enclaves left behind from the perceived glory of colonial days. I gave up on the idea of living in the old city of Casablanca. It was nothing like Fez and did not hold the same allure for me.

Still, Casablanca was a mix of worlds. My new neighborhood was dotted with Spanish colonials who had never considered Spain home and saw no reason to leave Morocco when the French and Spanish protectorates ended in the 1960s. An older Spanish couple who lived in the apartment next to my room insisted on speaking Spanish to me, even after I told them, in French, that I did not understand their language. They eventually gave up and accepted that the only common language we spoke was the monthly rent that was due.

My new position at a teacher training college in Casablanca presented a new set of challenges, expectations, and suspicions about my supposed intelligence background. The college was just a short walk from my apartment. Casa, as we called it for short, was a bustling metropolis, and the walk to school took me through a souk filled with all sorts of things being sold. But it felt more like walking through a small village than through a city.

I was saddened that I did not feel the same desire to blend in that I had felt in Fez.

One hawker caught my eye every day as I passed by: a man sitting on a blanket covered in human teeth. "Fifty cents!" he would call out. When I finally stopped to ask him what he was doing, he told me he was a dentist and the displayed teeth were evidence of his craft.

His only dental service was to pull teeth, so if I wanted a tooth pulled, I should lie down and he would put me in a headlock with his legs before pulling the offending tooth. He also performed circumcisions.

I declined.

JUST TELL ME WHERE IT IS

Casa certainly wasn't Fez, but it was filled with marvels of all sorts. French colonial architecture was just about everywhere, even abutting the souk where the dentist sitting on a blanket pulled teeth for fifty cents. Many wealthy merchants had moved to the city from Fez, seeking modern living and wealthier clients. But the transformation to a more French lifestyle, including the French language, posed a few problems for professors at the teacher training college.

Our first day of school took place on Throne Day, a celebration of King Hassan II's ascension to the throne in 1961. The king addressed the country without notes for a good seven hours whilst he twirled a beautiful gold pen, and we were required to listen, sitting assembled in the teachers' lounge.

To ensure that we were actually present for the speech, we were instructed to sign a guest book containing a list of all of our names written in Arabic script. My first big realization about life in Casablanca came when a colleague asked me to find her name on the list. She was Moroccan, but she couldn't read her own name in Arabic. Once I pointed out her name, she signed, sat down, and listened to a speech by her king—and understood not a word.

Language is more than the words that roll off the tongue. It shapes who you are and who others believe you are. The first words out of your mouth often shape the impression that sticks with your listener, despite any changes in your relationship. So it happened to me. Walking home after King Hassan's speech, I had a few letters to post but didn't know where the post office was. I stopped a young man on the street, and the conversation went like this, in Arabic.

"Excuse me, do you know where the post office is?"

"No, I'm sorry, I don't speak French."

"Oh, but do you know where the post office is?"

"No, I can't tell you because I don't speak French."

"But I am speaking Arabic to you."

"I want to help you, but I don't speak French."

"OK," I added hesitantly, "I know a little Arabic. If I ask you in Arabic, will you understand me?"

"Of course. I am Moroccan, and I speak Arabic."

"OK, here goes: Do you know where the post office is?"

"No, I'm sorry, I don't live around here."

He could see me but not hear me. To him, all foreigners spoke French. Apparently, he had never met a foreigner who could speak Arabic, so perhaps I was some sort of optical illusion that prevented him from hearing the Arabic words flowing from my mouth. My speaking the Moroccan dialect of Arabic surprised, delighted, and frustrated my interlocutors on a daily basis. I could be complemented and insulted in the same conversation.

Floating across time, as I had done in Fez, was more difficult in Casablanca. I could not separate linguistic worlds as I had done in the medina and the New City. Speaking English with my students also led me to a new yet unwanted profession: physician.

WHERE THERE IS NO DOCTOR

One day, after one of my students saw me speaking with the dentist sitting on the blanket covered in teeth, he jumped to the conclusion that I had a medical background. He arrived at this conclusion partly because he had also seen, on the floor of my apartment, a copy of a book the Peace Corps gave to all volunteers: *Where There Is No Doctor*, a type of survival guide that was useful when (you guessed it!) there was no doctor around.

I learned that my students were quite shy about sharing their ailments with me, yet they still wanted advice and they were too embarrassed to ask a parent or a doctor. Somehow, they thought that speaking in English about embarrassing situations was less embarrassing, so my unqualified physician visits were always conducted in English. I soon realized, when students began calling me "Doctor," that my casual advice was being taken too seriously.

My medical advice began innocently enough. Watching the amount of sugar young people were putting in their tea, I offered that there was too much sugar in my mint tea and I really needed to cut down. The next thing I knew, students were knocking on my door to ask whether I could speak to them confidentially about a medical problem. It didn't matter how many times I told them I was not a doctor; the transformation was already complete.

The male students were all living in dorms and left to their own devices. The concept of student services did not exist, so they relied on one another to solve most problems. Even though the students were in their twenties, they shared information as if they were just discovering the teen years.

My first patient arrived unannounced early one afternoon and began describing his symptoms. He had already followed the advice of his classmates, heating a knife over a flame and applying it to all his pressure points, which left numerous scars on his wrists, ankles, and neck. We consulted my medical journal. He was increasingly jaundiced and looked, according to page ninety nine, as though he may have hepatitis. My prognosis was that he needed to see a doctor.

In the dorms, word got around that I was a world-renowned surgeon specializing in all sorts of things, including anxiety caused by having sex before marriage. I thought back to my neighbor in Fez with the donkey, the condom, and the broom. I had a free supply of condoms the Peace Corps nurse had given me, and I suggested that the young men should use them if they knew how, but should leave the broom out of the operation. We also discussed the efficacy of other methods of birth control, such as women standing on their heads after sex.

It was hard not to laugh at their innocence at times, but there were also heartbreaking moments like when one young man broke down and cried because he felt so helpless not knowing why he felt sexually attracted to men. I could only hug him and tell him that he was a good person. Once he dried his eyes, he shared much more than I was ready to hear about his weekend sexual exploits in Marrakech. The AIDS epidemic was at its peak, and I tried to educate him the best I could about safe sex.

I felt, as these young people did, that there was no one else they could turn to—so I listened. I learned a lot about their lives, and realized that simply listening is often more helpful to a person than offering advice.

My life in Morocco was a circular voyage of repeating elements—including donkeys, marriage, languages, and the curse of Fatouma, over and over—with slight variations at each completion of the circle. Perhaps I never had the sense that I had learned something in its entirety, and so I repeated what may appear to be foolish mistakes.

Such was the case when two female friends from a past life travelled to Casa in search of the Rick's Café featured in the classic film *Casablanca*. They never found it.

ADAPTING TO MALE CHAUVINISM—MY OWN

With the curse of Fatouma and my nonexistent cheating wife in Zurich fresh in my mind, I was perhaps overly concerned about reputation—not my own, but that of my visiting female friends. My growing discomfort with public displays of affection between men and women—holding hands, greeting with a kiss on the cheeks, locking arms as we walked—played a part in how the adventure unfolded. My main concern was to avoid creating situations in which the two women faced aggression in the streets.

I wanted the visit to be fun, but I also wanted to make it clear that travelling in Morocco meant we had to adjust to local customs and expectations. I should have caught on earlier that the trip I had planned was not going to go well.

One friend warmed to the conversation of cross-cultural adaptation, while the other launched into a lecture pointing out that I had not been such a chauvinist when she visited me in Switzerland. In short, she stated that she had the right to do whatever she wanted regardless of what others thought. I didn't disagree with her, but I also knew that her first, European-like experience in Casablanca was not the same as what she would experience when we crossed the High Atlas Mountains and arrived in Zagora.

It didn't help the situation that I had students banging on my door late at night seeking medical advice. Immediately came the questions as to the identity of, and my relationship to, the women sleeping in my small apartment. If these young people, professing to be modern in their outlook, were asking about our relationship, then surely we would be questioned about it in the south of Morocco. I thought it reasonable that my travelling companions try to adapt on the trip, and it's not as though I ever asked them to don a burka. But they disagreed and said they would remain free of societal constraints.

The reality was that women were constantly harassed in Morocco. Foreign women travelling alone faced unwanted advances and many instant marriage proposals. Men travelling through the country, on the other hand, lived in a different world and didn't experience the same harassment or level of annoyance. Men could pretty much do whatever they wanted, without consequences, but women could not. It wasn't fair, of course, but that didn't make it any less true.

I should have planned an itinerary through the royal cities of Morocco, where tourists are ever present. Instead, I planned a wild adventure through the land of a thousand kasbahs.

MARRAKECH EXPRESS AND THE "REAL" MOROCCO

The trip to Marrakech was uneventful, and my two friends immediately felt at ease. They were delighted to meet people on the train who, they believed, were chatting amicably. The smiles of the other passengers, however, belied what they were saying among themselves.

Once it became clear that I needed a backstory, I began telling people that one woman was my sister and the other was my cousin. That calmed the waters until we entered the lands south of the High Atlas Mountains.

We boarded a bus, and I was immediately reminded of my voyage to Moulay Idriss on a souk bus. We fought for a bench seat for the three of us and headed onto the Route of a Thousand Kasbahs—a scenic road that winds its way through the desert and palm-strewn oases, past a stunning array of traditional citadels, part fort and part home. We travelled not only in distance but through time itself, slowly sliding back centuries.

The heat inside the bus was unbearable, but any attempt to open a window, even slightly, was met with howls of: "*Courant d'air! Courant d'air!* Close the window or we will all die of cold!"

Among Moroccans, a draft is the enemy. There is an obsession with the draft and catching one's death of a cold. On the bus, even people who did not speak French knew the phrase for "draft" and screamed it over and over, no matter how I protested that we could barely breathe—and that the air outside was not cold, but equally hot.

I thought the word for "breeze" would have sounded less dangerous than "draft," but I didn't know it—so we suffered, and sweated, in silence.

At times the bus would stop where there was no village to be seen, at a place bearing no indication of a reason to stop. Passengers would gather their things, exit the bus, remove bundles from the roof, and walk off into the distance. There was nothing for as far as the eye could see. The lonely travellers disappeared in the shimmering light and passed into another world of their own.

I was often tempted to walk off into the distance with them, simply to see where they were going. I didn't, of course, mostly because I had no idea when the next bus would come by or whether a fellow travel-ler would be welcome once they reached their destination. It seemed incredible that everyone else on the bus showed no interest as to where those people were going. Perhaps there was a *wadi*, a dry riverbed, at the bottom of a canyon in the fold of the heat waves. I was tempted to ask, but my ignorance would likely have been met with amusement, and my inquisitiveness with disdain.

I wanted my friends to see as much of Morocco as possible. They asked to see the "real" Morocco, but I never liked that phrase. My father used it often when trying to convince me to leave Switzerland and return to America. The more he said, "Switzerland is not the real world," the angrier I became. As he extolled the virtues of America, I heard in his voice a suddenly mythical place I had never heard him speak of before. I began to wonder what anyone considered "real."

Previously, I had only heard my father speak of Ireland with any cultural pride. Ireland was real, for some reason, but Switzerland was not. For my friends, the "real" Morocco must have meant a romantic place filled with handsome sheiks wandering the desert. Was the desert real, whereas the city was not? Perhaps the train to Marrakech was not real, but the bus rolling through the desert was.

I decided riding horses was real.

NO ROOM AT THE INN

My plan was to hire horses and ride through a magical place along our route, an absolutely beautiful trail running through orchards of almond and cherry trees in full bloom, after which the expedition would culminate in the gorge of Tinghir. Like much of my life in Morocco, however, the adventure—unplanned—would simply unfold.

We arrived in the town where we would start our equestrian trek. It was the height of tourist season, and even ordering a mint tea at the local café required reservations. We had none.

It was already very late at night when we walked up the path to the best hotel in the town. We requested a room and were greeted by the flummoxed receptionist and sniggering porters; we had no luggage and, hence, no tip for them.

"There are no rooms, sir," said the receptionist.

"Could you please phone another hotel in town for us?" I asked.

"There are no other hotels in this town, sir. This is the only one."

I had to break the news to my travelling companions and knew they would not take it well. The crying began early, and the one question I could not answer was repeated as we walked the rocky path down the hillside: *Where will we stay tonight?*

My faith in Moroccan hospitality was not shared by my travelling companions. Up the darkened path came a young Berber boy. It was late for him to be out, and he seemed to be simply wandering, as we were, in the dark. I asked if he knew of anyplace we might stay for the night. Without hesitating, he invited us to stay at his home.

I was thrilled.

My friends were horrified.

HOW TO BREAK THE CIGARETTE
HABIT IMMEDIATELY

We made our way down the path and entered his home, waking his parents. The boy's mother remained hidden but prepared tea and apologized for not having a proper meal for us. She offered bread and cheese, which we gobbled down. The young boy proudly introduced us to his older brother, who sat staring at us through sleepy eyes.

One of my friends was a smoker. She had done a good job of sneaking cigarettes when no one was looking, but it had been hours since her last one. I could see her eyeing the cigarettes in her bag. Despite my pleading, she pulled out the cigarettes and offered one to the sleepy host.

He looked sullenly at me and asked who these women were. I followed the script we had devised, telling him the woman holding the cigarette was my sister and the other was my cousin.

"Do you allow your sister to smoke?" he demanded.

"I have tried many times to get her to stop, but she refuses."

"Have you tried beating her?"

I tried changing the subject. "Please thank your mother for her kindness, and your father for welcoming us into your home. We had no other place to stay."

"Why don't you beat your sister and take those cigarettes away from her?"

I tried to reassure him. "She will not smoke that cigarette in your home."

"You are a weak brother."

I had nothing left to try, and simply said, "I think it is best we go to sleep."

THE DONKEYS AND THE BOTTLE OF COLOGNE

In the morning the boy's mother prepared a simple breakfast, after which we gathered our things and prepared to leave. My smoking faux-sister had given me a gift of cologne at the beginning of the trip. Having nothing to offer the family to show our appreciation for their hospitality, I presented the bottle of cologne, which was well received.

The regifting set my travelling companion on a tirade of public indignation, spitting out that the cologne had cost fifty dollars and was now wasted on people who would not appreciate its value. I pointed out that the family had opened their home to perfect strangers in the middle of the night. They fed us, gave us a place to sleep, and prepared breakfast for us without asking for anything in return.

The violence-prone brother eyed this exchange with a level of disgust and implied that he understood what was communicated despite not speaking our language.

My mood soured.

I was disappointed in my friend and thought her ungracious. True, the cologne was her gift to me, and perhaps I should have offered money instead. But I thought that would be insulting, a cheapening of their hospitality. My friend's dismissal of this hospitality angered me, and I imagined that few tourists would have had the experience we just had. It meant little to her.

Our next challenge was to find horses to rent so we could make our way up to the gorge. There were no horses to be had, but we managed to find two donkeys accompanied by a gaggle of teenage boys. The path we followed was bordered on both sides by irrigation ditches flowing with life-giving water. But my idyllic vision of travelling on horseback through an oasis of fragrant, flowering fruit trees was marred by the stench of the cologne bottle being regifted. The donkeys added their particular smell to our less-than-perfect outing, as did the drooling gaggle of horny teenage boys following after my pouting companions.

Disappointment, however, was the least of our problems.

After an hour on the donkeys, it was clear that hiking would be more comfortable than sitting astride. One of the boys took advantage of a vacated donkey, taking a run at him, launching himself upward, and spinning in midair before landing squarely on the donkey as if he had been sitting there all along. It was an impressive athletic feat, and my friends thought they would give it a try. The more athletic of the two easily made the landing, and the boys gave their applause. Not so with my other friend, the smoker.

The maneuver started out well enough. My "sister" began her run slowly but gathered speed as she neared the donkey. Her trajectory seemed a bit off, but I thought she would correct in midair as she twisted her body to land. The combination of gravity and lack of leg strength precluded any height to her launch, however, and her body simply turned whilst still on the ground before squarely slamming into the hapless donkey. Her backside met its flank, propelling our four-legged friend into flight instead of her.

The sight of a donkey's flight, in slow motion, is something to behold. As the poor creature gained an altitude previously unknown to it, the boys' jaws moved in the opposite direction, finding lower and lower depths. Their mouths remained open until the shock subsided and we all had to spring into action. The donkey had landed upside down in the irrigation ditch and was drowning.

We set about lifting the donkey out of the ditch. The flailing hooves proved to be an additional challenge, but we did manage to right the poor guy very quickly. Now it was the boys, not the donkey, who could not breathe, as they rolled in the dirt laughing so hard that it seemed they would pass out.

I tried not to laugh along with them, but I lost the battle and did no more to stifle the keening laugh of a banshee—a true laughing jag that would not subside. My "sister" forged ahead alone and did not speak to me for the next four hours.

As the day wore on, it was clear that what was meant to be a morning outing had turned into a ten-hour trek, with darkness approaching. The boys had begun to annoy the women more directly, first trying to pinch their behinds but eventually finding themselves unable to resist a fondle of the rear end that could take down a donkey with one sway.

Their unwanted touches turned increasingly aggressive, and I began to see the ten boys in a more ominous light. On the narrow path, I used my body to block the boys' access to their intended targets, both of whom were riding the donkeys. For a few more hours, it was a game of cat and mouse, with donkeys joining the fray.

We reached the gorge as the sky darkened. The tourist buses were filling back up with contented travellers who had made our ten-hour trek in just an hour. We could not see the gorge through the plumes of diesel exhaust, but I saw the busses as a way to escape the menacing boys, who were now circling the two women like an eager swarm of gnats.

I convinced one bus driver that my friends were in danger and that we had no way to get back to the village. He agreed to take the women, but he would not take me. The two women boarded the bus, and I was left standing there with ten frustrated teenage boys.

Before the women boarded the bus, we agreed that the trip was over and it was best to return to Marrakech the following morning. The driver promised to arrange a room in the village, and the bus disappeared down the mountain. I told my travelling companions to go to the room, however unpleasant it might be, and lock the door. Then the donkeys, the boys, and I set off down the path in the dark.

The questions began immediately. "Why did you let us pinch the girls?"

"I didn't let you! You did it without permission, and they were very angry."

"Where are their husbands?"

"They are not married."

"You are not a real man."

"Why do you say that?"

"You did not protect the honor of your sister and cousin."

"There are too many of you trying to touch them."

"You are not going to make it back to the village tonight," they warned. "We are going to beat you." We walked in silence for a few minutes, and a few boys began picking up stones.

My mind raced as I thought how best to fend off an attack, and it occurred to me that honesty is not always the best weapon. "In truth, the girls are not my sister and cousin," I confessed.

"Who are they?"

"They are some foreign girls I found on the bus."

"Did you have sex with them all night long?"

"Of course I did."

"Ah, so you *are* a real man!"

The stones dropped to the ground. The boys wanted nothing now save for me to regale them with my sexual exploits.

I had avoided a beating but had also inadvertently created a vision of sexual exploration in the minds of roaming teenagers, who now had high hopes of the rewards awaiting them upon our return. The boys were drooling in anticipation of their lost virginity.

After a long hike back to the village, I awoke the women and told them we needed to flee immediately. We jumped into the first bus with an open door and escaped back to the real world of Marrakech.

My last vision of the village was the smashed bottle of regifted cologne on the side of the road.

MARRIAGE, SPIES, AND THE MUSLIM BROTHERHOOD

The desire, sometimes by complete strangers, to marry me off was a theme that followed me for years. I increasingly viewed invitations for a couscous lunch with suspicion but still succumbed to their lure. When Mohammed, a student celebrating his graduation from English language summer school in Rabat, the capital city, invited me for couscous at his home in Salé, I accepted.

Salé sat across the Bou Regreg River and was long a haven for pirates, at least since the seventeenth century. Vague concerns about pirates kidnapping me and marrying me off to one of their daughters crossed my mind, but visions of a mountain of steaming couscous solidified my decision to accept the invitation.

Mohammed's home was in the old city of Salé, a much smaller version of Fes Al Bali, made up of many hidden alleys no wider than your shoulders. Mohammed had given me the address of his home, but it was of little use. I needed a guide to find it.

Mohammed was waiting for me outside the medina, and we walked the short distance to his home. Upon entering the house, I encountered the smell of the couscous wafting toward us, drawing me farther into the large salon. I had expected to see only the male members of his family, but a young lady was there, too, in a beautiful caftan, sitting in the center of the room and surrounded by a group of very serious-looking older men.

"Have you performed your ablutions?" said the eldest among them.

"Why, is it prayer time already?" I asked.

"No, for the ceremony."

"Is there a couscous ceremony?"

Mohammed's face grew red and there was an uncomfortable stirring in the room. I thought perhaps we were in the wrong house, but the elder gentleman continued. "Are you not ready to be married?"

"I don't understand what is happening."

"Mohammed told us that you had seen his sister at school and wanted to marry her."

"I thought we were having couscous."

"You can discuss your fascination with couscous with your new wife, once you are married and have a son."

"Are we having the couscous before that happens?"

My intended removed herself from the room, and the discussion turned to my trousers—more particularly, the status beneath my trousers regarding circumcision.

I calmly explained that I was a fully compliant Muslim but I had no intention of being engaged today. Mohammed had invited me to have lunch in celebration of his graduation from the English course. Mohammed was now able to say, in English, "Come to my house for couscous on Friday," but apparently not much more.

The marriage contract was quietly put away, and the couscous arrived.

The eldest gentleman, Abu Karim—Mohammed's grandfather—was kind and generous of spirit. He asked me to walk with him so we could discuss important matters in private. As we strolled through the labyrinth of the medina, he gently took my hands away from my back where I had clasped them. He instructed me never to hold my hands in that manner, or Satan would surreptitiously place evil there and I, unwittingly inhaling it, would be lost forever in a sea of wickedness.

We continued deeper and deeper into the medina, and I soon realized that I would never be able to find my way out of the labyrinth without him. Then we entered an impossibly tapered alley with no egress. The last door on the right required a deep bending of the entire body to traverse its threshold.

After navigating narrow stairs in the dark, I found, sitting in a circle on the floor, a group of men immaculately dressed in white djellabas. Abu Karim introduced me, asked me to recite a verse from the Quran, and explained that I was the new Muslim Brotherhood ambassador to the United States.

I was in the bowels of an underground mosque and the seat of the banned Muslim Brotherhood, a political force opposed to all forms of government aside from a reestablished caliphate. The organization's leaders were considered to be the architects of the assassination of Egyptian president Anwar Sadat just a few years earlier, so my new membership automatically entitled me to the potential of a long prison sentence in the center of the Sahara Desert, in the south of Morocco. Hamas, an offshoot of the Muslim Brotherhood, would take over Gaza years later and would touch my life in an unexpected way.

For the moment, however, I was just trying to figure out how to escape the ambassadorial role. If I was found sitting there with my host by the Moroccan secret police, my future travels would take a very different path.

I supposed couscous and the curse of Fatouma had led me to this moment. I had evaded marriage twice, but now I was faced with the prospect of a life of dark cells and waterboarding—not to confuse these two major life events.

I spent the day laying out the plans for my ambassadorial appointment. Then I bid my brothers goodbye, promising Abu Karim I would never walk with my hands behind my back, and walked out of the medina. I boarded a plane for Boston the next day.

Cambridge

The Somewhat Worthless Diploma

Where There Still Is No Doctor

Street Urchin Arabic and a Wise Mentor

The Butcher of Harvard

Marry Me, Blue Eyes

THE SOMEWHAT WORTHLESS DIPLOMA

On the flight from Casablanca to America, fleeing the pirates and the Muslim Brotherhood of Salé, a young man by the name of Aziz approached me and proudly showed me his diploma from an English language summer school. Brandishing his newly acquired academic credentials, Aziz informed me that he was going to study alongside me at Harvard.

Until very recently—the previous day, in fact—I had been the director of the Peace Corps pre-service training program for newly arrived volunteers in Morocco. Volunteers would spend the summer learning about Morocco, the Arabic language, and cross-cultural skills, before embarking on their assignment. Part of the training for teachers of English included teaching young Moroccan high school students in a three-week summer course, after which we held a graduation ceremony. I signed all the diplomas, which is how I know that the summer English course would not have gained Aziz entry into any American university.

The flight from Casablanca was long, so I had plenty of time to explain the true worth of the diploma and the unimpressive weight of my signature. Aziz was disappointed but undeterred. As he was actually going to Cambridge, I suggested that we try to find one another the following week in Harvard Square. Lacking any contact details, we set Au Bon Pain, next to the Harvard Student Union, as our meeting point.

When I had first arrived in Cambridge after returning from previous stints in Morocco, I immediately sought out the comfort of a Middle Eastern café. I found one with mediocre mint tea on Brattle Street, but it was the sounds of Moroccan Arabic on the terrace of Au Bon Pain in Harvard Square that caught my interest. Before the days of mobile phones, friends living on a student budget found one another by sitting in common spaces and at familiar places, waiting for a gathering to form, and the terrace of Au Bon Pain was just such a place. A gathering of Arabic speakers from around the world gathered there almost every evening.

After our first meeting at Au Bon Pain, Aziz quickly found other Moroccans and a place to stay. I was busy settling into my graduate student housing and bought a cheap landline phone. The phone was a marvel to me. In the old city of Fez, there was a seven-year waiting list for a landline. After living as a student in Switzerland and as a Peace Corps volunteer in Morocco, it had been ten years since I'd had one.

I gave Aziz my number and told him to phone me whenever he wanted to get together. His first call did not go over all that well. He spoke to me plaintively, asking why I would not answer him. Over and over again he shouted into his phone, asking why I would pick up but not speak to him, and insulting me for being so rude.

"Is this some kind of American joke?" he shouted.

He was talking to my answering machine.

Aziz and I connected later that day at Au Bon Pain. Agreeing that the answering machine was the culprit in this episode, we remained fast friends.

WHERE THERE STILL IS NO DOCTOR

Being accepted to Harvard was a great first step, but I quickly learned that there was an application process to be accepted into specific courses. As a Peace Corps volunteer, I had moved from teaching English in a typing class to designing courses at a teacher training college to directing the pre-service training of other Peace Corps volunteers. I wanted to build on that experience, so I chose a degree in administration, planning, and social policy. I did not plan to continue my profession as a well-meaning but utterly clueless physician stand-in, relying on my worn-out copy of *Where There Is No Doctor*.

To pay for my studies I took on a number of jobs, including that of a research assistant. Some people plan their entire life's route and pursue the envisioned path with determination. On the contrary, my path continued to unfold before me step-by-step, and I chose simply to follow it with the delight of an explorer. Still, there were regions that I had no vision of exploring, and being a physician's assistant was one. Despite my conviction, the Harvard student health clinic, located above the terrace of Au Bon Pain, is where I had my first job as a translator.

As a research assistant, I worked with visiting dignitaries from places like Egypt, Pakistan, and Yemen. One visiting scholar from Yemen was experiencing, on his first trip to America, severe hemorrhoid pain. I was the only Arabic speaker he could find, so could I please let the project director know that he needed to see a doctor?

Unlike my students in Casablanca, whom I knew very well and who asked me delicate questions in their stilted English, the scholar spoke no English at all. But this difference aside, it remains a mystery why I was yet again discussing—with recently minted acquaintances, in Arabic but never in English—the nether regions of the human body.

I had fallen back into the role of Doctor Without Any Personal Borders.

My program director instructed me to take time away from my studies briefly to bring the afflicted soul to a properly licensed physician at the student health clinic and remain there to translate for him. Stripping down in the doctor's office, the visiting Yemeni scholar did not seem to be embarrassed and showed no regard for my own dignity.

To my relief, though, the doctor informed me that I would not be required to stay for the examination. He knew where to find the offending swell.

STREET URCHIN ARABIC AND A WISE MENTOR

I realized that it was time to formally study Arabic, so I tried to enroll in a course called Modern Standard Arabic. The course wouldn't fit into my schedule, so the only alternative was to enroll in a course in Quranic Arabic.

The Quran is sacred, and the language in it remains unchanged throughout its history. There are no "versions" of the Quran; translations are merely educational tools to understand the Quran. No one actually speaks the language of the Quran in everyday conversation. It is very formal and considered the highest, most revered form of Arabic. And my studies in Quranic Arabic revealed that I had the vocabulary and manner of a street merchant, not a learned scholar.

My research assistant assignment introduced me to one of the most remarkable of men, Professor Russ Davis. During the week, we designed relational databases for the national ministries of education, and on weekends, we spent much time laughing and drinking tea—and there were no more visits to the Harvard student health clinic.

Russ asked me to spend time with Yemenis from all regions of the country and take them to places around Cambridge and Boston that they had never seen. Some of these places I had never seen either, but mostly I focused on outings that would be unfamiliar to them, like ice skating. I was touched when Russ wrote an evaluation stating that I accepted all assignments without rancor.

Russ was unlike other professors I encountered at Harvard. Through him, I had the incredible experience of writing the relational database manual, in English and Arabic, for visiting ministry officials to use when they returned home. The manual was published by Harvard and sold for ten dollars a copy. More important, the cover included my name as an author, a practice that was unheard of and not appreciated by other professors at Harvard.

I remained silent in the elevator one day, just as I had quietly listened in the darkness of Karim's carpet emporium in Fez, as two tenured professors—not knowing or caring who I was—lambasted Russ for allowing a graduate student's name to appear on one of his published works. But Russ, who was a fully tenured professor, insisted: all his students who had contributed to a paper would have their names listed in alphabetical order on the title page. So even though I was a lowly graduate student, there was my name printed on a publication.

Russ profoundly influenced my career path when he sat me down one day for a chat. Others at Harvard were encouraging me to stay and pursue a doctorate. I had applied for a graduate position that would have allowed me to earn money as I completed my coursework. But Russ told me that he thought I could accomplish much more by going back out into the world and doing good work rather than spending time on earning a PhD.

I didn't understand it at the time, but Russ was right, of course. I mourned his death shortly after finishing my graduate work. The main reason I would have stayed was to work with Russ and have him serve as my doctoral advisor.

Perhaps it was maktub and he knew what was written.

THE BUTCHER OF HARVARD

At another unplanned gathering at Au Bon Pain, I learned about a registered club for Muslims at the university: the Harvard Muslim Society. The club was in need of a volunteer imam to lead Friday prayers, and I was volunteered against my will. My brothers from Malaysia appreciated not only my ability to lead prayers in Arabic, but also my willingness to help cover with bedsheets the portraits of Harvard luminaries adorning the walls of our makeshift mosque. The congregation did not want the images of Harvard graduates leering down at us as we prayed.

I took on other duties as well, such as securing a sheep to slaughter for Eid celebrations. When the holiday arrived, we travelled in a caravan to a nearby farm that was known for celebrating with the Muslim community. We were all students living in tiny rooms that could not accommodate large gatherings, so celebrating at the farm was our best option.

The farmer accepted with a bemused look on his face all the various customs, clothing, languages, and requests coming from people with origins all around the world. When I explained to the farmer that we would encircle the room with salt to keep evil spirits from entering, however, he controlled his urge to run but passed the responsibility of the sacrifice (along with the knife) to me.

I had not planned on carrying out the sacrifice myself, but the farmer had been scared off by the thought of evil spirits invading his farm and was nowhere to be found. My Muslim brothers and sisters stood watching and waiting. No one else would carry out the sacrifice. Thus, through poor translations of a series of languages, I became known as the "Butcher of Harvard."

I tried to explain that it was not the ideal way of expressing my role in the holiday, but it was no use.

MARRY ME, BLUE EYES

As my reputation as the Muslim Butcher of Harvard grew, I thought it best to find a new mosque. The Islamic Center of New England was in an industrial area of Quincy, Massachusetts, and had a proper imam from Egypt who welcomed me into the community and never asked about the rumors swirling around Boston—rumors about a Muslim from the Old World who had a violent reputation at Harvard. The imam asked me to become a member of the mosque. Sheep were not a topic of conversation, but marriage was.

The office secretary told me that she needed to meet with me later in the week to sort out the paperwork for membership in the Islamic Center. We met over coffee on the terrace of Au Bon Pain, and she laid out her plan.

"You are a good Muslim," she said.

"Oh," I replied. "Thank you."

"You have blue eyes."

"Umm, yes."

"You are not married."

"No. Do you have the membership paperwork?"

"No. The paperwork I am interested in involves a marriage contract."

"How's that?"

"I was married. Now I'm divorced, and I have three children. I think you love children and you have blue eyes and you want to marry me."

I glanced down at the contract in question, which she had taken the liberty of filling out.

My coffee, and my blood, went cold.

Her name was Fatouma.

Fez, Kenitra, and (Eventually) Imilchil

Saïd the Mendacious

The Girl from Tangiers

What Happens in the Men's Room Stays in the Men's Room

The Endless Viewing of Photo Albums

Marriage Festival at Imilchil

SAÏD THE MENDACIOUS

In the year 1987, or 1408, my graduate work was complete, and I prepared for my return to Morocco and to the medina of Fez, where I could slide back to simpler times. But I also had an important stop to make upon my arrival, in Rabat.

The night before my departure from America, Aziz, whom I had met on the plane and befriended in Cambridge, met me at Au Bon Pain with a child's bicycle and a ten-pound bag of candy. He asked me to take the bicycle and candy to his little brother in Rabat. He also told me that I was invited to his father's home for couscous. I took the candy but regrettably had to leave the bicycle behind.

When I arrived in Casablanca, there was a crowd of people greeting their family members. No one came forward to greet me, despite Aziz having assured me that his father and brother would be there. At last, when the arrivals hall was nearly empty, I noticed two men standing alone and preparing to leave. The younger of the two held a Polaroid photo of me that Aziz had taken at a Halloween party in Cambridge. I was dressed as a Touareg Bedouin—a Muslim nomadic people of North Africa and the Sahel region of the Sahara Desert—with my face completely covered in a blue turban and face veil. Aziz had sent the photo to his brother, Abdelillah, thinking I would be easily recognizable at the airport upon arrival because I had blue eyes.

The ride from Casablanca to Rabat lasted two hours, and the conversation focused on clarifying that I had not called Aziz's other brother, Saïd, a hopeless liar. I had never met Aziz's brother Saïd, but I had met another Saïd, who was the greatest liar I had ever encountered (up to that point in my life). Saïd the Prevaricator, mendacious in all unimportant things, frequented the terrace of Au Bon Pain, and no tall tale was beyond the pale.

My vision of him, standing in Harvard Square, resplendent in a polkadot shirt mismatched with chalk-striped trousers and grease-covered shoes, remains to this day.

Saïd: "Aziz, tell this guy to give me a hundred dollars."

Aziz: "He speaks Arabic."

Saïd: "Tell him my father just flew in from Paris on the Concorde and gave me these latest fashion clothes and a check for ten thousand dollars, but I can't cash it until tomorrow."

Aziz: "He speaks Arabic."

Saïd: "Ask him if he likes clothes from Paris. If he does, tell him he can see more of my gifts tomorrow, but tonight I need a hundred dollars because I don't have any money."

Aziz: "He speaks Arabic and understands everything you are saying."

Saïd: "Tell him my father just got on the Concorde and flew to Tokyo for a meeting."

I gave Saïd ten dollars so he could eat that night. The next time I saw him, he was working as a sous-chef at Au Bon Pain, overseeing the burning of croissants. His employment there lasted all of three hours. In his interview, he had told the manager that he was a pastry chef in Paris and had just moved to America. When the manager realized that he was not telling the truth, he handed him a broom and told him to clean all the flour he had spilled on the floor. Saïd, in his version of a resignation letter, turned up all the ovens to 500 degrees and left the restaurant. The fire department wasn't able to save any of the croissants.

THE GIRL FROM TANGIERS

When I finally convinced Aziz's father (Mohammed) that I was not calling his son (Saïd) a liar, my perceived insult was quickly forgotten. We caught up on other news in the car and finally arrived at the family's home just in time for lunch. The topic of marriage arose as quickly as the steam coming off couscous. In fact, a call from Aziz in America prevented my spoon from digging in for a first bite.

"It is time for you to get married," he insisted.

"Can I finish the couscous first?" I asked.

"Don't you want to get married?"

"I do, but I don't know any girls."

"There is a girl in my family, a girl from Tangiers. I will talk to my mother."

It wasn't clear to me why Aziz was so vague about the girl from Tangiers. I didn't feel I could ask anyone in the room if they knew of a girl from Tangiers who wanted to get married. I tried to press Aziz for more information but he hung up the phone.

"Hello? Hello? Hello?"

I returned to the couscous, but my strength had left me. Morsels of meat fell, by the grace of Allah, to my section of the plate, but they remained there, staring at the hapless bachelor.

My mind drifted to the girl from Tangiers. Who was she? Was she a cousin? Why did she live in Tangiers? Where was Aziz's mother? I thought the mother in a family arranged marriages. Was I supposed to ask Aziz's father about the girl from Tangiers? I was too embarrassed to ask.

No one in the room acknowledged the telephone call, and conversation returned to a debate over the biggest lie Saïd the Mendacious ever told. Despite sharing my plan to return to Fez the following morning, I soon learned that a string of invitations awaited me. Ignoring my own plans entirely, the family laid out a proposal and agreed to fit in a trip to Fez along the way.

Abdelillah looked down at my feet and announced that I was badly in need of a new pair of babouche, and that he knew a guy in the Fez medina. He quipped that I surely had no bargaining skills whatsoever, so he would take care of all the shopping we might do. But when I introduced him to my glue-sotted cobbler friends, he was sorely disappointed and, unable to show off his bargaining skills, became sullen.

It seemed I was not who he thought I was. He found it odd that I knew cobblers sitting in an obscure hole-in-the-wall factory in the medina. Aziz had told him that I had been to Morocco, but clearly there was more to the story. Abdelillah made it his goal of the trip to find out what lay beneath the surface. He was still carrying the photo of me dressed as a Touareg, but he now realized that he did not have all that much information.

Meanwhile, I had no idea if Aziz had spoken to his brother about introducing me to the mysterious girl from Tangiers, so we were both at a disadvantage. Even so, when my cobbler friends offered Abdelillah a free pair of babouche, it was the beginning of a great friendship. But that friendship was not yet at the point where I could confide in him that Aziz was trying to broker my marriage.

WHAT HAPPENS IN THE MEN'S ROOM STAYS IN THE MEN'S ROOM

In the medina, time stands still for some. For others, it ages them before their time. A year had passed since I had left Fez, but I found friends sitting in the exact spot I had left them, arguing the same points their fathers had argued before them.

Politics were discussed in whispers, and knowing looks shared in silence, as the portrait of King Hassan looked down from every shop wall. The country was not calm. The young were restless again, and political dissidents, real or perceived, were disappearing in the night. I thought of my proposed marriage to the granddaughter of Abu Karim and the expectation that I would be an ambassador for the Muslim Brotherhood. I had declined to mention my secret ambassadorial position to anyone.

Our shopping and bargaining in the medina was interrupted by my need to work, and Abdelillah was left to his own devices. I had returned to Morocco to speak at a conference of teachers. Following my decision not to pursue a doctorate at Harvard, I had entered the world of consultancy.

Lining up work as a consultant required an entrepreneurial spirit. A friend once commented that the work of a consultant is not a career—it's a careen. Family members were always asking questions like "How do you just find a job in Africa?" and "Why don't you settle down?" But to me, it all seemed normal. Life was an adventure. I think Russ Davis saw that in me. He envisioned an academic path that involved sitting in a dusty room, staring at a computer screen, and knew that it wasn't for me.

My presentation in Fez, to one hundred assembled Peace Corps teachers, was interrupted by the regional security officer (RSO) from the American embassy. His intention was to give the group an update on the security situation in the country and to tell us that all was well. The room erupted. From there on, every sentence he uttered was challenged.

Pierre, the most vocal of the group, shouted out that the information being presented was absolute rubbish. "How can you know anything?" he demanded. "You don't speak Arabic!"

"I travel the country and have firsthand knowledge," replied the RSO.

"Your car has diplomatic plates on it, and everyone runs when they see you."

"There have been no arrests, and the situation is calm."

Pierre begged to differ. "My Moroccan brother was arrested last night, and we don't know where he was taken." The vitriol continued for an hour, with respite coming only at the coffee break.

In the men's room, I took advantage of an empty stall and was still there, pondering, when the RSO and two other embassy officials entered the bathroom to vent their frustration at how the security briefing was being received. The creativity of the insults they flung at the teachers was admirable. They discussed how to turn the meeting around and convince the teachers that the embassy had inside information about the security situation.

I considered whether it was better to hide and continue to listen, or to expose my presence. Choosing the latter, I washed my hands as the three embassy officials stared and considered the implications for the rest of their briefing.

We have all spoken in anger. We have all shared our inner thoughts aloud when we believed we were alone. As I left, I said, "Gentlemen, you had a private conversation in the men's room. It won't be part of any questions I have during the rest of your security briefing."

Oddly, my lack of anger, when they believed I should have been angry with them, was not entirely perceived as disinterest. They knew that information is valuable, whether it is used immediately or saved for a later date. Years later, when the RSO and I crossed paths in Romania, he reminded me of that parting comment. The narrative that I was a covert agent for the CIA continued to follow me, transforming from what I perceived as an amusing canard to a more serious view (however incorrect) of me and my work.

There are moments in life that seem trivial but in fact shape our paths. My respect for their privacy was one of those moments that repeated itself a number of times in my career.

THE ENDLESS VIEWING OF PHOTO ALBUMS

After the conference, Abdelillah and I continued our travels, arriving in the city of Kenitra just in time for a couscous lunch with his family. Introductions were made, although I was just as confused about the various relationships as I was before they were made. I noticed one woman from Kenitra who sat quietly in the other room, having couscous with undetermined relatives. Abdelillah's uncle introduced her as his daughter. Nadia and I did not speak at the lunch, and I was so focused on finding the girl from Tangiers that I didn't consider that Nadia, from Kenitra, was anyone but a cousin who liked couscous as much as I did.

Ever since my telephone call with Aziz, there had been no mention of the girl from Tangiers, nor had I broached the subject. There were no marriage interviews that day, however, and the train ride back to Rabat was short and sleepy.

Couscous is not a light meal, and it's a mistake not to schedule time for digestion. The gentle rocking of the train put me into a deep, dream -saturated sleep. Fatouma reared her monstrous head, threatening to expose my deep cover as an ambassador for the Muslim Brotherhood and my covert CIA operations in the men's room of the teacher conference. Sadly, in my dream, the girl from Tangiers never came up.

A major pastime for Moroccan families is presenting a stack of family photo albums to honored guests. So it happened that evening. In one of the many stacks sat a photo of Nadia, the young woman I had seen in

Kenitra. But as the photo was not of the girl from Tangiers, I didn't think too much more about it.

I was still trying to figure out the relationships among the parade of people continuously flowing through the house when the phone rang. Aziz was on the other end of the line, asking if I still wanted to get married.

I told him that I did, but whilst I considered myself adventurous, I still wanted to see the person whom I was supposed to marry. Aziz said he would speak to his mother and hung up. I was still looking at the photo albums after the rest of the family had gone to bed. In one of the photos sat a young Nadia with a caption written on the back. "Nadia, daughter of Mohammed." The mystery grew. At lunch, Nadia was introduced to me as the daughter of the uncle from Kenitra, but here she clearly was identified as the daughter of Mohammed, which would make her Aziz's sister. And still the question remained: Who in the world was the girl from Tangiers?

The word of my possible marriage soon spread throughout Morocco.

MARRIAGE FESTIVAL AT IMILCHIL

Many Moroccan marriages are arranged after young people see one another at the weddings of family members. Berber tribes from across the mountainous region gather once a year at a wedding festival, where they arrange meetings of young men and women, agree on a future marriage, and then return to the following year's festival for the next round of weddings. The courtships take place entirely at these massive public festivals complete with young people who are both excited and terrified. Coarse hair tents, slung low to the ground, are populated with the betrothed, musicians, tourists, and sheep. Like the sometimes-hapless brides and grooms, the sheep are led to slaughter. The newlyweds may indeed have a happy life, but that remains unknown.

I was invited to attend a wedding festival in Imilchil, a town high in the Atlas Mountains. Visions of Fatouma jumping out from behind a tent, having me tied up and married before I could object, weighed heavily on my mind, but I decided to stiffen my spine and agreed to go to the festival. My habit of not putting too much effort into a plan was firmly established by this point, so I headed off with friends on a crowded souk bus to the nearest town in the mountains. From there, we planned to hitchhike the rest of the way.

You will remember I also had a bad habit of eating roasted peanuts from street vendors? Well, this time I wound up taking an unwelcome travel companion along for the ride: dysentery. After I managed to grab the steering wheel and force the bus to veer off the road a fourth time for a visit to the nearest bush, my intestines slept and so did I.

We finally arrived at the base of the mountains as the sun set.

Hitchhiking in the mountains is more a case of flagging down a vehicle rather than passively waiting with your thumb out. When a lumbering dump truck stopped to pick us up and the driver said he was heading to a wedding, we were thrilled with our luck. We congratulated ourselves on securing a ride all the way to the Imilchil wedding festival and settled in to a five-hour bumpy ride up the rocky path that most would not even call a road.

When we stopped outside a small house nestled into the side of the mountain, we were greeted with young children screaming, "Nassareni!"— implying that the Nazarenes had arrived. For some reason, it was assumed that any foreigner was from the village of Nazareth in the Holy Land. The driver explained to the growing crowd that ours was a group of strange Nazarenes who could speak Arabic but not Berber, so therefore it was best to insult them in the local language. The driver also invited us in for the wedding. The only problem was, he had not taken us to Imilchil but rather to his cousin's wedding.

The women in our group disappeared into the house and were not seen again until the next morning. We men were seated on the stairs that led to the bedroom of the groom to await the results of the couple coupling. The musicians played throughout the night, and the rest of the men danced, drank mint tea, ate cookies, and looked up to the balcony in anticipation of the groom emerging triumphant.

I thought of the poor couple trying to concentrate on the task at hand and sensed that the whole affair was taking too long. As the music began to die down, the father of the groom extolled them to play louder in order to drown out any ecstasy occurring above. The groom eventually did emerge, looking as if he had been in a car accident. I never saw the bride, but another round of mint tea and cookies was served, and the dancing continued until we all fell asleep on the stairs.

In the morning, we learned that we were not even on the beaten path to Imilchil, but we agreed that we should not feel defeated—at least we had attended a wedding. A few hours later, the driver let us know that his cousin would be leaving with his truck, and we were welcome to jump in. He failed to mention the other guests in the truck with us for the eight-hour drive up the mountain: sheep.

The upside of travelling with twenty sheep in a truck is that there was no possibility of any prospective bride showing interest in me once I arrived at Imilchil. Arriving exhausted, dirty, smelly, and single was all I could offer, and no young maidens came forward.

All the boys and girls at the festival were bright-eyed with rosy cheeks and great hopes. But it seemed there were forces working against us having an enjoyable time at Imilchil. Once again there were accusations regarding our wretchedness for travelling with women who were not our sisters, cousins, or lawfully wedded wives. Had we been ignorant tourists, we may have received a warmer welcome. The fact that we all spoke Arabic made us suspicious rather than a delightful oddity. In short, we should have known better.

I found another sheep-filled truck and headed back down the mountain, still a single man.

Mauritania

SAND AND TEA FOR THREE

I left the next day for an assignment in Mauritania, with no further discussion of marriage in Morocco. My plan was to be back in Morocco in a few months. I was already growing weary of the life of a consultant. Always on the road, I found it hard to develop any lasting friendships. I thought ahead to my future with a wife and beautiful children whom I would hug and kiss and whisper that I loved them, as my father had always told me that was the secret to raising children.

Windblown sand, polished through millennia, resembles talcum powder. It lodges in parts of the body previously unexplored. My first night in Nouakchott, the capital of Mauritania, I brushed my teeth seventeen times throughout the wee hours. I made the mistake of leaving clothes exposed to the dust storm that found its way inside the house. The dust was everywhere. I would never again wear the orange wool sweater—which previously had been natural-colored—that I'd left lying on the dining room table of the empty US embassy guesthouse where I was housed.

In the morning, a rumbling of the house was caused by the plow passing by my window as it cleared the road of the sand, forming a massive dune that blocked traffic. There was a smell in the air that reminds me to this day, forty years later, of Mauritania. It was a smell completely unfamiliar to me.

My meeting at the Mauritania Ministry of Education began with tea being served. I slowly sipped my mint tea, savoring the aroma and trying not to dwell on the smell that continuously assaulted me that morning. The young man serving the tea shifted uncomfortably as he stood in front of me with a teapot, waiting to expel its contents. I noticed that everyone in the room had already finished their small glass of tea. So I gulped mine down, assuming that the glass of tea was perfunctory and we needed to get right down to business.

Then everyone gulped the second glass of tea, and I did the same. It wasn't until the third glass had been poured and consumed that I realized the custom was three quick shots of tea, and then the tea boy could dis-appear. There was to be no savoring of tea during the meeting.

We discussed what the Ministry of Education hoped to achieve from my consultancy. The minister made it clear he wanted to implement an English language program in secondary schools throughout the country. Together, we would develop a curriculum, a training program for teach-ers of English, and a plan to implement the new initiative. I provided the officials with a sample of work I had done previously at the teacher training college in Casablanca.

I left out the part where I diagnosed sexually transmitted diseases of students who showed up on my doorstep in the middle of the night.

MORE COUSCOUS AND MARRYING FATIMA

The meeting adjourned, and I was whisked off to my first Mauritanian couscous. The home of my host, Mohammed, resembled very much a typical Moroccan home, with the exception that the salon was filled with the entire family: men, women, children. All the women were dressed in traditional Mauritania gowns, and gold glittered anytime they moved their hands. There seemed to be much discussion of what exactly I was doing in Mauritania and, most important, my marital status.

I wondered if any of the women were named Fatouma, but my new friend assured me that was not a common name in Mauritania. He did feel free to announce to the assembly that I was not married.

The tea was served quickly, and conversation danced around the level of my interest in marrying during the months I was in Mauritania. I was having trouble understanding the Mauritanian dialect, Hassaniya, but did manage to grab snippets: a girl named Fatima was of marrying age . . . she was too thin right now but would be quite plump before the wedding night . . . and would I like to meet her?

It was the plumpness that caught my attention. When the laughter subsided, I got the answer to my question: Fatima would sit in a small room and eat to her heart's content so that she would be alluringly fat on her wedding night. It was hard to concentrate, thinking that Fatima might be in the room with us and hearing the whole conversation.

The amount of couscous consumed during lunch was staggering.

TEATIME AND SLAVERY

When Mohammed, my host, asked a woman sitting at the end of the room for more tea, she turned to a young boy and told him to run to the kitchen and get it. Much more laughter erupted when I asked Mohammed if the woman was his mother. I was trying to figure out the pecking order of the room and it seemed that this particular woman was very much in charge.

"No, she is not my mother," Mohammed said. "She is a slave."

"A slave?" I asked.

"Yes. She belongs to our family."

"A slave?"

"Yes, she was born in our family and has lived her entire life with us."

"A . . . slave?"

"Yes, why do you ask?"

"Is the boy getting the tea a slave too?"

"No, he is my little brother."

I could not get my head around this. "The slave just told your little brother to go get the tea?"

"Oh yes," Mohammed replied, "and if he doesn't, she will give him a good slap."

Slavery in Mauritania was outlawed by presidential decree in 1981, yet no laws to enforce compliance were passed until 2007. Mohammed's little brother brought the tea while Mohammed identified the slaves in the room. I stirred the tea while my head spun. Everyone seemed to be having a great time. The couscous gurgled up a storm in my stomach.

I returned to the guesthouse, still trying to comprehend that there were slaves in Mauritania. It was the calmness, the level of unawareness in casually mentioning slavery, of referring to family members as slaves, that unnerved me. Only when I kept asking for clarification did my colleague sense I was uncomfortable and begin insisting that slavery was now outlawed—that his family really wanted their slaves to take their freedom seriously and strike out on their own. It was the slaves themselves, he claimed, who didn't want to do so. Why would they? They lived in a comfortable home, with clothes and food paid for by the family.

His additional comments did not ease my mind

The guesthouse was empty, so there was no one to help me navigate the time warp into which I had stumbled. I didn't bother to dust off my bed and just lay in the talcum powder sand, thinking.

I was unmarried, and therefore available.

Fatima would be fattened for marriage.

I had eaten couscous with slaves, who not only existed but bossed the family around.

Mohammed struggled to get his family's slaves to accept their freedom and pay for their own clothes.

And there was that smell that seemed to linger.

Mauritania was not what I had expected.

In the morning, we drove through sand dunes to the airport where I was to board my flight to Nouadhibou, in the north of Mauritania. Along the side of the road were a number of animals that had succumbed but, because of the very dry weather, did not decompose. Instead, with the wind blowing sand in bone-dry air, the corpses turned to bone and leather.

I had discovered the source of the mysterious odor: desiccated animal corpses.

The smell of a corpse that has never rotted remains with me today. At the scent of a poor animal killed on a highway, I am transported to Mauritania. It is an inescapable memory.

Like the smell of a camel lying frozen in death, it was hard to get the vision of having lunch with slaves out of my mind.

POLITICAL FAUX PAS

The flight to Nouadhibou followed the Atlantic coastline. The ocean meeting the desert landscapes was a beautiful sight, except for the carcasses of ships littering the beaches. The size of the ships ranged from fishing trawlers to large-scale container ships, like a family of desiccated camel carcasses along the roadside. All that was left of each ship was a rusted skeleton listing in the sand. There were no flags of convenience flying from their sterns, but Mohammed told me they were all Russian. No further evidence of their origin was offered. The ship graveyard has grown every year since.

My first meeting was with the mayor of Nouadhibou. Sipping our tea, we chatted about Mauritania and Morocco. I asked him how far Nouadhibou was situated from the Moroccan border.

After a short, awkward silence, he answered, "For you, we are twenty kilometers from the border. For me, we are two thousand."

If you look on a map printed in any country other than Morocco you will see a "country" called Western Sahara sitting between Morocco and Mauritania. If you look at a world map published in Morocco, you will see that Morocco stretches from the Strait of Gibraltar in the north all the way to the border with Mauritania.

In November of 1975 King Hassan convinced 350,000 Moroccans to peacefully march into the Spanish Sahara, a disputed territory occupied by Spain but claimed by Morocco. With the promise of free land, houses, and Saharan landscapes, the parade of Moroccans in trucks, cars, and horse-drawn wagons was a jubilant affair that quickly escalated into a sixteen-year-long war with the Polisario—an insurgent group (from the Moroccan perspective) made up of people from the Sahara but also from Algeria and other countries of the Sahel region. Known as the Green March, this event lived large in the eyes of many Moroccans, despite the fact that everyone just went back home afterward with no new land or house. It did accomplish one important goal: Spain evacuated the Western Sahara but left Morocco with the parting gift of a long war.

After a whirlwind of meetings with local officials, we boarded the plane back to Nouakchott. Flying over the desert, I found it curious to think of people fighting for so long over what seemed to be barren land. The short answer: under the sand was a wealth of phosphates, used in everything from fertilizer to food and cosmetics. As in so many seemingly unfathomable events around the world, all roads lead to someone making money.

THE BREAK-DANCING CONSULTANT AND THE CAMEL BAR

We landed back in Nouakchott, and Mohammed dropped me back at the embassy guesthouse, saying he would pick me up the next morning for meetings with the minister of education once again. I had been the only guest staying at the cavernous house, so I was surprised to hear noise inside.

The laughter of boisterous boys greeted me as I opened the door, but the group fell silent as I introduced myself. They had been enjoying the dormlike atmosphere of the empty house, and I was viewed as the older guy who was going to spoil all their fun.

When I asked them what they were doing in Mauritania, one of the boys broke into a dance move. There was a popular American film at the time called *Breakin'*. Break dancing was entering the mainstream, and the US ambassador to Mauritania was intent on importing American culture. He had invited the dance troupe to perform at a twenty-thousand-person soccer stadium in the capital city.

The boys would be staying with me in the guesthouse. Their first question focused on food. "Are you fixing something for dinner?"

"Am I fixing dinner? No, why would I be fixing dinner?"

"Are you the guy who is supposed to take care of us?"

"Umm, no. I'm the guy who is working on a project with the government."

"Who is going to feed us?"

"Well, who is supposed to staff you?"

"Staff us?"

"Who is supposed to take care of you?"

"They picked us up at the airport, and then they just left us here."

"Are they coming back?"

"We don't know anything. We just came from the Bronx today."

Suddenly I was living with a group of teenage break-dancers from New York City who were told that someone would look after them, and I was the only person standing in front of them. I broke the ice with the only break-dance move I could muster, and soon became "Papa Break-Dancer."

I later learned that the boys were victims of tension and infighting at the embassy, between the ambassador and cultural attaché. The attaché wanted a string quartet to perform classical music for Mauritanian VIPs, and the ambassador wanted to fill the stadium with Mauritanian youth who would love truly American culture. But right now, these boys were hungry and looking to me to get them fed.

Mohammed picked us up in a van, and we headed to the beach. Like the road to the airport, the road to the beach was littered with weathered carcasses, and the smell was pungent. The boys thought that was cool and reminded them of the Bronx. Teenagers have vivid imaginations.

After a good meal at a beachside restaurant, Mohammed announced that we would finish out the night at a camel bar. So once we convinced the boys that they needn't go back to the house to change clothes, we headed into the desert.

The boys wanted to "make the scene" and look cool at the Camel Bar—they thought it was a club and were anxious to show off some moves that were featured in the break-dancing movie. In reality, "the camel bar" was a herd of camels sitting in the sand. The tent was listing to the right, the bonfire was fading, and the camels chewed their cud. We could feel their breath as we inched closer to the fire to ward off the chill of the Saharan night.

"Milk all around!" called Mohammed to the waiter.

As she was milked, the camel did not protest too much. The enormous shallow wooden bowl, filled to the brim with warm milk, was passed from one patron to the next. The fire cast a dancing shadow across the faces of the men sipping the still-warm milk. We stared in horror as the bowl came closer and closer to our group, and the boys began to fidget. The darkness prevented a true counting of the number of flies sitting on the lip of the bowl.

My eyes told the boys: *Do as I do, or you will regret it in an hour or two.*

When the bowl reached me, I lifted it slowly to my face. Because the vessel was now half-empty, I could tilt it to completely shield my face and, more important, my lips from view. The lip of the bowl never touched my lips, but all present applauded my bravery for taking such a great gulp of fresh camel milk.

The flies never revealed my lie.

SWEET SIXTEEN AND ALONE

Back at the embassy, I warned the boys not to leave any of their clothes lying around lest they find them covered in talcum powder sand in the morning. One boy, Alex, never heard that warning, just as he had not heeded my warning at the camel bar and was now spending the night in the bathroom reviewing that decision. The rest of us headed off to bed for a good night's rest. It wasn't until three in the morning that I heard the crying.

The youngest of the boys was sixteen years old. He sat in the living room weeping and made no attempt to dry his eyes when I appeared in the doorway. He continued sobbing, and I sat next to him to offer what comfort a stranger could without intruding. He told me he had a medical problem and needed my advice. Any attempt I had made to escape my role as Doctor Downes had failed, and I was thrust back into a role I had not chosen for myself. Was it my premature graying hair that inspired ill-placed trust in my medical expertise?

The story spilled out as the boy begged me not to tell anyone. I explained that all doctors are required to adhere to a strict code of confidentiality and, while I was not a doctor, I would keep his medical problem secret. He confessed that his problem was about sex. He thought he was too young to make a baby, but apparently girls can have babies at sixteen—which was news to him. He had only done it once, so the baby couldn't be his, right? What should he do?

"Please don't tell my father," he begged.

As with many problems, a good night's sleep often makes it seem less ominous in the morning, so my advice was to try to get some sleep and we could talk tomorrow. I explained that jet lag causes extreme fatigue and that he would think more calmly in the morning.

"Will she still be pregnant in the morning?" he whimpered, before crying himself to sleep.

FATHER OF THE ENGLISH LANGUAGE IN MAURITANIA

In the morning, I headed to the Ministry of Education for my meeting. I expected to give the minister a brief update on my meetings in Nouadhibou, leaving out the Moroccan border discussion, and then meet with technical advisors to begin framing the national curriculum for high school students learning English. Great expectations aside, towers of paper stood on the minister's desk, and a smile spread across his face as I entered.

"Never have I seen such progress so quickly," he praised. "Congratulations! I am very pleased."

"Oh! That's wonderful," I said. "But . . . what happened?"

"The national curriculum is completed in record time!"

The towers of paper were copies of the sample curriculum I had left with the minister the day before. Each copy was stamped in blue ink with *The National Curriculum for English Language Teaching in Mauritania.*

Two responses raced through my mind. First, I could protest and say that it was not acceptable to simply photocopy the sample curriculum I had given them. Or, second, I could accept that I was now the author of a national English language curriculum and put that on my resume when looking for my next consultancy. I am not sure I heard much of the rest of the conversation, but the fog lifted a bit when I heard my name and the question, "When do you start working on the teacher training curriculum?" The meeting was deemed a great success, and a second and third round of mint tea was offered.

Both the future of the English language in Mauritania and teen pregnancy in the Bronx were on my agenda for the afternoon. In the light of day, my young friend was more embarrassed about crying than he was about his lack of understanding how his girlfriend got pregnant. He was in a better mood now and had already begun wedding plans.

HOW TO EAT A CAMEL

The boys were very excited about the luncheon the embassy had planned for them. They were heading to the desert for a Bedouin lunch of roasted camel and goat in honor of their arrival in Mauritania. After firing off a barrage of questions about how they were supposed to eat the camel, they fell silent when I told them they most likely would eat with their hands while sitting on carpets or mats.

For the young father-to-be, that came as a disappointment. "I thought we would be having camel sandwiches," he said.

"I don't think you will be having sandwiches," I replied.

"Then how will we be eating with our hands?"

"Well, you will pull off pieces of meat that you find under the gobs of fat."

"What gobs of fat?"

"The fat that covers all the meat."

"Where did all the fat come from?"

"You will see," I said. It seemed he was ignorant about not just human anatomy, but biology in general. "But it most likely will be very hot, so you should be careful not to burn your hands."

"Wait a minute, are you saying that we are going to eat an actual camel?"

"Yes, and a mountain of rice."

"I'm not going to eat a camel. You didn't drink the camel milk."

"Well, just pretend you are eating so you don't insult your hosts."

Despite the many cultural clashes, the real difficulty came not from the Mauritanian people or the break-dancing troupe, but the embassy staff, who seemed determined to manifest their displeasure with the ambassador. Those who had supported the string quartet proposal did little to make the cultural tour a success, and the boys from the Bronx were the ones to suffer.

Still, we were having a great time. Struck by the fact that the boys seemed to be largely abandoned by the embassy, I decided to join them for lunch.

MICHAEL JACKSON IN MAURITANIA

Teenagers live in a world of their own. The connection between American teenagers and Mauritanian teenagers was immediate and frenzied.

The morning following our luncheon date, we piled into the van to visit the embassy. I felt a sudden tug at my sleeve, from a hand that belonged to the first of a swarm of boys and girls crushing closer to get a glimpse of the celebrities from America. I found it amusing that I was suddenly a member of the dance troupe, but my smile faded when I realized that the swarm was growing and now blocked our departure.

This was long before the age of selfies, so it wasn't clear at first what the kids actually wanted. When my shirt sleeve ripped away, their intent was exposed along with my torso: they wanted any article of clothing that they could salvage for a souvenir. It was a mini frenzy, the type of screaming and pushing The Beatles must have experienced on a larger scale, complete with ululations thrown in to add local flavor. We were being mobbed.

As word spread that the *Breakin'* movie stars were in town, it became harder to move around the city. Even when I was alone, teenagers approached me—not to get my autograph, but rather to ask for an introduction to the boys. I was now, apparently, either a bodyguard, their manager, or just some old guy who knew the dancers. The dance event was still two days away, but the hype had already kicked in. The ambassador had won: the American cultural event of the century had arrived in Mauritania.

When the big day arrived, I climbed into the van with the boys again, and we headed to the stadium. The combined sound of music and the screaming crowd reached us before we arrived, reverberating in my chest— enthralling but also frightening. The stadium was full, and I imagined the same twenty thousand teenagers waiting for an unknown string quartet, sitting in silence and falling asleep. Waiting for the break-dancers, the anticipation was intoxicating.

The boys were not the first act. Mauritanian dance groups warmed up the crowd. As the first group of dancers, young women in flowing Mauritanian caftans, took the stage, I looked forward to seeing traditional dancing and music. Instead, Michael Jackson's "Thriller" blasted from the speakers, and the crowd began their own personal version of break dancing.

Couscous with slaves, diplomatic blunders, camel milk, and a teenage pregnancy could not have prepared me for the spectacle, and yet there I was, part of the spectacle. The ambassador smiled at me, knowing he had brought the real America to Mauritania.

UNINTENDED CONSEQUENCES

There was a particular sadness to my time in Mauritania. There was tension in the air, as was often the case in North Africa and the Middle East. Fighting erupted in the Western Sahara, and all Americans were advised to keep a low profile. Travelling with the break-dancing troupe was hardly keeping a low profile. But when I spoke to the boys about security concerns, they looked around and laughed it off, comparing Nouakchott to their home in the Bronx.

I also had an uneasy feeling about the suddenness with which I had become responsible for the English language teaching curriculum in Mauritania. The English language guide being used back in Morocco at the time was a British book published in the UK, which focused on Jane, her life, and especially her kitchen. I imagined a generation of

Mauritanians running around the country speaking about such weighty topics as Jane's kitchen and asking tourists if the cooker could be found on the left or the right.

I had left the sample curriculum with the minister of education only as a starting point, to show what I had developed in Morocco—and had never expected it would be sent around the country with no further discussion. And I had already experienced the impact of learning about Jane's kitchen as I travelled in the southern desert of Morocco.

Stepping off a souk bus, I had been immediately met by a young man who wanted to show me the sights. His first utterance was, "Hi, my name is Anas. I speak English and the cooker is on the right. Shall we have tea?"

"Ah, so you speak English?"

"Yes, why not?"

"Well, I could think of many reasons why not. We are in the middle of the desert."

"Ah, but the fridge is on the left, and the cooker is on the right."

Mauritanians with English language skills may have been able to navigate the geography of Jane's kitchen, but the intricacies of sorting out the geography of the conflict in the Western Sahara likely would require linguistic capabilities that went beyond a cozy domestic scenario. Still, I can claim that I launched English language teaching in Mauritanian schools almost by accident.

THE CLUB IN NEW YORK CITY

The break-dance boys were headed to Morocco on the next leg of their world tour, and I promised we would see each other again. When I got back, however, I was no longer part of the inner circle. The embassy in Rabat was taking good care of the boys, and I was stopped at the door of the clubs where they were dancing. We never managed to connect in Morocco.

A year later, I was in New York visiting friends at Columbia University, and we decided to go see Youssou N'Dour, the Senegalese icon once described by *Rolling Stone* magazine as "perhaps the most famous singer alive in Senegal and Africa." The club was jammed with people from all over North, South, East, and West Africa, but any sense of feeling out of place quickly evaporated when I heard my name shouted from somewhere in the crowd. After a few minutes, a growing chorus of "Azzedine!" reached our group. My wards from Mauritania had found me in the crowd. I left my graduate student friends, their mouths agape, and danced my way back into temporary fame.

The baraka had followed me to America.

The Moroccan Mountains

"Now" Is Not What You Think It Is

Mick and Keith in a Trance

Dancing for Grandma at the White House

"NOW" IS NOT WHAT YOU THINK IT IS

Upon my return home from Mauritania to Morocco, the topic of marriage came up again and again, with inquiries coming at me fast and furious from all angles. Being invited to weddings in Morocco is a common occurrence. These days, my Moroccan family always laughs when I share that observation, pointing out that I was dragged in off the street mostly to add an air of mystery to the proceedings.

One of the first invitations upon my return came from a Berber family I had met when hiking in the mountains. I was pleased to accept their invitation, even though they were virtually strangers.

The hike up to the village of Jajouka, perched high in the Rif Mountains, was not difficult, but it was a slow slog given all the sugar we had to lug up. A cone of sugar, wrapped in purple paper with an abundance of string tying it all together, was a gift much appreciated by the host. The sugar usually disappeared without comment, and I always assumed it reappeared in syrup form, as the mint tea was served after the couscous feast.

We also lugged large sacks of couscous up the mountain—enough to feed an army. The amount seemed excessive even as a gift to our hosts, who were celebrating the wedding of their son.

A group of Moroccan friends, also invited to the wedding, joined me on the hike. The air was festive as we slowly made our way up, but my friends ignored my questions about what was going to happen and what a wedding in the mountains would be like. Did they not want to tell me, or did they simply have no better idea than I did? It remains a mystery to me.

Their evasiveness was typical—not just about major events like a wedding. They could be equally evasive when I asked what time a bus was expected to arrive. The stock answer in English: "Now, it's coming." It was the "now" that was confusing.

Even in the simple event of leaving a room my friends would announce: "Now, I am coming." I would point out that they were not coming; they were going. They found my confusion hilarious, and I would be the butt of jokes for the rest of the day. Determining whether someone was physically coming or going seemed beyond my abilities to comprehend, so I decided to leave that one alone.

But I did try to explain the meaning of "now," to no avail. To my friends, time had different meanings that only an Einstein-type mind could explain.

One would think some questions are easy to answer, and others are very difficult—so one would expect to hear, once in a while at least, "I don't know." I have met many people who didn't know whether they were coming or going, but for my friends, even the most complicated astrophysical questions regarding the mysteries of the cosmos were treated in the same nonchalant manner. Responding to any question, even regarding the true nature of a black hole, could never include the words "I don't know." It was unthinkable.

They used the same logic when stating, with unwavering certainty, that "Now, the bus is coming."

"Somewhere in time and place, the bus is on its way," I would counter, "but not necessarily *now!*"

Such discussions could occupy hours at a time, and so it was on the hike up that mountain.

MICK AND KEITH IN A TRANCE

When we arrived at the Berber wedding in the mountains, there was great commotion near a large cave facing the village. Villagers were building a bonfire that seemed out of place for a wedding celebration. Perhaps the bride had been convicted of being a witch and would not see the morning after the wedding—an outcome that seemed more plausible in Salem, Massachusetts, four centuries earlier than in the mountains of Morocco today. But the excitement of building a large fire was palpable nonetheless. It was also a little unsettling.

That excitement among the villagers was matched by the lethargy of several older men sitting in a smoky haze, warming up their musical instruments. These were members of the Master Musicians of Jajouka. The group had played for sultans for centuries, passing down the traditions of their haunting music through generations of family members. We took our places as guests, ready to embark now on an astral journey via secondhand kif smoke.

Perhaps it was the kif, but at first I did not understand why everyone in the village kept telling stories about "Mick" and "Keith." Of course, the constant repetition of Western names in my presence was not uncommon. Someone was always asking, "You were in America. Do you know Joe?" Maybe they thought I was friends with some guys named Mick and Keith and wanted to share stories about our mutual friends.

As the day progressed, mysteries unfolded. I allowed myself to be lost in the music and began to experience what it feels like to enter a trance state. The billowing clouds of kif may have helped. Sipping at my mint tea, my eyes drifted to a photo hanging askew on the wall behind the musicians. The music from their pipes grew more frantic, and the photo became clearer. It showed the very man sitting in front of me, alongside Mick Jagger and Keith Richards. "Now," these Moroccan villagers were chilling with The Rolling Stones.

The drums grew more insistent. The couscous was served, and the wedding feast began. Yet for me, there was no question of eating. The drums called to me, and they had to be obeyed.

One musical piece by the Master Musicians of Jajouka, "Up to the Sky, Down to the Earth," best describes the imaginary heights I reached while dancing that night. The hand of a friend holding the back of my waistband was the only thing anchoring me to the earth. To this day, hearing their music makes my heart race, and even "now" I am in a trance. There was no sleep that night.

The next day, the pyre grew, and a new festival emerged as the sun set. The wedding (what I remember of it) was a happy occasion, but the gathering around the bonfire took on an eerie, menacing tone. Out from the cave came Pan, Greek god of the mountains, accompanied by shepherds and rustic music. A second figure emerged, and what appeared to be a battle between good and evil ensued. The pipes turned strident, and the only other sound was the crackling of the fire. Time in this small village seemed to have paused.

It all seemed out of place, from an Islamic perspective. Families brought forward their children "possessed by evil spirits," hoping the music would relieve their young ones of their torment. Music has a long history of being used in various ceremonies, some nefarious and others medicinal. Centuries earlier, one genre of music was even the prescribed remedy for mental illness.

In 1492, when Muslims were forced from Spain and resettled in Fez, they brought with them Andalusian music, which was played in the insane asylums of the day in order to soothe the patients. Mental illness was considered a form of possession, and the cure was both intoxicating and frightening. That night at the wedding, I'm sure there were disappointed parents who had hoped beyond reason that their child would "return" to them healthy and happy.

But to me, there was nothing soothing about the music of Jajouka being played that night. It continued to dance in my head many hours after the musicians stopped playing. As the fire died, I'm not sure that any evil spirits had departed, but some disappointed parents and their children in the crowd certainly had.

DANCING FOR GRANDMA AT THE WHITE HOUSE

Not long after the Berber wedding, I headed to Tangiers to meet with Aziz's family. No further mention was made, however, of whether I would ever meet the girl from Tangiers. I was becoming frustrated and phoned Aziz. I told him that I was an adventurous type but I at least needed to see the person that I was to marry. I insisted he tell me her name at the very least. He divulged the name of the mysterious girl from Tangiers: Nadia!

I was relieved but I was also jittery. I had only seen Nadia briefly and was very relaxed at the time. Now, I wondered if Nadia had known about the arranged marriage and if she had been checking me out as a possible husband!

I was still a bachelor, and it remained unclear to me what was supposed to happen in order for me to get married. Simply by acknowledging my future hopes of a family, I had set something in motion, but I couldn't even observe how it was unfolding. Of course, it was written—maktub—so I wasn't overly concerned. There would come an inflection point in my journey where I would gain control of my betrothal—or so I convinced myself.

Before visiting the family in Tangiers, I went by the old American embassy, now a museum, and heard great stories that would intersect with my life in later years. Morocco was the first country in the world to recognize the newly declared United States of America, on December 20, 1777. Thus, the first American embassy was established here, when Tangiers was the capital, and in 1821 the Sultan Moulay Slimane provided a home for the American ambassador. That home is still standing—the oldest American diplomatic property in the world.

After leaving the museum and rummaging around in the souks of Tangiers, it was time to find the White House. I thought of my conversation in Casablanca (which also means, in Spanish, "white house"), where I sought directions, in Arabic, to the post office. If I began asking local people where to find the White House, would they give me directions to Casablanca or perhaps even Washington, DC? I had no choice, as I had no other address for the home of Aziz's family. The more I had asked them for a specific address, the more frustrating the conversation became.

As with many things in Morocco, all would be revealed in time. So I set out, with no clear direction, to find my next couscous lunch.

As it turned out, the White House was not difficult to find. Everyone in the neighborhood seemed to know where it was and pointed me closer and closer in the right direction. A number of people also felt compelled to accompany me to the house, many carrying straw baskets filled with towels, soap, and a fresh pair of clothes. The reason became clear when we ended up at the local hammam.

Presuming a mistake had been made and assuring my guides that I was not in need of a good scrubbing, I realized that the family's house sat atop the hammam.

Upon entering the White House, I was still focused on meeting the famous Nadia from Tangiers and thought if the first encounter did not happen on this visit, I most likely was not getting married anytime soon. The missing piece of the puzzle was, who was going to introduce me to Nadia? I had no idea how it was supposed to happen.

As it turned out, it would happen that very afternoon, in the same way many events in Morocco revealed themselves to me: through a plan that was unknown to me, and in which I ended up being the entertainment.

Despite the kindness and hospitality of Aziz's family, I felt the need to break the awkwardness of sitting with an entire family who were strangers to me. So I took a short walk in the alley outside the house, where I encountered a man with a tray of glasses and a piping hot pot of mint tea perched on his head. He stopped at the door of the White House, looked me up and down, and asked if I would like to have musicians liven up the gathering. It seemed like a good distraction.

I paid the man the requested fee, and he disappeared down the alley with the tea still on the teetering tray, steaming. Miraculously, he returned within minutes with four musicians all warmed up from a wedding that had just run out of energy.

When I reentered the house with a band and hot mint tea, the room sprang into action. At first I was relieved, until I learned that for the family, "action" meant preparing the room so that I could dance for the entire family. As soon as I had completed my first gyration, the matron of the family screamed in delight, announcing that I must be a good boy and would have many children.

It was a festive afternoon, with much music, dancing, and laughing. But what of my impending engagement? I scanned the room again and again, looking for a girl named Nadia. The men in the family appeared to be utterly clueless, as is often the case, and the women never alluded to Nadia or marriage.

Finally, the couscous arrived. And so did Nadia.

At lunch, I was seated on one side of the eager family matron, who turned out to be Nadia's grandmother, and Nadia sat on the other side. Any private conversation that might have taken place between us, however, was conducted among the entire family as well as the many unknown guests who floated in and out of the house, curious as to the nature of the festivities.

After the meal was finished, Grandma sent Nadia and me to the store for more sugar whilst the rest of the family passed out for a post-couscous siesta. Nadia's youngest brother accompanied us as a chaperone, a tradition that I still found amusing. I am not sure what inappropriate things could have occurred between us as we walked through the crowded streets to make a small domestic purchase at a public shop—or what this nine-year-old boy would be expected to do about it. But there he was, dreaming not only of sugar and mint tea, but also of all the candy he hoped I would buy him.

That walk with Nadia was the extent of our interaction, and the topic of marriage was never brought up. We chatted amiably about buying the sugar and how much we should spoil her little brother with candy. Nadia never gave me any indication that she was interested in meeting me, let alone marrying me.

The sugar ran out, and the day ended. Everyone said their goodbyes, and I perceived no hint of knowing glances from anyone. Had the gathering, and my dancing for Grandma, sealed the marriage arrangement—or doomed it? I had no idea.

The next morning, I left for the United States to take on another consultancy assignment, and more followed after that. Thoughts of getting married faded. But once a work assignment was finished, I always returned to Morocco. By this point in my life, I considered it my home.

Boston, Philadelphia, and Washington, DC

MARRIAGE, THE DOWRY, AND *ZULU DAWN*

The telephone call from Aziz came on a Friday afternoon while I was sitting in the kitchen of my father's house in Rhode Island. As with other calls from Aziz that dealt with sensitive issues, the call was short and to the point.

"My mother wants to meet you," he insisted.

"Where is your mother?" I asked.

"She is in Philadelphia."

"Why is she in Philadelphia?"

"Get on the train tomorrow and come to Philadelphia with me. I'll explain on the ride down from Boston. She wants to speak with you."

"Speak to me about what?"

"About marrying Nadia."

I'll admit that I was beginning to think I might be biting off more than I could chew. I didn't think the events in my life were all that unusual, but I supposed that an arranged marriage was shocking to my father. Sitting across the table with his cup of tea, my father watched me on the phone. He was shaking his head ever so slightly. "Now what's going on?" he asked calmly.

"I'm going to Philadelphia tomorrow."

"Why?"

"I'm not really sure, but when I get back, I might be engaged."

His eyebrows shot up. "You don't even have a girlfriend. Or a date."

"I said I'm not sure. What more can anyone know?" I responded enigmatically.

"How could you not be sure whether you are getting engaged to someone?"

"Well, we went to the store to buy sugar together," I explained matter-of-factly, "but I don't know if she is interested in getting married."

My father's eyes narrowed. "Is this a prank?"

"On me?" I asked.

"No, on me!"

THE SAD STORY ON THE TRAIN

Getting aboard an Amtrak train is not like riding the trains in Switzerland. Swiss trains are very tidy; there is order to everything that happens. On my Amtrak train ride, the people walking down the aisle to find their seat resembled drunken sailors, and those already seated lived in fear of being splashed with hot coffee or having a stranger suddenly plop down in their lap. I saw Aziz come down the aisle looking for me, with a big smile on his face and a few croissants from Au Bon Pain. I was anxious to talk about what I would be discussing with his mother, but he evaded every question. I also wanted a full debrief on who was who in the family. He finally admitted that Nadia was his sister and he was too embarrassed to tell me that when he first asked me if I wanted to get married.

"Men do not get involved in discussing marriage," he explained. "The women will deal with the details." He then began to tell me the story, as promised, of why his mother was in Philadelphia.

It was a sad story. His mother had been diagnosed with breast cancer. She was originally told by a local doctor in Morocco that she should just use a cream to ease the pain. My own grandmother had died of cancer many years prior, and the word "cancer" could never be uttered in the house. I understood why families cannot bring themselves to acknowledge the seriousness of a cancer prognosis. The Moroccan doctor, not wanting to say the prognosis was terminal, sent Nadia's mother home with some hope of surviving.

Their mother had an urgency about her that went beyond her medical condition. She wanted to see her eldest daughter married.

As I listened to Aziz tell the story and thought about our impending visit, I imagined a scene of the two of us: mother and future son-in-law sitting in the kitchen, drinking mint tea and talking of love, children, and lives spent together in harmony. My vision was right out of a romantic comedy. It ignored the fact that I didn't really know Nadia and had no idea what I was doing.

How could I know what the future held in an arranged marriage? Aziz turned out to be no help whatsoever, only because he was as clueless as I was. So we threw ourselves on the mercy of his mother, trusting her to arrange our lives.

COMING TO AMERICA

Nadia's family and all its various members were becoming clearer to me. Aside from Aziz, the honest Saïd, and the little brother with the sweet tooth, Nadia's brother Youssef had a very interesting life—one which is perhaps best understood by watching the Eddie Murphy film *Coming to America.*

Aziz told me his father, Mohammed, had begun his working life in the first American embassy in the world, located in Tangiers, Morocco. While working for the American ambassador, he caught the attention of Prince Moulay Abdallah, the younger brother of King Hassan, and left the employ of the ambassador to begin working in the palace, in Rabat.

As a young boy, Youssef was summoned by Prince Moulay Abdallah to live in the palace and be the companion to his young son, Moulay Hicham. Living as a prince is not the same as being the prince, however—something the family would learn over time. Still, Youssef had gone to America with the prince to study at university in Philadelphia and remained in America once Moulay Hicham returned to Morocco.

Now their mother was being treated at the University of Pennsylvania medical center where she could be close to Youssef.

When we arrived at Youssef's house, I also learned about Nadia's sister, Amina, who was there to help take care of her mother. I came from a family of six children, so the ever-expanding number of siblings didn't concern me. But I did wonder how Nadia's mother had managed to have so many children when she was still so young.

I also realized that I was extremely nervous. How could I possibly have the private conversation I had imagined in my rom-com scenario?

Conversation was polite, and I didn't sense that there were any whispers behind my back about the impending marriage discussion. That observation may not have been quite true, because the family spoke a very odd Tangiers dialect that I couldn't quite figure out. But the main focus was on the impending couscous lunch and how Amina was the best cook in all of Morocco.

I was looking forward to the couscous, but not so much to the discussion of marriage. I imagined that we would spend most of the day getting to know one another, and then the following day would have a quiet moment when I could reveal my intentions.

In the post-couscous stupor, we watched television in silence as the 1979 movie *Zulu Dawn* blared on, with no one but me watching or paying attention. I was engrossed in the struggles of the Zulu in defiance of the British, when Amina suddenly stood up, switched off the TV, and announced that it was now time to speak to her mother.

"About what?" I innocently asked.

Amina's reply was swift and stern. "You are to discuss marrying Nadia." Panic set in as swiftly.

Nadia's mother sat on the couch and waited for me to start.

I couldn't really think straight, and for some reason, my high school Latin came flooding back. I blurted out the Moroccan Arabic version of Julius Caesar's "*Veni, vidi, vici*": "I went to Morocco, I saw Nadia, I want to marry her." There was no romance involved, no profession of love, no rom-com moment—only sweat dripping down the small of my back.

With a broad smile on her face, Allela—as I was instructed to call Nadia's mum—said, "I love your blue eyes, I love your name, the wedding is on August 25."

With that, Nadia's sister switched *Zulu Dawn* back on.

My high school Latin teacher had been right after all: Latin did end up serving me well someday.

But where was the profound conversation? Where was the tender rom-com moment when I would lay out my life together with Nadia? Where was Nadia?

THE BOOK AND THE LETTER

Moroccan Arabic is filled with French words. Many words have the same meaning as they do in French, whilst others have taken on a life of their own. I speak French, so it was never an issue to understand when someone switched between Arabic and French, but the Moroccan Arabic spoken in the north of Morocco also has a lot of Spanish words thrown in. To make it more confusing, people from Tangiers also add extra syllables to the end of words whilst cutting out syllables in the middle. "Tongue-tied" would be the best way to describe how the conversation unfolded from here.

Allela continued to smile, waiting for me to say something else. I didn't. But it soon became clear that she wanted to know about "the book." She used the French word "*carnet*," which to me meant the small book that held my residency permits in the various countries where I had lived. So I quickly assured her that I would arrange a visa for Nadia.

The volume of *Zulu Dawn* suddenly rose as if to drown out the silence. All in the room were looking down at the floor; no one was following the war drama.

Allela asked again what I would write in the book.

I explained that Nadia could have a visa once we were married and, if we lived in the States for five years, she could get a green card.

From Allela's reaction, I knew something was wrong, but I didn't know what it was. It was becoming harder to hear what she was saying, because Amina kept turning up the volume on the television. The Zulu war cries also were drowning out my assurances that a green card would not be that difficult once we were married.

What's more, no one had mentioned anything about Nadia. So I turned the television off and changed the subject, asking, "What does Nadia think?"

Amina turned *Zulu Dawn* back on. My own unfolding drama was becoming increasingly hostile.

I pressed on and asked again what Nadia thought of the whole situation. Allela smiled and said that she really loved my blue eyes and hoped that our children would have jet black hair and blue eyes. "They would be so beautiful," she insisted.

Amina suggested we have more mint tea and try to find an Egyptian film on the cable channel. She explained that one of the favorite pastimes the family had as children was to watch a melodramatic film and weep over the forlorn lovers whose lips would come so close to kissing but would never meet. The censors would not allow such licentiousness.

Now I was panicking. "But wait a minute, does Nadia want to marry me?"

Allela reached over, took my hand, and smiled. She told me not to worry, because a letter would soon be sent to Nadia. Then she turned back to the TV.

Nadia from Tangiers will get a letter soon, I told myself, *and it's all settled.* But the panic didn't subside. I had bared my soul in front of strangers in a strange land while the Zulu chanted their war cries, yet my tender moment was nothing more than an intermission. Any further mention of my burning question about Nadia's feelings for me was met with assurances, once again, that a letter would soon be sent. As we drank mint tea and ate leftover couscous, I cried silently inside.

When it was time to leave for the train, everyone seemed so happy, but I had a sinking feeling that the curse of Fatouma was finally taking hold. I had lost any sense of control over my own marriage.

Aziz and I boarded the train, and he faked falling asleep for a few hours. The third time I saw him peeking at me with one eye open, I told him I knew he wasn't asleep and wanted to know why he was avoiding talking to me. He then laid out the afternoon from his vantage.

He had watched in horror as his mother asked me about the book and I kept responding about getting Nadia a visa and then a green card if we ever lived in America. His face reddened as he explained that his mother was not asking me about immigration; she was asking what I was offering for a dowry.

I chuckled and told Aziz he must be mistaken, because "writing in the book" is not the Arabic word for "dowry."

He explained that in Morocco, when a parent asks what a prospective groom will "write in the book," they want to know what will be written in the marriage contract.

I had little more to offer than a visa. When pressed for a more generous dowry, I could throw in a green card. What was to become of me? I was a total disaster. I had met my own Zulu dawn.

Agitated, I asked Aziz why he had not helped me out. He said he could not overcome his own embarrassment and simply repeated that it was up to the women to arrange all these matters. He didn't want to get involved.

But I needed to step up my game in the next round, so I began plotting two strategies: one to get out of the whole affair (based on my belief that it was all happening as a result of the curse of Fatouma), and the other to figure out what I could offer for a dowry.

Even worse than the dowry issue, I could not shake the feeling that Nadia had no interest in marrying me. I had not been asked to write the letter to Nadia. It was clear to her mother that I was not capable of closing the deal, so I was sidelined early in the negotiations.

What, then, would the letter say? What if it was filled with all sorts of promises that I could not keep? Was I supposed to follow up with a love letter to a stranger? The beginnings of a draft letter floated around in my head: *Dear Nadia, how are you? By the way, we are getting married on August 25. I have blue eyes. See you then.*

When I arrived back at my father's house, he wanted to know all the details. I had no details to share but suggested we invite Allela to meet him. This was partly so he could see that I was not on some sort of LSD trip and imagining the whole thing, but mostly to correct the damage of the dowry discussion.

My father's only response was to ask if he needed to build a Wailing Wall in the cellar to make everyone feel at home. Historical and religious inaccuracies aside, I told him that would not be necessary.

His comment about Jerusalem did portend another shift in my life, about five years later. But what to do about the letter remained a mystery.

THE CONVERSION

My extended family gathered to witness the spectacle. Aunt Mary arrived early to get the best seat on the sofa, next to Allela. I apologized to Allela for the dowry faux pas, and she put my mind at ease: she had not mentioned the insult in the letter that had been sent to Nadia from Tangiers.

I explained that in Fez, the groom brought gold and the bride brought the home furnishings. The conversation ended quickly, with Allela explaining that in Tangiers, the groom provided everything. I really needed to find a full-time job, and quickly.

Translating is not the same as interpreting. If you are a translator, you are bored and sitting in a room quietly, with time on your hands, as you turn one document into another document in a different language. Interpreting, on the other hand, is live translation of ten different conversations, jokes, and couched insults, all at the same time. It is exhausting.

Jokes are the most difficult to interpret, and poor delivery is met not with mirth, but with anger. The Downes family loves to tell jokes and to laugh at their own jokes, sometimes so heartily that they can't finish the joke. They also enjoy telling the same joke over and over, for years on end, while laughing just as much as they did the first time. Translating into Arabic, and watching as the room waited in anticipation, was tiring. But my attempts to shorten a story or skip a joke were quickly challenged by the youngest members of my family.

Allela and Aunt Mary had no such problems, spending the next three hours engrossed in conversation. The fact that neither of them spoke the other's language did not deter them from having a wonderful time while speaking simultaneously, one sipping mint tea and the other sipping Manhattans. When their mystical dialogue petered out, Aunt Mary announced that it was all settled: "Nadia will convert to Catholicism."

Allela smiled broadly and asked me what Aunt Mary had said.

I translated for her: "Aunt Mary said she can't wait to have a nice couscous someday."

All agreed.

Aziz started to say something, but my dagger eyes instructed him to smile and nod approvingly, which he did.

He owed me that much.

A LETTER ARRIVES

I avoided all the questions as to when everyone would meet Nadia. I had no idea. I still did not even know if the letter had arrived, not to mention whether it was well received—or even what was in it or who had authored it. I was riding the wave of fate.

I was able to pry from Amina that she had set up the couscous lunch and dance party with Nadia's grandmother in Tangiers. Nadia had been told that she needed to come to the house to give cash to a foreigner who would then bring it to America for her mother. She was not aware of meeting me for any other reason. Watching me dance was a bonus.

The very day that our two families met, three pieces of news arrived. First, Nadia remembered who I was. Second, she agreed to marry me. And third, I had been offered a new job.

The letter to Nadia faded from memory as preparations for the wedding and a new job accelerated. Complications began immediately, and the specter of "the book" returned when it became clear that Nadia and I would need to be married before I left for my new job assignment. And for that, she would need a visa to enter the United States.

I fought the vision of Fatouma drugging me with couscous in order to lull me into marrying her, providing her with US citizenship, paying her mortgage, and then eviscerating me in my sleep. Nadia didn't seem like the eviscerating type, so I arranged for a visa for her to come to America.

THERE WAS COUSCOUS AT THE WEDDING

In February 1988—or the year 1409 for my-bride-to-be—my orientation to marrying someone I did not know and my orientation to a new job began simultaneously. I don't think the term "bridezilla" had been invented yet, but it would not have made any difference in our case, because Nadia was not involved in any of the wedding planning or implementation.

The visa was fast-tracked, and so was the wedding. There were to be two weddings, in fact: one in America and one in Morocco. The major event was to be in Morocco, but in order for me to leave America for my new job with Nadia as my wife, we had to be married. I put together a wedding at the local yacht club and said that it would be small, with a few close friends and immediate family. That left us with one hundred and fifty people attending, with Aunt Mary presiding as the matriarch along with Allela. My friend Ray threw in a white stretch limousine.

To make things colorful, friends from my Harvard days came to the wedding in traditional dress from their home countries. We debated how my Aboriginal friend from Australia should handle the nudity issue, but she decided to wear something flowing with ostrich feathers tickling the naked bits, so it all worked out.

The Egyptian imam from Quincy, Massachusetts, presided, and two friends witnessed the marriage contract, which stipulated I would pay a dowry of two diamond rings, fifteen gold bracelets, and five thousand dollars. My sister swears there was no food at the wedding, because I didn't let her plan the whole event, but there was couscous and a fine time was had by all.

Wedding planners have created an industry that seems to have as its primary goal to cause anxiety and amplify dysfunction in families. It is a very successful industry. One uncle swore it was the best wedding he had ever attended. He loved the kimono of a Japanese friend who is now a minister of state in Japan. He also loved the ostrich feathers of my Aboriginal friend; I could tell because he kept cleaning his glasses.

There was no alcohol served at the wedding, but somehow the door to the adjoining bar of the yacht club was pried open. Once a steady stream of revelers had slipped through the crack in the dry, Islamic plan, an even greater time was had by all. The Irish singers, dressed in Moroccan garb stolen from my suitcase by my brothers, were in full form—belting out drinking songs that half the room knew by heart and were singing along to.

My brother Dennis had a penchant for drinking alcohol from a shoe. That dubious activity took hold when my Aunt Anne cried out that I faced eternal damnation for leaving the Catholic Church. She quickly decided that we may as well steal one of my yellow babouche and have Dennis drink out of it for a while, hoping that Satan would be appeased and leave us alone.

To me, this day wasn't my real wedding, and so I had not given much thought to how best to meet the expectations of people attending a Moroccan-style wedding in the United States. It was never clear, for example, what I was supposed to do with the wedding cake. Was I supposed to smash it into Nadia's face, or just cut it and start passing it out? Honestly, it was never clear what either one of us was supposed to do.

I had to admit that a bit more planning would have been a good idea.

The imam managed to get everyone to stop singing the latest Irish ditty long enough to actually marry us. Nadia and I, clueless, sat down with him, and he began explaining to the crowd what was happening. I listened with rapt attention, just as curious as anyone else.

Nothing like a rehearsal dinner had taken place. If anything could be considered any preparation at all, it would have been the moment I said to the imam at the mosque in Quincy: "Oh, by the way, Nadia speaks no English, so don't ask her anything in English. Also, is there anything I need to say in Arabic? If there is, I should learn it before the wedding."

We had arrived at the moment of truth, and the imam asked Nadia, in English, if she agreed to marry me. I thought back to that moment at the mosque, and I was certain that I had shared with him that Nadia spoke no English at all.

The room fell silent. I began to feel faint.

I turned to ask my friend to pass me a glass of water and saw Nadia smiling and staring at the imam. She was the only one in the room smiling.

He repeated his question, in English: "Do you accept to marry Azzedine?"

Nadia smiled again and looked to me for a translation.

My mouth was dry, and the room began to shift into slow motion. The remaining beer in my yellow babouche started sloshing around. "Just say yes," I blurted out.

She did.

The room burst into laughter and cheers, and the band straightened their turbans and struck up "When Irish Eyes Are Smiling."

CONSUMMATION ANTICIPATION

The honeymoon was planned equally as well as the wedding, which is to say, not at all. The wedding night began with the hotel manager congratulating us on our marriage and asking how we had met. *Cringe.*

I had not thought about this part of the wedding. Let me just say that there are few moments less awkward in one's life. There also seemed to be a number of things Nadia was doing in preparation for her private chat with her mother in the morning. Like most men, I suppose, I had no idea what was going on. Lucky for me, all went well and, like the wedding party, a good time was had by all.

At brunch the next morning, the seating arrangement had shifted significantly as a number of amorous couples had formed during the course of the wedding. Nadia and her mother were whispering quite a bit and looking at something hidden in Nadia's purse, but I didn't follow up on what was going on—something about Nadia no longer being a girl.

I was busy trying to convince my new wife that the restaurant menu was not some type of practical joke. She didn't think it was possible that steak could be on a breakfast menu, and the French onion soup she had ordered was clearly a joke: it was filled with cheese, bread, and onions—all of which she removed.

We left for Washington, DC, that afternoon, newlywed and newly met.

NADIA COOKS

I had accepted the position of associate Peace Corps director in Yemen, but first we moved temporarily to a government apartment building while

I prepared for the assignment at the DC office. My friend and professor at Harvard, Russ Davis, once told me that one should never do three things at the same time: take a new job, get married, and move somewhere new. It wasn't as though I had planned to do any of those things simultaneously, but clearly . . . maktub—it was written. And so it was. I was relieved not to have to look for more consultancy assignments. Off we would go to a new land. We would discover it, and one another, together.

An urgent call came in for me shortly after my first meeting began. There were no mobile phones in those days, so three people had passed along the message by the time it reached me—about a woman screaming into the phone in an unknown language. Someone, somehow, managed to understand that the government apartment building was on fire, and the front desk confirmed that the fire alarms in the building were indeed blaring.

Nadia had made her first toast as a married woman.

When the smoke cleared and the fire engines left, Nadia went to do some shopping in the George Washington Hospital gift shop across the street. She figured it was a safe place to shop, in the event that she was either admitted for smoke inhalation or fainted when her new husband came running home after leaving the first meeting of his new job.

Later that evening, I assured Nadia that I thought the whole situation was funny and that she would not have to pay for any damages out of her dowry.

This reminded her: When would I be making the first payment to the dowry? It seemed to be in arrears.

HOUSEHOLD EFFECTS AND THE UNKNOWN BIRTHDAY

For my part, I wondered when I would be receiving my first paycheck and whether Nadia would be a casual shopper or addicted to gold, clothes, and shoes. One good sign on that front was when she went to an American supermarket for the first time and felt overwhelmed. She had to leave the store quickly, having realized that there were one hundred and seventy-nine varieties of mustard on the shelves.

When I was told somewhat casually by my new boss that most any item Nadia might want in our adopted country would not be available, it was clear we had to go shopping before we left for our overseas assignment. Everything we bought, he explained, could be shipped with all our other household effects.

We didn't have anything to ship, and furthermore I was not sure what a "household effect" actually was. But I nodded knowingly as the administrative officer explained in great detail, with no irony at all, that what goes in must come out, and that included household effects. There was no mention of any digestive system analogies.

My first formal request in my new job was to apply for annual leave so that I could attend my own wedding in July. The administrative officer was somewhat flummoxed. There was a great deal of paperwork to fill out, and she had already uncovered a number of irregularities in my documents. We would need to spend most of the day clarifying those irregularities, such as why I did not have any household effects.

The administrative officer explained, in a heavy southern drawl, that she needed to know where our household effects were. When I said we had none, her face replied that all men are morons and she would need to speak with my wife to get any real information.

Her first meeting alone with Nadia lasted four minutes before I was called in to interpret.

Nadia has a great smile, and in later years she would use it to create greater levels of confusion as part of her strategy to get anything she wanted. These were the early days, however, so she could only smile and make knowing sounds as if she understood what anyone speaking English was saying.

"What is Nadia's birth date?" asked the administrative officer.

"Nadia, when is your birthday?" I asked my wife.

"Wait a minute, don't you know her birthday?"

"No."

"Why not?"

"Because we just met."

"You just met your wife?"

"Yes."

"Is this a joke?"

"No."

"OK, when is her birthday?"

"Nadia, when is your birthday?"

"I don't know," Nadia replied.

"She doesn't know," I told the officer.

"Nadia doesn't know her birthday," the officer repeated flatly.

"No."

"Well, who knows her birthday?"

"No one knows it."

"Well, the form here says it's July 29."

"That's what I wrote on the form, yes."

"You filled out all these forms?"

"Yes."

"Why?"

"Because she doesn't know her birthday."

"Are her parents alive?"

"Yes."

"Do they know her birthday?"

"No one knows her birthday. I did the best I could filling out the forms."

"Why did you say her birthday was July 29?"

"Because her mother said it was a hot day when she was born."

By then the birthday discussion had gone on too long, and Nadia was wondering why I wasn't translating anything. When I explained the confusion, she said she thought it must have been in September.

But I couldn't say it was September now. It was too late. I had written July 29 on our marriage contract, our marriage license, and the form that allowed us to ship household effects.

"Ask Nadia where the household effects are," continued the administrative officer.

"We don't have any household effects," I said.

"You must have household effects, so please just ask her."

"Nadia, where are our household effects?"

"What are household effects?" Nadia asked me.

"Stuff," I replied.

"We don't have any stuff."

"That's what I told her."

"What's Nadia saying?" asked the officer. "Stop talking and just translate."

"She says we don't have any stuff."

"I asked about household effects."

"Aren't household effects just stuff you have in your house?"

"Well, we don't say it like that in the government, but if that is the only way I can communicate with you—just this once, yes, it's the stuff in your house."

"We don't have a house."

"Where do you live?"

"We don't live anywhere."

"Are you homeless?"

"Well, you know the telephone call you got about the woman who was screaming in a strange language and set the apartment building on fire?"

"Yes."

"That was Nadia, and that is where we live."

"That is a government-owned property!"

"Yes. It has weird household effects, and the toaster has been destroyed, but otherwise all the government-issued household effects are still intact. But none of them belong to us."

THERE MUST BE A CONSPIRACY TO UNCOVER

I quickly learned that government officials live in another world, where everything must fit into a form in the proper order. Any deviation from that form means there is likely fraud occurring or a contrivance of unknown intent. In the mind of a bureaucrat, the reality of anyone living in the gray areas of life cannot be. All life forms must comply with the form.

Nadia did not know her birthday because her parents did not know her birthday and because birthdays in Morocco were not celebrated, so there was no clear record of her birth date. Her younger siblings were considered very modern and westernized; they knew when they were born and, in fact, even went so far as to have a piece of cake on that day.

There is a fatalism to not knowing your birthday. Nadia would only answer that we will never know when the day has arrived for us to die, so why should the day we were born be so important? The government official did not share that view and vowed that she would get to the bottom of the conspiracy to defraud the government. To my knowledge, however, no fraud concerning our household effects was ever uncovered.

The next stage of our orientation to government life was to have a full physical examination at the US State Department, to confirm that we were in good health and able to travel to disturbed areas. The casual inclusion of phrases like "disturbed areas" was something I would come to accept as the years went by. It was akin to someone saying, "By the way, you could be killed at any time," and your response would be, "Oh, you don't say? Please pass the salt."

It was the words "State Department" that threw the receptionist off. When I went to the doctor's office to have my eyes examined, I presented the forms at the front desk. The sullen receptionist asked me where the results of the test were to be sent.

"To the State Department," I replied.

"The state department of what?" she asked.

"No, just the State Department."

"The state department of motor vehicles, the state department of health . . . ?"

"No, the Department of State."

"Just saying it backward doesn't help me," she scolded, "so if you want the exam, you need to start speaking English and stop being a wise-ass."

I left without the exam and was relieved to find out from the form-obsessed bureaucrat that both Nadia and I had in fact been approved for top-secret security clearance. So our physical examinations would take place at the Department of State, located in the Foggy Bottom neigh-borhood of Washington, DC.

No Arabic translator was approved for Nadia's visit, however. And when we entered the State Department's maze of hallways, we went our separate ways in order to be prodded and poked into good health.

As I lay naked on the examination table, the office phone rang. The doctor excused himself, explaining that the phone never rang during a physical examination so it must be urgent. He nodded a few times and looked over at me, shivering on the table. "I know this is awkward," he said, "but you need to take this call." He asked me not to get dressed, because we needed to finish the exam quickly due to his busy schedule.

I stood in the middle of the room, stark naked, with the phone cord dangling dangerously close to the source of my future family, and calmly explained that Nadia did not know her birthday and it might be best for me to clear up any other details once I had clothes on.

The doctor, and the female nurse, did not seem fazed and continued their important work, carefully documenting any birthmarks by drawing on the outline of an anatomical male figure on their forms. After all, there was no sense in wasting time, and in fact standing upright made an otherwise sensitive measurement easier to complete.

I was pronounced healthy and capable of fathering children. And if anything unfortunate should happen to me in Yemen, my corpse could potentially be identified thanks to a very thorough documentation of my birthmarks.

Sana'a

You may remember my only previous experience with Yemen was when I had to look up the Arabic word for "hemorrhoids" in order to interpret in English for a visiting Yemeni government official. It crossed my mind to get in touch with him, as I didn't know anyone else in the country. But I hadn't spoken to him since that day, and I thought the first telephone call would simply be too awkward: *Hi, it's Azzedine from Harvard. Remember, we met when you were having your hemorrhoids examined by the doctor? And how are they?*

So rather than go that route, I decided just to make new friends as soon as I got settled.

A THIN VENEER OF MODERNITY

Nadia and I arrived in Yemen as newlyweds, strangers in a strange land. Yemen is an ancient civilization, thought by some to be the source of the frankincense and myrrh brought to the infant Jesus by the three kings. Whether or not this is a myth, the mysterious nature of stories from Yemen persists.

Time travel had become a fixture in my life by then, so leaving Washington, DC, in 1988 and arriving in ancient Yemen was accomplished through modern flight. The veneer of 1988 was thin in Yemen, and it was easy to get lost in the past, something still very much alive there. Admiring the Yemen Gate in the ancient city of Sana'a, the capital of North Yemen, we saw pockmarks left by cannon fire. The gate is a thousand years old, and stepping inside transports you back to the day it was built. To the left of the entrance is a tiny, darkened room that serves as a grist mill. Inside the room is a camel who spends his life walking in a tiny circle as he turns the stone that grinds the wheat. He and his ancestors have been turning that stone for a thousand years.

Continuing forward through the gate, we saw that the stone street was littered with small green leaves. If you followed the trail of leaves, you would walk by men sitting atop piles of branches looking off into the distance, eyes glazed and faces deformed, one cheek pushed out by a giant wad of those leaves that stretched the eye so taut, they could not see out of it. In some cases, a tiny stream of green liquid oozed from the corner of the mouth. This was my introduction to qat, the intoxicating leaf that was chewed daily and around which much of daily life revolved.

I needed no introduction to the bureaucrat we encountered in Sana'a, as he was the overseas equivalent of the administrative officer back in Washington, DC. Bureaucracy is as ancient as the Yemen Gate. This bureaucrat's first question was: "What is your name?"

"Azzedine," I replied.

"What is your real name?"

"Azzedine."

"Let me see your passport."

"Why?"

"I want to know your real name."

"That is my real name."

"I refuse to call you Azzedine."

"Why?"

"Because you don't look like an Azzedine."

"What should I look like?"

"You should not have blue eyes."

"Are you a student of history?"

"Why?"

"Just wondering if you have looked into the Crusades at all."

"Stop talking nonsense and give me your passport."

In the end, the administrative officer had to admit my name was Azzedine. But our run-in spelled trouble, and his suspicions continued to grow. To him, I was not what I appeared to be. He was very suspicious of the seeming unfamiliarity I had with my own wife and her paperwork. He clearly believed he was in charge of the embassy, and he was confident that he would uncover my deception.

DISCOVERING QAT

The people working at an American embassy represent two worlds: the world of the Americans, and the world of the people from the country in which the embassy is located. In many ways, it was a class system, and not just with two levels for Americans and Yemenis. Within those levels were multiple classes as well. At the top of the American class system, for example, sat the ambassador. At the bottom were the administrative staff—like the officer who was determined to cause trouble for me.

The ambassador loved Yemen and all things Yemeni, including qat. The only problems he had with qat were that his tongue would swell so much he couldn't talk (which was not always a bad thing) and sometimes he had trouble breathing (which was more of a problem).

At our first home in Sana'a—a stone, one-story building surrounded by high walls, barbed wire, and beautiful bougainvillea bushes—we had a guard who opened the gate in our high wall and watered the bougainvillea. He tended the tiny strip of flowers and lived in a small room in the garden. As we got to know Abdullah, I asked him if he was married.

"Yes, of course," he replied. "I am a man."

"Yes, I know you are a man, but are you married?"

"Yes, I am a strong man with many children."

"Where is your family?"

"They are in the mountains."

"Why don't they live with you?"

"Because I don't have any money."

"But I pay you."

"I have too many children."

"How many children do you have?"

"Five."

"But when do you see them?"

"I go to the mountains and do my duty."

"How often do you go do your duty?"

"I told you I have five children, so obviously I have gone once a year for the past five years. Can't you do math?"

I learned a lot about Yemen from Abdullah. It became clear early on that his daily salary was entirely consumed by his qat addiction. He outspent his entire salary on qat, and nothing I said to convince him to budget his money had any effect. He usually countered by trying to convince me to buy the qat so we could share it and spend the afternoon chewing.

I knew nothing about qat but was learning quickly that if I did not chew, I would be missing out on a huge part of Yemeni cultural life. My first priority, though, was dealing with the administrative officer at the embassy.

THE UNDOCUMENTED MAID

The administrative officer insisted that my paperwork was not in order and that I had simply failed to fill out the forms for the shipment of my household effects. I repeated the litany of reasons why we had no household effects, but he insisted that we did and were trying to hide something.

I tried to explain the logic: there was nothing to hide because there were no household effects because there was no home.

He persisted, countering that any man with a wife had to have household effects, so having no household effects meant that Nadia was not my wife. The discussion turned ugly, and the class system at the embassy began to show.

The first official correspondence from the embassy hit my desk the first week we arrived in Yemen. The administrative officer informed me, in writing, that no mail for my "maid" would be forwarded through the diplomatic pouch from the United States.

The diplomatic pouch is basically the internal mail system used by diplomats around the world to send things among one another. The pouch is a large canvas bag that is secured with a seal and can never be opened by anyone else but an authorized person who has diplomatic immunity. There are plenty of movies where the diplomatic pouch is used to transport top-secret documents, spy secrets, and sometimes even spies who stuff themselves into the pouch and survive the journey in the cargo bay of an airplane.

It was true that Nadia did not know her birthday, did not have any household effects, and did not know me very well. But most certainly she was not my maid. She was my wife.

I marched over to the American embassy, a traditional old palace and a magnificent example of Yemeni architecture, to confront the bigoted offender. The mud skyscrapers of ancient Yemen stood proudly behind white painted archways and stained-glass windows. The embassy compound was made up of such buildings, and the American ambassador loved these buildings and the embassy gardens. He would fight to the end when, a couple of years later, Washington, DC, decided to build a new embassy for security reasons.

To enter an embassy, one must pass through a series of security checkpoints. Back in the days when bombings were rare, it was not such an arduous process. I had the proper identification, so I made my way to Marine Post One, where a US Marine stood watch over everyone coming and going through the front door. Not everyone who works in an embassy is a diplomat, nor are they necessarily diplomatic.

There were moments when some people forgot they were in a country not their own and made comments, in front of their Yemeni colleagues, that would never meet the standards of a diplomat. The administrative officer was one such type. There is a reason that Dilbert cartoons are so popular. We all live with a Dilbert in our lives, and this guy gave the word "officious" a new meaning.

"I got your message about the diplomatic pouch," I began.

"There are no exceptions," he insisted, "and my decision is final."

"What is your decision exactly?"

"That no mail is allowed in the diplomatic pouch for maids."

"I don't have a maid."

"Mail came in for an Arab, and she is not on my list."

"Mail came in for an Arab?"

"Yes, there are no Arabs on my Form 29-dash-B."

"We live in an Arab country called Yemen."

"You are on American soil in this embassy."

"Are you a diplomat?"

"I am in the embassy, and that is all you need to know."

"Please give me my mail."

"You can have your mail, but you cannot have the mail for the Arab maid."

"I don't have a maid. What is the name of the person getting mail?"

"Nadia Ben Khayat."

"Nadia is my wife."

"This person does not have the name Downes."

"She kept her last name as Muslim women do."

"You cannot marry a Muslim woman."

"Why not?"

"Because you are not Muslim."

"But I am Muslim."

"You can't be Muslim. You have blue eyes."

"Have you ever lived in another Muslim country?"

"No, this is my first time."

"Nadia is my wife. Give me her mail, or I will take this up with the ambassador, who loves Yemen and loves to chew qat. When he is flying high from the qat, I will mention you and watch his face cringe at the sound of your name."

That was enough to do it. But even though I walked out with Nadia's mail, I knew he would live to fight another day.

THE GLARING TRUTH

In my new job in Sana'a, I managed fifty-four Peace Corps volunteers. The big boss was the country director, an Armenian American named Hrand who had grown up in Iraq and spoke Arabic in the Iraqi dialect. I was an associate director. We had both arrived in Yemen at the same time.

Hrand loved Moroccan food, so Nadia and his wife, Shaheen, enjoyed having low-key cooking competitions. We men were the beneficiaries, although we never entered the kitchen because there were so many knives lying around. One evening we started out with two competing dishes, couscous or biryani, and I thought the silverware was just for eating—but the conversation began to drift toward the topic of marriage, and the knives were out.

Hrand's wife, Shaheen, was an Indian American who dove right into the details of my marriage, starting her assault in English: "How long have you been married?"

"Three weeks."

"But you have only been here for two weeks."

"Right, we got married right before we came to Yemen."

"Why isn't Nadia answering?"

"Because she doesn't speak English and has no idea what you are saying."

"Well, when did you ask her to marry you?"

I couldn't answer her question.

Shaheen was pressing for details that I could not provide. I was beginning to get the feeling that she must have been a cog in the wheel of the Indian bureaucracy during the Raj. She soldiered on. "Where did you meet?"

"What do you mean, when we first spoke to each other?"

"Do you speak English?"

"Yes, I do, but I don't understand the level of detail you are asking about."

"When did you meet? It's a simple question."

"Well, I saw her in Tangiers, Morocco—"

"I didn't ask you when you saw her. I asked you when you met her."

"Well, she came to America a month ago—"

"You just told me you have been married for three weeks."

"Yes, that's right."

"Well, just tell me how you asked Nadia to marry you." It was Shaheen's last command that stopped the lunch being cordial.

A feeling of dread crept over me—the same feeling as when I had asked Nadia's mother if Nadia wanted to marry me. Allela had dismissed my question and mentioned that a letter would be sent to Nadia, and shortly thereafter we got married. But I had not written the letter. I did not know what was in the letter. And, in fact, I had never seen the letter.

Somewhere in our house, as far as I knew, was a letter that contained the secrets of my marriage proposal, but Nadia had never shared the letter with me.

I fell silent, embarrassed, as the three of them—Hrand, Shaheen, and Nadia—sat staring at me, waiting for a response. My brow began to perspire. The glaring truth was, I had never asked Nadia to marry me.

The curse of Fatouma popped into my head. For a split second I wondered if Nadia and Fatouma were long-lost friends, part of a cabal that had spiked the various couscous luncheons and had succeeded in luring me into marriage. Perhaps the nefarious letter contained a contractual promise of paying the mortgage on Fatouma's condominium in Fez, in exchange for releasing the curse once Nadia and I signed the marriage contract.

Where was the letter?

Why had Nadia hidden it from me?

Did the letter even exist?

DELVING INTO THE DOWRY

Desperate to change the subject, I considered turning the tables to interrogate Shaheen about her wedding to Hrand. Armenian weddings fascinated me, thanks to Armenian friends who would regale me with stories of the fights that had broken out at their own nuptial celebrations. The Armenian diaspora spread its seeds all over the world, and like all immigrants, visiting cousins often brought their political baggage. Add in the mélange of languages and dialects, and these weddings sometimes resulted in hurt feelings—and stab wounds. Carried out in the Arabic spoken variously in Iraq, Syria, Palestine, Lebanon, France, and New Jersey, these "friendly" arguments never seemed to be resolved by eating the delicious foods at an Armenian feast.

But I resisted this topic and instead explained that Nadia and I had been married by the imam in Boston. We had a marriage license from America and had signed the marriage contract, I said, which included the promised dowry.

Shaheen's eyes lit up. "How much was the dowry?"

"Two diamond rings, ten 18-carat gold bracelets, and five thousand dollars," I replied.

"What else?"

"That's all."

"What a bargain! Nadia, you are so cheap!"

Hrand tried to jump in, but Shaheen carried on with her inappropriate remarks, divulging that in Yemen, some dowries were 250,000 dollars, and repeating her comment that Nadia was "a real steal."

Shaheen didn't sense that I was growing more uncomfortable by the minute. Nadia, however, sensed that I was not interpreting truthfully.

I decided this was not the time to tell the story of how I had offered a visa and a green card as part of the dowry, but the mood had turned sour anyway, and Hrand and Shaheen left with a story to tell.

Meanwhile, I was no closer to seeing the all-important letter.

THE MYSTERY OF THE WHITE CLOTH

In Yemen, TGIF became TGIW: Thank God It's Wednesday. The weekend there consisted of Thursday and, of course, Friday—the day for prayers at the mosque. Nadia would prepare couscous for lunch, and I would set off to the mosque.

There are many mosques in Sana'a, but I decided to attend the small mosque closest to our house. The building held no real architectural interest compared with the far grander mosques around the city, but being a newcomer, I thought it best to stay close to home in the hopes of meeting my neighbors.

A taxi was often stationed outside our house, the half-asleep driver feigning disinterest. I always found it curious that undercover security agents were so obvious, but I was assured by the embassy security officer that most foreigners were under surveillance, so I should regard the taxi as a comfort rather than an annoyance. The not-so-undercover agent did not follow me to the mosque and apparently went back to sleep.

Our street was not paved, and the dust floated up as I walked. I was accustomed to going to the hammam before prayers, but it didn't seem to be a custom in Sana'a, so I had performed my ablutions at home and put on white clothes and my yellow babouche from Fez.

The mosque was already full when I arrived, so I removed my babouche in the courtyard and looked for the small boxes on the wall that typically are there to hold shoes in all the mosques I have visited. I stuffed my babouche into one box that still had some space and found an empty spot to sit on the ground in the courtyard.

As I was sitting silently waiting for prayers to begin, I noticed that the small boxes on the wall contained not only shoes but pieces of white cloth. I didn't think much of it but stored away this detail to ask someone about this Yemeni custom later, so I could be sure to follow suit.

OUR HOUSE IN SANA'A

On the way home from the mosque, I often saw a long line outside the public oven at the end of our street. The daily life that revolved around ovens and bread was not like in Fez, however. The bread here was of the pita variety, and there were no symbols pressed into it. People did not make their own dough at home and then bring it to the oven to be baked. The sale of the bread in Sana'a was more transactional. It was also delicious.

The oven being so close to our home was habit forming. Once the smell of fresh bread wafted near, our neighbors would rush to the oven before all the bread was sold. I soon learned to join them. It was best to eat this bread hot and straight out of the oven.

Nadia would have the couscous all ready when I got home, and we would sit together, just the two of us, in the *mufraj*—the traditional Yemeni lounge full of sofas that are more like soft mattresses on the floor.

Many Yemenis have the mufraj on the top floor of their home, and if there is a great view, it includes many windows. An abundance of pillows against the wall and hard boxy pillows upon which to rest your elbows allow you to talk and slowly sink into an afternoon siesta. Eating on the floor is not all that difficult after years of going to the mosque for prayers and sitting cross-legged or with one leg folded under you for hours at a time. Over time, I also learned that people in Sana'a did not linger over a meal but moved quickly to the qat-chewing sessions to begin their hours-long daydreaming.

Our house had only the ground floor, so there was no view to be had, but we spent many hours in that mufraj and mostly ignored the rest of the house. As in many houses in Yemen, a multitude of doors separate the living room, the mufraj, the dining room, and the kitchen. The homes are designed that way so male and female guests can be sequestered—men never see the women, and vice versa. The outside world and the inside world always remain separate.

In all the years I lived in Yemen, I never saw beyond the veil of my female neighbors, although Nadia was always invited and would disappear into the inner sanctum. She was soon relegated to the young girls' area of one neighbor's home because she never partook in chewing qat. There was no qat in our home. The Yemeni women found this quite funny and silly.

THE STORY OF THE LETTER

As we sat together one day in the mufraj, I asked Nadia to tell me the story of the letter—to go step-by-step through how she learned that we were going to be married. Sana'a did not offer much of a social life, so we definitely had time on our hands—enough for the story to unfold.

She began her story by saying she packed a suitcase to come to America. I have learned over the years that Nadia is not the greatest storyteller. She often starts a story in the middle and everyone is immediately lost. She even starts a joke with the punch line and then explains why the joke is funny without ever actually telling the joke. I stopped her and asked her to tell me when she had received the letter. I wanted to know her reaction to it, but I also wanted to know what was in the letter, as I had never seen it. She started the story again.

The letter had arrived in Tangiers, she said, and she had read it before hiding it under her mattress for a few days. In fact, she had read the letter over and over, and she would treasure it always. She couldn't provide any more details than that.

Eventually she showed the letter to a cousin, who congratulated her on her impending marriage. She then showed it to her grandmother, who asked if I was the same boy who had danced for her; hearing the answer, she advised Nadia to marry me immediately. So Nadia started packing a suitcase for America.

I asked her to show me the letter. She looked for it amid her belongings—but even to this day, she has never found it. So we agreed that it must have gone missing in the move to Sana'a.

Nadia told me not to be upset about losing the letter. She repeated that she would treasure the letter forever. I wanted to point out that she could not really have treasured it all that much because it had gone missing in the short time we were married, but then again, I wasn't really sure how much of my feelings I should share with someone I hardly knew. More importantly, I realized in that moment that I had never personally asked Nadia to marry me. There was no romantic moment of a proposal. There was only a missing letter.

THE SHEIK

Heading to the mosque one Friday, I fell in with a group of Sudanese men walking to prayers. They were extremely tall and wore the most brilliantly white clothes that made my white robes seem dingy. Atop their heads sat enormous, impossibly high white turbans that I imagined must have been constructed with a heavily starched bolt of cloth at least ten feet long. Even though dust clouds jumped from under their sandals, they somehow remained spotlessly clean.

When we arrived at the mosque, we removed our babouche, stepped inside, and looked for empty spots in the shoeboxes on the wall. As during my previous visit to this mosque, I found pieces of white cloth stuffed in among the shoes. I asked my new Sudanese friends what the cloth was, but they only chuckled and gave no answer.

It was a hot day, and I was happy to find a spot on a bright red carpet inside the mosque rather than sitting outside in the courtyard. Once men are settled in their place for prayers, they generally don't change places unless there are so many people stepping over you that you are forced to shift positions. When prayers begin, straight lines are formed with brethren standing shoulder to shoulder and feet to feet. If a space opens up in the line in front of you, the two people on either side of the empty space will signal with their hands that someone should fill the empty space. No empty spaces are ever left open once the prayer begins.

As I sat waiting for that moment, two men approached me and whispered something in the ears of the two men sitting beside me, who then immediately jumped up and found other places to sit. An elderly man then approached and sat beside me, so that the two whispering men had spots on either side of us.

I soon noticed two newcomers sitting in the line in front of us and another two newcomers in the line behind us. I thought it odd that these young men would practically surround the elderly one but figured he must be their father and deserving of respect. Perhaps I, inadvertently, had taken a chosen spot.

The elderly man and I exchanged whispered greetings and then sat in silence. As prayers began, all the men in attendance performed them by standing, bowing, kneeling, and touching their foreheads to the floor. Throughout this process, there was the normal forming and reforming of the lines as men departed, empty spaces opened up, and other men moved forward to fill them.

When an open space opened up in the line directly in front of me, I took a step forward to fill the space. But the elderly man grabbed my arm, pulled me back, and said, "My son, you stand next to me, please."

I nodded and remained by his side.

During the next part of the prayer when I pressed my forehead to the floor, I glanced quickly sideward and found myself looking into the barrel of an AK-47. I slowly looked to the other side and met the barrel of another AK-47. I'll admit I was distracted at that point and don't remember if I performed much of the remaining prayer. I was more focused on the details of the guns.

My prayer was that the men with the guns would lay them down gently so they would not go off accidentally and blow my head off. Dying during prayers had its advantages, of course, and I made a mental note to research this in the event I encountered such a fate.

Prayers ended, and I remained sitting quietly, waiting for something to happen. It didn't. The elderly man bade me farewell, and his posse got up and left with no further ado.

I waited until the mosque had cleared of the crowd and then asked a nearby man if he knew the elderly man. I was told that he was a well-known sheik and the men with the guns were his bodyguards.

The sheik had chosen to sit next to me not at random but with good reason, my new acquaintance explained. Anyone attempting to assassinate the sheik would hesitate if a foreigner might be killed in the crossfire. For this reason, it was always best to keep disputes contained to killing fellow Yemenis and not get families of foreigners involved. Gunfights were fairly common, he explained, and the sheik would always seek me out and sit next to me at prayers.

I made a mental note to find a new mosque.

GUNS, DRUGS, AND MARITAL HONESTY

Driving through mountainous Yemen was incredibly beautiful, but not for the faint of heart. Jumping in the car to take an unplanned ride through the countryside was not an option. Foreigners were required to secure a permit even to leave the city. There were checkpoints on every road in and out of Sana'a as well as some, manned by military personnel, along the road. If you had not planned ahead, you would not have the permit in hand by Wednesday afternoon—a critical point because the weekend was Thursday and Friday.

In theory, you received the permit, kept it with you at all times, and showed it to the soldier at every checkpoint. In reality, we photocopied the permit, making twenty-five copies to hand out as we went. The original was kept in the glove box and rarely saw the light of day. I suspected that most times, the permit was tossed into the bin or used behind a bush in a way that clearly demonstrated how much the soldier thought of the bureaucracy that produced it. Many a young, bored, illiterate soldier inspected the permit, examining the proper authorizations, all whilst looking at it upside down. Pulling away from the checkpoint never left me with the sense that the nation was safer as a result.

Agriculture in the countryside was undergoing incredible shifts away from the beautiful mountain terraces filled with fruit trees. The country had been a great producer of peaches, but when qat became so popular— and so expensive—farmers began ripping out fruit trees and planting qat trees.

In addition to causing all sorts of gastrointestinal problems, qat is an appetite suppressant and contributed to the rise in malnutrition among Yemeni women and newborns. Despite this and a host of other problems caused by the national addiction to qat, there was much discussion questioning its narcotic nature, and all my Yemeni friends did their best to convince me to start chewing with them. They assured me that it was not a drug.

I pointed out that being caught selling qat in Saudi Arabia brought a five-year prison term, and did that not mean qat was a drug?

The typical refrain was that by chewing qat, I would see America in an astral projection trip, and that qat was just like drinking Lipton tea. My assertion that I had never astrally projected to America while drinking tea held no sway.

The shift in land use across the country brought much activity at the Ministry of Agriculture, which was located in a building very close to our house. Disputes often resulted in shots being fired from the array of guns that everyone seemed to carry into the building. When one American embassy official was shot whilst driving by the ministry, we were warned by the regional security officer to alternate our route to the office. He described in detail the characters who might want to shoot us but never specified the reason for the assault.

I thought perhaps I could also ask the sheik who sat next to me at Friday prayers to ride along with me, based on the premise that proximity to each other meant we would not be shot. I wasn't sure if the same logic applied to being shot in a car.

Using my imagination, I went over the shooting of the embassy official in my mind and decided that it was the result of a stray bullet that had ricocheted off the ground. The bullet had then punctured the floorboards of his car and entered his foot, causing him to punch the gas pedal and plow through a fruit stand. Clearly, I assured Nadia, the shooting was a one-off occurrence and there was no need for concern.

I decided not to tell Nadia what happened next.

NIGHTMARE TRAFFIC

The official workday at government offices started at eight o'clock in the morning and ended at one o'clock in the afternoon. In practice, however, it was rare to find anyone in the office before ten thirty or after noon. The vast majority of "work" was conducted in the afternoon and early evening whilst chewing qat. That meant everyone basically had an hour and a half to go to a government office and get anything done.

The morning after the American embassy official had been shot, the crowd outside the Ministry of Agriculture was larger than normal. I figured, as was normally the case, there must be a serious land dispute going on. When two armed men jumped onto the hood of the Toyota Land Cruiser I was driving, I sensed the dispute was a bit different today.

Time slows at dramatic moments. As the bullets whizzed by, I watched calmly. It occurred to me that I would not be shot in the foot, because the bullets were maintaining a healthy height; most likely they would not ricochet off the soft body parts of the men firing back from the hood of my car.

Next I thought it best to switch on the windshield wipers in order to get the combatants' attention. I could remind them that shooting me, a foreigner, may cause problems down the road.

Did the incident last a few seconds, or was it an hour-long firefight? I can't say, but the windshield wipers did the trick. The two men stopped shooting, looked at me, and smiled, offering their apologies. Then they slid off the hood as I drove away to make my first meeting of the day.

The meeting began on time and was uneventful.

THE CRYING

One night Nadia asked me to return to the mufraj whilst she prepared dinner. I said I liked to cook and was happy to help. She started crying and explained that she did not want me in the kitchen—that I should go and sit in the mufraj. It was the crying that convinced me to do what I was told.

As I sat alone, I wondered what young married couples did with their time. I had not thought about bringing books in my household effects, and we had no television; I had not owned one for the past ten years. We had no children yet, so I'd imagined that we would spend time together just talking. I protested that it made no sense to have me sitting alone and her cooking alone in the kitchen.

Meanwhile, Nadia thought it made perfect sense for the husband to sit in the mufraj and the wife to be in the kitchen. Kitchens were not really a place for families to gather, in her eyes, and most kitchens in those days were not a place anyone would want to spend all that much time in anyway. She had the habit of talking to herself, so she had company of a sort. I, on the other hand, didn't talk to myself, so I felt ridiculous sitting alone.

The house was empty, so I began pretending that we had children and would call out that they should be quiet and get back to doing their homework. Nadia was upset by my antics, saying that I should never pretend to know what Allah would give us and I should just sit quietly waiting for dinner.

One afternoon, I insisted I was going to help cook. But Nadia took away everything I was working on, saying that I clearly did not know how to make Moroccan dishes. She suggested I go to the shop to buy spices, and it seemed like a good compromise—until she started crying again.

"The shopkeeper was a nice man," Nadia whimpered.

I agreed and said I would go and chat with him.

Nadia repeated that he was a nice man, and I repeated that I agreed. "No, he was, was, *was* a nice man," she said through more tears.

After a moment, I asked if he was no longer a nice man because of something that had happened at the shop. I was ready to storm out the door and defend my wife's honor. Exasperated, Nadia finally explained: the shopkeeper was dead.

The shop was next to our house, and I stopped by most days to say hello. It was much like the ones I knew from my life in Fez. The shopkeeper sat behind a counter, which served as the entrance to the shop as well as where all your items were placed in order to begin the calculations of how much you owed. You never entered the shop; there was no door, and all shopping was done via the shopkeeper, who fetched anything you asked for. There was no concept of "browsing."

My first encounter with the shopkeeper, and his two grown sons lurking in the darkness at the back of the shop, had not gone well. I had thought it best to start out simply and ask for items I could see from the street. I figured that there would be differences in Yemeni dialect and that the names of some things in Morocco would not be the same as in Yemen.

Greetings in Arabic can go on for quite some time. The better you know a person, the longer the greeting lasts. The crescendo builds, delving into health issues, the children, the parents, and back to health, and then it finishes up with a blessing that Allah will aid us all in our struggles. And then, finally, "Please give me a liter of milk."

Ending a conversation with a shopkeeper in Morocco also followed a script and ensured that everyone was polite, happy with the purchase, and most important, accepting of the price paid. Conversations could be formulaic, repeating the same words over and over. The exchange ensured that everyone strived to be a good Muslim. There were times when people buying items would become angry, so it was best to have a formulaic expression at the ready.

I quickly learned that the formula was different in Yemen, and I was not prepared for the argument that broke out at the end of my first purchase with my neighbor.

When I had finished pointing out all the items I wanted to buy, the shopkeeper asked, "Any work?"

"Work?" I repeated.

"Any work?"

I shook my head. "No, I have no work for you."

"I don't want to work for you."

"Why did you ask me for work?"

"I didn't ask you for work, I asked you if you have had enough."

"Had enough? Why are you being so angry?"

"I'm not angry, but I've had enough, have you?"

"I'm getting pretty close to having enough if you keep wanting to fight."

"Fight? What are you talking about?"

"Forget it, that's enough."

"Blessings for what?"

"What blessings? If you want to fight, I will find another shop."

"I've had enough. Any work?"

Clearly, there was a communication breakdown. He was not following any formula I knew, and now I wasn't sure if he would be pulling his *jambiya*, the Yemeni dagger, from his belt or giving me a discount for the groceries.

Language can sometimes be a reflection of spirituality, and you hear what you expect to hear. It goes far beyond ways of expressing the same exact thing. Husbands and wives know this to be true, even when there are no linguistic or cultural differences between them.

When a wife says to a husband that the grass is long, he hears: "You need to mow the lawn right now." She will respond that she never said to mow the lawn. He will retort that he doesn't have time to mow the lawn, and then she will push back by saying she was just making an observation. Neither of them believes their spouse's argument, but over time, they learn to live with the ambiguity.

So it was with the shopkeeper and me. We never came to blows. We made friends in the short time we knew one another. Through him, I learned the Yemeni formula was much more to the point than the Moroccan formula. I also learned that more French had crept into the Moroccan Arabic dialect than I, a French speaker, had even realized.

The shopkeeper was, as Nadia had said, truly a nice and patient man.

DEATH AND THE TAXI

I walked over right away to see if the shopkeeper's sons were at the shop so I could offer condolences. The true home of the three men was in the mountains, and like Abdullah the security guard, they visited the village once a year. The three men had no home in the city but lived in the shop. When it was time to close up shop, they made beds in the very back and slept there with their father. It seemed a sad existence, but they always had smiles on their faces. I suppose their lifestyle was not all that different from many men living away from their families in order to send money home.

The boys were sitting in the shop now, and I relayed my condolences and told them that Nadia had just given me the sad news. They thanked me and said that it was good timing that I arrived just then, because they were about to take their father home to the village. In Islamic tradition, the deceased are buried within twenty-four hours of passing, and there is little time for preparations. Visits to the family often take place after the burial occurs.

Awkward questions can be forgiven when ignorance of traditions is the cause, and living in the constant state of being a foreigner allows license. So I asked the boys what needed to be done and if I could help somehow in this difficult time. They expressed appreciation for the gesture, but the taxi beside me was there to take them home to the village.

I didn't know the word for "hearse," so I awkwardly asked where their father was.

Without hesitating, one of the sons pointed to the taxi. "My father will come home with us," he said. Sure enough, in the back seat of the taxi sat the corpse of their father.

The boys climbed into the taxi and waved goodbye as I stood there trying to process what I had just seen. This could not possibly be normal, even in Yemen. Yet people were passing by as they drove off, and no one seemed to take any particular notice. It was not just the fact that their dead father was in the taxi that struck me as odd, but that he was sitting up.

Getting back to the village before sunset was the priority, and a taxi was the best way to adhere to the Islamic practice. The boys had done their best.

RAMADAN

Ramadan is the month in the Islamic calendar in which Muslims around the world fast from sunrise to sunset every day, for twenty-nine or thirty days, depending on the sighting of the new moon that year. The Islamic calendar is a lunar calendar, so the months move eleven days earlier each year and drift across the seasons. One year, Ramadan might fall in the middle of summer, and the days are long and hot, so fasting is more difficult. Another year, Ramadan will fall in the middle of winter, so the days are short and cold, and people spend time snuggled under a mountain of blankets. Depending on where you live, sunset—the time when you can break your fast—moves later or earlier in the day. During Ramadan, there is obsessive clock-watching to make sure you are where you want to be when you break the fast.

During the fasting hours, Muslims can't eat anything, can't drink anything (including water), can't smoke cigarettes, and must refrain from sexual activity. If you live in the Netherlands, for example, the sun in the summer months doesn't set until ten o'clock in the evening; then it rises very early in the morning, so there are only a few hours of the night in which you can eat, drink, and get busy.

People who regularly smoke or drink ten cups of coffee a day outside of Ramadan are miserable for this whole month. And they make everyone around them miserable. One of the goals of Ramadan is to experience the daily struggle of poorer people who suffer from hunger and deprivation every day of their lives. It is not acceptable to be angry and lash out at people because of the thirst, hunger, or headaches you experience during the day. Ramadan teaches us to practice patience. Many people fail the test.

My first test of patience was suffering through the endless stream of people asking to see my tongue. "Are you fasting?" was a common question asked of people with blue eyes. People with brown or black eyes were assumed to be fasting and did not submit to the tongue inspection ritual.

In Morocco, random people would stop me in the street and ask if I was fasting. When I confirmed that I was, they asked me to stick out my tongue to see how dry it was. The first few times I found it amusing, but then I grew irritated and didn't want to stick out my tongue. Refusing to submit to the tongue inspection, however, resulted in a tongue lashing. My commitment to fasting was called into question. Once they accepted that I was fasting, people were somehow both complimentary and incredulous.

Many people around the world look forward to Ramadan, which confuses nonfasting friends, who say something like: "So let me get this straight. You can't eat or drink water from sunrise to sunset every day for thirty days? And that is something you look forward to?" As odd as it might sound, Ramadan is a time to reconnect with faith, patience, self-awareness, and empathy.

The disparate Ramadan routines in Morocco and Yemen helped create my first impression of my new country of residence as a very different world. In Morocco, it would be apparent even to the uninitiated that Ramadan had arrived. Ramadan life was a clear departure from everyday life. The foods we ate, as well as the attention to prayer, altered the daily routine. Breaking of the fast was a very festive time to gather with family and friends, and nighttime was a visual celebration with strings of lights hanging from trees, streetlamps, and houses.

In Yemen, I didn't get the same sense that life was altered in a substantial way. There didn't seem to be special Ramadan foods or treats when we broke the fast. When I was invited to join friends in Yemen, the focus still seemed to be getting through eating as fast as possible so that the qat chewing could begin.

Qat remained a central focus of daily life in Yemen, and not wanting to chew qat began to affect social life for Nadia and me. My focus for Ramadan meals was the Moroccan soup *harira*. There was no Ramadan without it. Perhaps less important, but a remarkable difference, still: no one in Yemen ever asked me to stick out my tongue.

During Ramadan everywhere, the mosques are full. Prayer is a form of meditation, and the sense of brotherhood and calmness within a mosque helps inspire patience. I had not yet found a new mosque in Sana'a, however, so I went to Friday prayers again in the mosque closest to my house. I hoped the sheik and his bodyguards would not be there, but I soon found myself peeking once more into the barrels of AK-47s during prayer. It is odd what you can become accustomed to.

What I couldn't get used to were the pieces of white cloth stuck in the shoeboxes on the wall. The mystery was finally solved during that first Ramadan, when I asked a fellow supplicant about the cloth. He said it was underwear that men had taken off along with their shoes, in an attempt to be really clean and make sure there was no pee on their clothing when they were praying.

I recommitted to my search for a new mosque.

Time seemed to slow down during Ramadan, and thoughts of getting any serious work done seem to fade even more. Work schedules were often adjusted, mostly to shorten the workday, and for most Yemeni bureaucrats, that meant not working much at all. The American embassy was struggling with how to handle the time-off requests coming from the Muslims working in the embassy.

Ramadan fell in the hot summer months that first year, and workers were asking the ambassador, a qat chewer, to shorten the workday. The ambassador phoned me and asked what we were going to do in our office; he wanted me, as a Muslim, to offer my opinion.

I was young and in good health, I worked in an air-conditioned office, and I had not altered the normal workdays. So I advised the ambassador that the people working outside in the hot sun should have a reduced work schedule, as they could not drink water during the hot summer days, but people like myself, working in air-conditioning, could continue their normal workday without much suffering.

The ambassador took my advice. All hell broke loose.

The general consensus was communicated to me by my administrative assistant. She stated boldly that, in her opinion, American Muslims must be much stronger than Yemeni Muslims and that if the ambassador took my advice and the Yemeni staff had to work normal business hours, they would go on strike.

To show leadership as a foreign Muslim, I shortened the workday and went home and took a nap.

Morocco

A CHIPPED TOOTH + A BOILING KETTLE = PREGNANCY

Remember the administrative officer in Yemen who would not believe my name was Azzedine? To make up for his refusal to call me by my name, he got in touch with his cousin who worked at Saudi Airlines and arranged for Nadia and me to fly to Morocco via Jeddah, Saudi Arabia. He even got us tickets in first class so we could arrive at our second wedding—the "real" wedding—in style.

When we boarded the plane, the only other person in first class turned out to be a Jewish Moroccan comedian who kept telling jokes that I couldn't understand. When the stewardess brought out a wedding cake, the comedian's only comment was: "Wedding cake? But Nadia, aren't you pregnant?"

This did nothing to quell Nadia's anxiety about the little baby bump she was showing. She worried about her mother making sure that everyone attending the wedding knew we had already been married for three months and were living together in Yemen. She didn't want any tongues wagging, saying we'd been fooling around before the wedding.

Nadia had never even told me she was pregnant. I found out from the embassy doctor. I saw him in the snack bar, and he asked how I was finding married life. I confided in him that Nadia seemed to burst out crying for no apparent reason, and I couldn't figure out whether it was me or living in Yemen. He told me to come to the embassy infirmary together with Nadia.

"What seems to be the problem?" I translated for Nadia.

She said she wasn't aware there was any problem, but admitted she liked crying from time to time—for example, when I chipped my tooth while changing a flat tire. Watching the kettle boil also made her emotional.

"Sounds like you are pregnant," the doctor said casually.

My first thought was of Russ Davis at Harvard, and his list of important life events that one should not seek to achieve simultaneously. I forgot to mention earlier that there was a fourth item on the list: have a baby.

Well, I had ticked all those boxes and then, for good measure, was headed off to tick another one, at a second wedding for me and my already wife.

SALLY AND MOROCCAN JEWS

As with the first wedding, I did no planning. Nadia's family arranged everything, and our friends and family flew to Morocco for a three-day extravaganza. All the women loved having their hands and feet hennaed, and all the men loved eating while seated on the Moroccan banquettes— long couches along the walls—and then falling immediately asleep as some loving mother covered them with a blanket. My brother told me that he had only ever dreamed that you could live in a place where you eat and sleep in the same place without ever moving. His dream had come true.

Some of our guests had a more difficult time acclimating to Moroccan culture. One of these was my friend Sally, from my Harvard days. Sally loved to be in charge of, well, everything. She often reveled in bossing us around and fancied herself a great organizer and traffic cop. Nothing had changed since graduation, and upon arriving at the Casablanca airport, even the smallest of details did not escape her eye. She immediately took it upon herself to comment loudly that she was deeply offended that Jews had to go through a separate line at immigration.

Before I could point out that there was no separate line for Jews, she announced that she did not wish to attend a wedding in a country that discriminated against Jews, and she would stand in the Jewish line as a protest to the affront. As she was escorted out of the line by armed Moroccan border agents, I explained the truth to her: the line was for Moroccan citizens, and the Star of David she was screaming about was actually the Moroccan flag.

The handcuffs were not all that tight, and the marks on her wrists had faded by the time we arrived at Nadia's father's house, inside King Hassan's palace in Rabat.

Despite this misunderstanding, Sally did not back down and never missed a trick throughout the wedding week. She immediately bonded with my sister in planning their attack on the palace guards. The two of them marched down to the palace doors whilst insisting that they should be allowed to tour the king's private quarters, just as they had done in Washington, DC, when visiting the White House.

"What kind of democracy is this?" exclaimed Sally as she was brought to the palace police station, where the meaning of monarchy and how it compared to democracy was explained to her. Fortunately, she immediately became distracted by the tiles on the sidewalk, which she found fascinating as she was dragged across them and away from the entrance to the king's palace.

The exasperated palace guards had their revenge on Sally years later when she ascended to the position of city manager in a western US city. Sally had never forgotten the look of those sidewalk tiles pressed up against her face. She so loved the tiles that she had some of them imported from Morocco and installed throughout the city.

Sally had overlooked the detail that such tiles were not meant for a city that experiences rain. People in her fair city began slipping on the tiles, falling, and breaking their arm. The city was sued time and again. Poor Sally was ousted as city manager, and the tiles were ripped out at great cost. For Sally, the impact of attending my wedding continued to ripple through time.

MY FATHER AND THE TIME WARP

My father told me he was looking forward to singing Irish songs and dancing up a storm at our wedding. Nadia's father had arranged to have King Hassan's private band play at the wedding, and I warned my father that I was quite sure they would not have any Irish tunes in their repertoire.

I also told him that there would be no alcohol at the wedding, something he found hard to believe. But then, he rarely believed much of what I told him about my daily life. He often remarked that I seemed to be describing life as it was hundreds of years ago.

For me, life was still that way when I was deep in the medinas of the

Old World. Hawkers still walked through the streets sharpening knives, selling fish, peeling fruit, and repairing shoes. If you needed something quickly, for example, you could ask one of the kids running through the streets. Going to the public oven and bringing you back some bread would bring them a reward: coin enough to buy themselves some candy.

It was only when he tasted his first Moroccan orange that my father began to believe I was living in a time warp. Eyes tearing up, he said, "I feel as though I am tasting fruit for the first time in my life."

EVERYONE IS BORN A MUSLIM

As family and friends arrived for the wedding, it became clear that they all had different ideas about travelling around Morocco. The first challenge was getting everyone to accept the idea that lunch would last for hours, a nap was nonnegotiable, and waking up to mint tea and pastries before dinner was the order of the day. The combination of those endeavors was each day's primary activity.

My sister wanted to know where all the museums were and why, as her recent run-in with the palace guards made abundantly clear, she couldn't visit the inside of the king's palace. I explained that if she kept approaching the guards at the gates, she would indeed see the inside of a building—but it would not be the king's private quarters.

The thought did cross my mind that having her disappear for a while would be an elegant solution to her attempts to plan the wedding, but I thought better of it. Considering the connection between Nadia's father and King Hassan's family, having a somewhat eccentric sister arrested and thrown in a dungeon, however enticing, would have caused a diplomatic incident.

The seeds of various problems had been planted, and as for Sally, the impact of attending the wedding rippled across the globe. Yoko, another school friend, flew in from Japan wearing a face mask to protect her from catching a cold. Nadia's family was delighted that Yoko had converted to Islam and was covering her face with a veil.

It mattered not that the veil looked like something you would see in a hospital. It mattered not that, as I explained, Yoko was just doing what so many people in Japan did on a regular basis, and it had nothing to do with being a Muslim. No, Nadia's family insisted, everyone is born Muslim, and some rediscover their roots and wear a veil because they are so devout.

When Yoko eventually removed the mask, the mood turned against her for being so brazen as to expose her face to men who were not her husband or part of her immediate family. She did regain some respect for covering her sensuous mouth with her hand whenever she laughed.

At university, Yoko had even used a second hand to cover her first, for added decency. But over time, she had all but dispensed with this habit, moving her hand farther and farther away from her mouth as she became more and more comfortable with the rest of us, until at last both hands were a good two feet away from her mouth whenever she giggled. I teased her about the impression this gave: that she was clawing at the air as she fell off a cliff.

Years later, Yoko became a minister of state and told me that her main focus was work-life balance. She took her revenge on my mirth over her clawing when I visited her in Japan, forcing me to sit through endless hours of government meetings conducted entirely in Japanese. She also arranged for me to march in a parade in a small Japanese village celebrating the arrival of black tea from India one hundred years before. My place in the parade was among a cadre of elementary school girls, and Yoko laughed without covering her mouth, so all could see.

WITHIN THE PALACE WALLS

King Hassan's palace in Rabat is an enormous complex surrounded by high walls and is accessible only through massive gates. The gates are closed at night, much as they were in the Middle Ages. The area where all the servants of the king live is called Touarga, a name derived from the Tuareg tribe, Muslim nomads of the Sahara Desert. Many of the original inhabitants of Touarga were slaves beholden to the king. Over the generations, families were freed but never left the employ of the king. Today, everyone still knows everyone within the palace walls.

So my comings and goings at night raised some suspicions, and I spent a number of hours in a small room while a guard looked through a very thick file. The file apparently contained vital information about me. I did my best to peek at it but didn't get a good look before it was slammed shut and I was sent on my way. I might have been the first foreigner who had family members staying inside the palace walls, but I can't confirm that.

I did my best to serve as interpreter for the wedding guests, but I did grow tired of explaining that jokes were actually funny if you understood the context. No one understood the context.

Despite her mother's best efforts, there were a few questions about Nadia's baby bump. I had to translate more questions than I had patience for concerning the exact date we were married in the United States. I was happy when Nadia's aunt lifted this burden, telling me that I would no longer need to sit there and answer questions about the first wedding night. She had all the answers anyone needed and was happy to supply them.

As during our first wedding, I had no idea what I was supposed to be doing. Just as no one explained to me how I was to be engaged, no one thought it was important to explain the wedding to me. When the guests began to arrive in force, I was told to stand in the doorway and greet them. I had the sense that the women in the family just wanted to get me out of the way so they could get Nadia ready for the many gowns she would be wearing that evening.

An army of unknown women called *ngeffas* flitted about. They were in charge of dressing Nadia and helping her walk around in the increasingly heavy gowns with their gold belts and matching crowns. I, on the other hand, was assigned just two suits of clothing: first a white Moroccan djellaba, and then a dark blue suit and tie.

As it was summer, I had brought a light-colored suit to wear at the wedding. When the ngeffa squad saw it, however, they flew into a tizzy. I had already broken an unknown, unwritten rule, and that's when I was shunted off to the front door of the villa to greet people I did not know. They did not want anyone to see me in the wrong color suit.

When the last guest passed through the door, I decided it was time to join the wedding. The couscous arrived—a huge bowl sitting in the center of the table—and everyone looked around, wondering if they should start digging in. But by then, my father was missing.

My brother told me that our father had been missing for half an hour already, and no one knew where he was. Our first clue came shortly thereafter: shouting from the kitchen, which could be heard over the dinnertime chatter. When I heard Irish songs being belted out, I rushed to the scene.

In the middle of the kitchen was a very conservative guest—a member of the Muslim Brotherhood, with a long, flowing beard—screaming at my father and the band, all of whom seemed unfazed. On the counter was a bottle of Johnny Walker Red Label scotch. My father was having the time of his life and loudly declared that I was completely wrong to tell him that Muslims don't drink alcohol. The proof before us was that the band was half in the bag and wanted to continue singing.

The infuriated bearded guest began shoving the offending band members out of the kitchen and told them that the wrath of God would rain down on them if they did not abandon their wickedness. He agreed that the music could continue at the wedding, but the drinking had to stop.

My father thought it was all part of the great fun he was having. But when I told him the couscous had arrived, he agreed to head to the table.

MY UGLY HANDS

When Nadia disappeared to change into yet another caftan, my American brothers informed me that their plan was to meet beautiful Moroccan girls that night and marry them. Meanwhile, all my Moroccan brothers wanted to know if I had any *other* sisters they could marry. The one who was at the wedding seemed to be already engaged to be married to the guy who was with her.

To get away from the interpreting job for a bit, I went and sat on the dais. Nadia had returned, and she looked very much like a queen. Not knowing the proper wedding etiquette, I copied Nadia and sat very formally with my hands on my knees for an hour while guests danced. Nadia's aunt sat down next to me and said it would be best if I took my hands off my knees and move away from the dais. Nadia's hands were decorated with beautiful henna designs, she explained, and mine were not.

"No one wants to see your hands," she informed me, "and everyone keeps asking why you are sitting up here like a sphinx."

I moved down a few steps, and the gap was filled with girls wanting to take photos with Nadia. I looked out at the dance floor and saw my father doing a version of a belly dance with a young woman who had hiked up her gown so far that naked skin never touched by the sun danced along with them.

Nadia's father sat down beside me and pointed out the gyrating couple.

"They seem like they are having a good time," I offered.

Grim-faced, Nadia's father agreed. "That's good, because tomorrow she is fired," he said. "She's the maid, and she should not be dancing in public with the father of the groom."

My father came to her rescue by intervening the next morning. The maid got back to work but gave him a bigger portion of everything the breakfast table had to offer.

Yemen and Saudi Arabia

TWICE MARRIED YET STILL STRANGERS

Nadia and I left for Yemen the next day. On the plane ride home, I thought about the long journey that had brought me to this point. I had been so focused on the *getting married* part of the journey that I had not thought all that much about the *being married* part of our life together.

Life in Sana'a offered few distractions, and there was little for Nadia to do during the day. She was invited to chew qat with the neighbors, and even though she refused to join in, she did get to talk with the people on our street, which is more than I had ever done. I made friends with colleagues, but it seemed clear early on that I would have few casual acquaintances or friends like I had in Morocco, if any.

Nonetheless, we experienced the thrill of a brand-new country, a new culture, and a new life—and we explored it all together.

SON, POINT MY CAR IN THE RIGHT DIRECTION

From 897 until 1962, Yemen had not a king but an imam: a religious leader who ruled the country. I was often told that during the time of the imam, there had been only one paved road and one car in all of North Yemen. That one short road led from the house of the imam to the mosque of the imam situated less than a mile away. True or not, this story stuck with me.

The 1962 revolution to overthrow the imam had been simmering since the 1940s, and in all that time, little progress had been made to alleviate poverty across the country. The revolution descended into a long civil war that flared on and off until 1972. Nadia and I arrived in Yemen in 1988, and it was fair to say that in those short sixteen years, the country had only just emerged from being frozen in time. Walking in and out of the old city of Sana'a was measured not in distance, but in time.

The same was true with driving in Yemen. Word on the street was that the government had no control of the country beyond sixty miles north of the capital city. There were paved roads linking the major cities, but any travel to small villages in the mountains was accomplished by driving through bone-rattling riverbeds and trails along cliffs. The road from Sana'a to Hodeida, on the Red Sea, was a beautiful winding road descending from the heights of the mountains to the sands of the coast. The preferred beast of burden, known for its ability to climb straight up a rock face, was the Toyota Land Cruiser.

In theory, everyone driving the roads had a driving license. In reality, that was a dubious claim. My first visit to Hodeida exposed the level of driving experience some new car owners possessed. At the port, I witnessed Toyota Land Cruisers being taken off the massive ships. There was great excitement as the vehicles cleared customs and the proud owners drove off with no plates and, apparently, no driving experience.

An older gentleman approached me and asked if I could point him in the direction of Sana'a. He didn't mean he wanted me to indicate whether he should take the road north or south; he meant could I literally point his Land Cruiser in the right direction because he didn't know how to put the car in reverse and just wanted to take off moving forward.

I obliged and made a mental note to avoid being present when a shipment of cars was being unloaded at a Yemeni port.

NOT AFRAID OF DYING QUICKLY

I had a regular schedule of visits to teachers whom the Peace Corps had placed in small villages. Some of these villages could be reached only by driving through rock-strewn riverbeds at a maximum speed of seven miles an hour.

I always chose to be in the driver's seat. A passenger had nothing to hold on to. Being a passenger resulted in arriving at one's destination battered by a jostling that could only be remedied by visiting a chiropractor. Being the driver meant you could hold on to the wheel and would not suffer your head being bashed against the window as the Land Cruiser rolled over the riverbed rocks.

To be clear, I am not referring to a riverbed rolling lazily across a fertile plain. These riverbeds were often in canyons. Driving to villages high in the mountains was akin to a mountain-climbing expedition.

I once picked up an older gentleman walking up the trail to his village. As we bumped along, I asked whether he had a car. He told me that he had never owned a car. Not only that, but when he was young, the only way to arrive at the village was to walk or to ride on camelback.

Perhaps the story about only one car in all of North Yemen was true after all.

The man then told me that we needed to get out of the riverbed as soon as we could, because it was raining farther up the mountain. I looked up to see dark clouds looming and tried my best to hurry. The water arrived as a trickle but steadily increased. By the time we reached the point where we could climb out of the riverbed, the dry river had become a stream—thankfully, not yet the raging torrent that thundered past as we drove alongside the river in relative safety just minutes later.

Safety is a relative term. Farther up the path, we crawled along the edge of a cliff that provided stunning vistas but also brought us inches from a thousand-foot drop to the bottom of yet another canyon.

When asked if I was afraid to drive so close to the edge of death, I answered, "No." This was half true. I wasn't afraid of being killed instantly when the car completed its plunge to the bottom of the canyon. I was only afraid of surviving the fall and lying at the base of the cliff, shattered but alive, knowing that death would come slowly because no one would ever find us.

THE KIDNAPPING TOURS

Poor drivers and natural hazards were not the only concerns when driving in Yemen. Carjacking occurred not infrequently, but it was not just the vehicle that some bandits were after. Kidnapping of tourists—German tourists in particular—became a lucrative pastime.

Tour buses that ventured into tribal areas were often captured and the tourists brought back to be guests of the local sheik. Once released, the tourists reported that they had been treated very well and enjoyed learning about the local culture in ways that no other tourist could experience.

Kidnapping German tourists became so popular that tour companies began advertising "Guest of the Sheik Kidnapping Tours." The German ambassador in Sana'a, never having been kidnapped himself, eventually got involved and shut them down.

During a day trip to see an amazing Yemeni house that sits atop a rock near the city of Sana'a, a friend and I got out of the Land Cruiser to admire the view of the valley below. A young boy, cradling an AK-47 in his arms, approached nonchalantly. We exchanged polite greetings, after which he said he was sorry, but he was taking my car and leaving us stranded.

He waved the gun at us a bit and asked for the keys. I hadn't noticed how he had arrived, but then saw another Land Cruiser with an older gentleman sitting in the driver's seat looking over at us.

I wasn't ready to give up the car so easily. "Listen, my son, please just let us go on our way."

"No. I am taking your car. I have a gun and you, oddly, do not."

"You are quite right about the gun, but I am your older brother, and you are not showing me respect."

"I don't know you, and you are not my family, so I don't need to show you respect. Give me the keys."

"The man with me is my guest, and you are embarrassing me. Please just leave us alone."

"No. I want your car."

"Who is the man in your car?"

"That is my grandfather."

"Well, before you take our car, I would like to speak with him."

"He will just say that you should give me the car, but go ahead and talk to him."

I approached the boy's grandfather and exchanged greetings. "Sir, please don't take my car. It will cause us all problems."

"True, but it will be a bigger problem for you than it will be for me."

"True, but look at the car. It has diplomatic plates on it. If you take the car, the ambassador will call President Ali Abdullah Saleh, and you know what problems that will cause."

He thought for a bit and then called to his grandson. "This man is your brother," he said, "so leave his car alone."

The boy didn't hesitate and told his grandfather he would obey. He then turned to me and suggested we do something fun, given that he was not going to steal my car. As giant buzzards flew overhead, he screamed with delight and shouted, "Let's shoot the birds!"

With that he opened fire and began spraying bullets in all directions.

I jumped behind a boulder and watched as the bullets ricocheted off the road in front of oncoming cars. His grandfather told the boy to get back into the car and then, as they drove away, invited us to chew qat with him sometime.

The birds, the car, and my friend and I all escaped unscathed. Perhaps it was maktub that we were to return safely to our homes. I was quite proud of myself, in fact. I had remained much calmer during the attempted carjacking than I usually did in a Sana'a traffic jam.

THE ADVANTAGE OF CALM

I learned through these experiences that remaining calm could be disarming. It was not the expected response, so it invited curiosity. It also invited speculation (once again) as to my true identity, which was at times amusing and at other times rather exhausting.

During the carjacking, I simply didn't care all that much about the government-issued car and figured we would find a way home. There was also something amusing about how nonchalant the boy was in announcing he was going to steal the car. It may be a fault of mine, but I find humor in most things.

Traffic is not one of them.

Drivers in Sana'a had an interesting habit of viewing empty space as a lane. It didn't matter if the lane was a sidewalk or the opposite side of the road full of oncoming traffic. It never occurred to the intrepid drivers of Sana'a that driving up onto a sidewalk filled with pedestrians would eventually impede the forward motion of any and all cars in the vicinity.

It didn't matter that driving head-on toward cars would eventually mean that no one could move in any direction. It didn't matter that AK-47s appeared and were fired into the air in frustration. All that mattered was that other drivers, and the traffic, just could not be allowed to prevent anyone on the road from getting to their desired destination in order to chew qat that afternoon.

How had such a situation evolved? I couldn't figure it out.

I did learn that the Egyptian government, as part of its economic development foreign aid, had sent hundreds of driving instructors to Yemen right after the revolution. Thinking back on my first driving experience in Cairo, it all made sense: the driving in Egypt's capital is some of the most chaotic in the world.

OUR UNEXPECTED SAUDI HONEYMOON

Nadia's crying about my chipped tooth—a vital key to her pregnancy diagnosis—is a story born from car troubles that provided not just a challenge but also an unexpected respite. When I was changing that flat tire on my car, the tire iron slipped off the nut and I whacked myself in the mouth. My lip split and my mouth filled with blood as well as what felt like a lot of sand. Had it flown off the tire iron and into my mouth? Upon inspection, I discovered no sand in my mouth. What I thought was sand was actually the remains of a tooth.

The upside of hitting yourself in the mouth with a tire iron in Yemen is that you get sent to Saudi Arabia to fix your tooth. Nadia and I were authorized to have dental work done in Jeddah, on the Red Sea. It might sound odd, but I was happy to be getting on that plane to see a dentist in Jeddah. My wife and I had never gotten a chance to take a honeymoon, so this would be a romantic getaway—our dental honeymoon.

Checking in to the Red Sea Palace Hotel in Jeddah caused immediate confusion. I put my American passport and Nadia's Moroccan passport on the desk at registration. The Saudi man checking in next to me put up five passports: one Saudi, and four Moroccan. He looked at me, and

I at him, and then we turned around to see Nadia talking to the man's four Moroccan wives.

He smiled and asked, "You only have one?"

The clerk asked if we were all together. I told him we decidedly were not.

Telling people you were having a great time in Saudi Arabia got strange reactions. When I phoned my brother-in-law to tell him where we were, he asked me how soon we would be able to leave. I laughed and reported that we were having a great time in Jeddah—sitting outside in cafés, sipping ice-cold juice. He questioned my grip on reality and said that he had never heard of anyone going to Saudi on a honeymoon.

This trip, I explained, was more the result of an assault with a tire iron than a true honeymoon. That didn't seem to improve his opinion much. But when I told him we were going to Mecca, he switched gears and congratulated us on the plan.

NEOPHYTE PILGRIMS

The hotel was advertising a day trip to Mecca, so we booked a car and headed off as religious pilgrims. As you approach Mecca, the highway divides into lanes for Muslims and non-Muslims. Only Muslims are allowed into the city of Mecca. I'm not sure where the non-Muslims are headed.

When our driver stopped at the tollbooth, we did our best to look holy. I had brought my marriage contract with me to prove that I was Muslim, as I thought the blue eyes would be a problem. But the wonderful thing about Mecca is that you will see the greatest variety of humanity ever assembled. All it took to pass through the tollbooth was a greeting in Arabic, and we continued on our way.

When the sight of the Great Mosque of Mecca appeared, the driver said, "Here we are. Please be back at the car in an hour."

"There must be some mistake," I protested. We had planned to spend the entire day in Mecca.

The driver grew angry and said the hotel excursion was for one hour, after which we needed to head back to Jeddah. So we told him to leave without us and said we would find a taxi back to Jeddah. We had become religious pilgrims and were no longer simply on a dental vacation from Yemen. Honeymoon or no honeymoon, we did not come all this way for a one-hour tour of the center of the Muslim world.

Millions of people visit Mecca every year. Making pilgrimage to Mecca is one of the five pillars of Islam, and every Muslim with the means to do so is expected to make the pilgrimage once in their lifetime. For many wealthy people, the pilgrimage is something they can do—and want to do—more than once. It is also a blessing to send someone to Mecca, and I was happy to do that for my Moroccan mother: to fulfill her dream by financing her once-in-a-lifetime pilgrimage. For her, it was truly a blessed religious obligation.

It is common to see people returning home from Mecca to great fanfare and delight. The pilgrim earns the right to be addressed as *Haj* or *Haja*, a great sign of respect used when addressing a person who has fulfilled their obligation. Many pilgrims also return with gifts from all the shopping they did in Mecca.

Throughout history, Mecca has always been a trading post. Still, the shopping seemed out of place to me. I had imagined a quiet, reverent ambience, but that idea was quite inaccurate.

With throngs of people circumambulating the Kaaba, the very center of the Muslim world, there was no time for quiet reflection. Originally, Muslims prayed in the direction of Jerusalem, still the third holiest site in Islam after Mecca and Medina, but starting in the year 624—year 3 in the Islamic calendar—Muslims were expected to face Mecca instead. Political tensions between Israel and Palestinians still prevent most Muslims from ever visiting Jerusalem and the holy mosque at the Dome of the Rock, but all dream of making the pilgrimage to Mecca.

Although pilgrims came from all around the world, there was no difference in what they wore: all white cloth with no stitching. The simplicity of the garb ensured that there were no indications that might signify wealth, social status, or country of origin. One difference that did become apparent quite quickly was that most pilgrims seemed to know what they were doing.

Nadia and I, on the other hand, were utterly unprepared.

BURNING FEET AND THE CRUSH OF HUMANITY

Our first challenge was the heat. On the day of our unplanned visit to Mecca, the heat reached a staggering 53 degrees Celsius—that's 127 degrees Fahrenheit. As I looked out over the massive white marble floor, and then down at my bare feet, I wondered how we would survive the experience.

The Kaaba sits in the very middle of the mosque. Pilgrims walk in a circle around the structure, reciting specific prayers. Some people prepare their whole lives for that moment. Nadia and I were in awe, but we were also on a hotel-sponsored, extended one-hour tour and had done no preparation. The floor reflected the blazing sun. Our feet would soon burn.

I must have looked frightened, because a kind man approached and asked if there was a problem he could help us solve. I told him I thought my feet would be burned if I stepped out onto the stone. He assured me that Allah would cool the stone with the water of the Zamzam, the spring that has been flowing in the very epicenter of the holy mosque since 2000 BC. It has medicinal properties that are mentioned in a number of holy books.

Sure enough, as I stepped onto the stone, I found it cool to the touch.

I pondered the miracle of Zamzam water as we joined the throngs of pilgrims. I later learned that Saudi engineers had installed air-conditioning below the marble floor, but nonetheless it was hard not to be emotionally overwhelmed by the experience.

I was amazed by the waves of humanity circumambulating the Kaaba, but I also was struck by the frenzy to touch the cloth covering the structure. It is forbidden in Islam to worship idols, which—along with idolatry— were destroyed in Mecca with the advent of Islam. So I found it odd that a physical structure incited such desire to touch it.

Similarly, pilgrims jostled to kiss the black stone embedded in the corner of the Kaaba. The desire to kiss the stone has its roots in the tradition that the prophet Muhammed kissed the stone. Millions of pilgrims trying to do the same meant that people were crushed and cried out in pain. I preferred the serenity of areas where quiet reflection on the import of our visit could take place.

Our visit to Mecca was so rushed that we didn't really have time to reflect. The last taxi of the day leaving for Jeddah was at six o'clock in the evening, and it was now five thirty, so our unplanned pilgrimage was at an end.

The pilgrimage to the taxi stand, along with hundreds of other people, seemed equally rushed. We did get to know a Muslim family from Senegal intimately when they piled along with us into that last taxi of the day leaving for Jeddah. We had arrived in luxury, riding in the hotel Mercedes, but we left Mecca with a family of nine sitting on our laps in a taxi built for three.

THE IMAGINARY BABY

Nadia was happy that her tummy was growing larger and larger, so I thought it would be a good time to bring up the issue of me sitting alone in the mufraj. She still insisted that I should sit alone and have a coffee or tea while she was doing things around the house. It was never really clear to me what exactly she was doing. When I asked, she declined to share those details with me.

She also did not want me in the kitchen, even though I continued to insist that I enjoyed cooking and would prefer to at least sit with her while she cooked. No, she insisted, I had to sit in the mufraj alone and wait for her to arrive with dinner.

I never minded being alone, but it didn't make sense to me to have the two of us alone whilst living together. I was used to being alone and had already lived a solitary life for many years with neither a phone nor a television.

Our new home did include a television, but it only worked with the old VCR that sat beside it. Apparently, there was no television antenna on the roof, and it didn't occur to me to have one installed. You will remember that I had not owned a television for many years, nor did we have any household effects, which meant we had no videos to watch.

To entertain myself, I continued the habit of pretending that the baby had arrived, had grown immediately to the age of seven, and was a little rascal who had to be brought under control by his young father. We never wanted to know the baby's gender, but I pretended it was a boy named Aziz. I would call out to Aziz and tell him to be a good boy.

Nadia would come running in from the kitchen and ask if someone was in the house.

No, I would explain, I was just practicing to be a father and telling little Aziz to behave himself.

She said only Allah would determine if we had a baby boy, rascal or angel. The first part of her argument I understood, but the part of Aziz being a predetermined rascal did not sit well with me, and we had our first disagreement. Our arguments usually evaporated along with the steam coming off the delicious tajine that Nadia prepared for supper, however, and soon we were laughing about the kind of parents, God willing, we would be.

FUTURE CITIZENSHIP

In 1988, Yemen had one of the highest infant mortality rates in the world. It also had one of the highest maternal postpartum mortality rates. The reasons for such a dire health situation were hotly debated, but the issue of qat chewing always came up as a possible factor.

Since qat is an appetite suppressant, the theory was that neither the pregnant women chewing qat nor the fetus were getting adequate nutrition during pregnancy. Once a baby was born, it was still not getting adequate nutrition via breast milk because of the effects of the appetite suppressant. Anemia and malnutrition were serious problems then that persist today in war-torn Yemen.

This was now a very real issue for us. Our baby was due to arrive in Yemen. Did that mean the baby would be Yemeni?

Despite my first miserable attempt to present a visa as part of Nadia's dowry, I had never arranged for her to acquire a residency visa or US citizenship. So it was not only the infant mortality rate in Yemen that weighed on my mind, but also the baby's future: he would have a difficult time explaining that he was born in Yemen to parents of different nationalities. In essence, he would be a man without a country.

When we looked at all the factors that affected the baby being born in Yemen, we decided to take the advice of the embassy doctor and send Nadia to the United States. So Nadia went off to America alone, with no English, to live with my father and my brothers.

A HAUNTED HOUSE AND A REAL BABY

Nadia's first challenge with living in America was her fear of going upstairs in a wooden house. During our telephone calls, she would tell me that the house spoke a lot at night. At first, I thought she was saying the house was haunted. Then I realized that the house was just creaking in the wind.

I convinced her that wooden houses creaked all the time and there was nothing to worry about. We talked about her going to live in Morocco instead while waiting for the baby to arrive, but we decided that it was too late to change our minds. Most airlines don't allow women to travel beyond the seventh month of pregnancy. Plus, my father loved having her stay with him, so there she stayed.

She was in labor at the haunted house for a full day before she mustered the courage to say, "Daddy, baby," whereupon she was driven to the hospital and gave birth within the hour. I got the news whilst sitting alone in Sana'a that my imaginary child was now real.

I was the proud father of a baby boy named Abdulaziz.

BROKEN ENGLISH AND THE LANGUAGE
OF MOURNING

After making arrangements to fly home that week, I arrived at my father's house to be greeted by my father and brothers all speaking in broken English and odd French-ish accents. Nadia had not learned English per se, but my family had learned to speak a new Nadia language.

One brother said everything to Nadia in English with a cartoonish French accent, even though he did not speak French. He explained to me that Nadia understood him better that way. My father opted for an approach that leaned more toward pidgin English, somehow thinking that speaking in very broken English would help Nadia learn the language. My other brothers simply smiled and ate whatever Nadia prepared for them.

I had arrived from Yemen for a joyous occasion, but it was also one of the most difficult times in my life. The birth of our baby was darkened by the death of Nadia's mother from breast cancer.

Nadia was well aware that her mum was ill and that the treatment she had received in America had not been successful. Allela had arrived in America too late. The anger surrounding the dismissal of the severity of her condition, despite its early detection, had never subsided for Nadia and the rest of her family. Allela had returned to Morocco to be with family and await the inevitable.

When Nadia got home from the hospital, we sat together on the bed with our baby son cradled in her arms. I struggled to find the words to tell her that her mum had passed away just as the baby was born. Nadia's mother had dreamed of seeing her daughter married, happy, and with beautiful children. Nadia had accomplished the first two goals in time, but sadly her mother did not live long enough to learn of Nadia giving birth to Aziz.

The desires of a mother for her daughter weighed heavily on me as I considered how to break the sad news. I had no idea how Nadia would react. We hadn't known one another for very long. The only experience I had with Nadia conveying the news of a death was when she told me that the shopkeeper in Yemen had suddenly passed away. I also wanted to make sure that I was expressing myself in Arabic in an appropriate way.

Before I could begin speaking, however, tears started rolling down my face. Nadia sensed what was coming and let out a scream. When I finally got the words out that her mother had passed away, her first reaction was to deny it. She said that she had just spoken to her mother, so it was not possible that Allela had died. I told her that her brother had travelled to Morocco and that, in accordance with Islamic tradition, Allela had already been buried on the day she had died.

I didn't expect the wailing that came. Nadia scared me, holding the baby tighter as she wailed and flailed on the bed, and I took Aziz in my arms. Her cries grew louder and became moans of anguish, and I could do nothing to calm her. The baby began crying too, but nothing I could say soothed either my wife or the baby.

It was only when she saw my own tears flowing again that Nadia suddenly turned to me, in her moment of grief, to offer comfort. Her act of kindness shocked me, and I knew at that moment that I would love this woman.

Now there was silence throughout the house. I recalled what my father had told me about the tradition of professional mourners in Ireland, who were hired by Irish families to wail convincingly at funerals or wakes. The same show of emotion is common across many countries in the Middle East. The rawness silences everyone.

I learned much that day. Is anyone truly comfortable with expressions of grief? Nadia's grief was tumultuous. My brothers seemed flummoxed and remained silent. My father showed his grief through an act of kindness.

He came into the bedroom. "Hold your baby," he said quietly to Nadia. "Know that we love you and know that your baby will love you as you loved your mother. So sit up now and hold your baby."

I don't know if Nadia understood much of what he said in that moment, but she knew that he loved her, and that he wanted her to take the baby and cuddle him. And that is what she did.

LEAVE SOME NAPPIES FOR US

The few weeks that I had with Nadia and the baby in America were spent arranging paperwork, passports, birth certificates, and the shipment of the all-important household effects that were authorized when we first left for Yemen. We went shopping for anything we thought we would need for the baby. While Nadia focused on clothes, I searched for the critical item: Pampers.

As I transferred the mountainous display of nappies into the five carriages I was filling, the manager of the store approached me and asked if I was a new father. I proudly told him that, indeed, I was. He gently pointed out that I did not need to buy all the Pampers at once and asked if I could leave some for other customers—some of whom were looking on in awe.

I explained that we lived in Yemen and were shipping them in our household effects. He looked puzzled, muttered something about new parents, and ordered a nearby employee to restock the mountain of Pampers. He never asked me what "household effects" meant. I was disappointed to have missed an opportunity to explain the inanity of bureaucracy.

When everything was prepared for Nadia and Aziz's eventual return, I headed back alone to the land of Sheba, a claim Yemen disputes with Ethiopia. After a month, Nadia and Aziz followed, and the process of getting the Pampers through customs began.

Yemen had adopted not only Egyptian driving habits but also Egyptian bureaucratic norms. As I learned during my later travels to Egypt, bureaucracy, like cockroaches, could survive any attempt to destroy it.

On one trip to Egypt, when I was attempting to leave the airport in Cairo, the last bureaucratic hurdle appeared at the exit of the parking lot. The taxi driver stopped, rolled down the window, and gave my details to a police officer holding a massive book in which he wrote my name, my passport number, and the color of my eyes. The system had been in place from Ottoman times, and the mountains of dusty books were hidden away in long-forgotten crypts in the bowels of bureaucratic buildings, never to be seen again. To be fair, there may indeed be scholars sitting there as well, and perhaps their research into the number of travellers with blue eyes arriving in Cairo will someday prove invaluable.

I knew that getting anything approved at government offices in Sana'a took a great deal of time and a great deal of detective work. The workday at a government office was very short, and much business was conducted during the qat chewing sessions of government officials dispersed throughout the city, in private homes.

To avoid wasting time chasing paperwork, we had one staff member, called an "expediter," whose sole job was to chase down government officials and get the required signatures. Don't imagine a neat sheet of paper with two signatures at the bottom. Multiple signatures were required in order to prevent, for example, a possible criminal ring of Pampers smuggling.

During the process of getting approval to import diapers, it was clear that no one actually read the document. The content of the document was not important. It was the signature that mattered. Each bureaucrat only looked for one signature. It was not a random examination of the document to find the previous signature; the signatures always appeared in the same place on the page. Each bureaucrat knew the exact bureaucrat who was supposed to sign before he signed.

This made the process all the more difficult because the expediter had to find the officials in the exact order in which they would sign. If you ran into one of the bureaucrats on the street, there was no chance of getting them to sign out of order.

Most government bureaucrats, as I learned through this process, were filled with a bloated sense of self. For the most part, at the top of the bureaucracy were people who believed the system was designed to be efficient and transparent—ethical officials who were invested in rules and felt that everyone should be treated equally. At the bottom of the bureaucratic pyramid were the petty bureaucrats. These were people who used the bureaucracy for their own benefit and would simply open their desk drawer, stare at the pile of money sitting in it, and wait for you to drop a gift into the drawer before they would sign.

American officials considered this a form of corruption. Most anyone needing to get something done viewed it as merely petty bribery of petty bureaucrats. It was the cost of doing business, and it was my turn to pay.

VANQUISHING THE PETTY BUREAUCRAT

As my first bribe floated into the drawer of the feckless official, a tall, blue-eyed man standing nearby introduced himself in Arabic. He explained jauntily that he worked at the Dutch embassy and was at that moment working to get a shipment cleared through customs in the port city of Hodeida. After that first meeting, we would run into one another from time to time, and I complimented him on his good Arabic. He complimented me on my good English. I thought he was Dutch, and he thought I was Syrian. It turned out he was a Syrian working at the Dutch embassy, and I was—well, you know, confusing.

My new friend broke the news to me: I would never get the Pampers cleared through customs. Once he took a look at the growing number of signatures on the customs clearance form I carried around, he warned me that the final person on the list would be responsible for blocking the importation of these critical bum coverings.

The signature page was a work of art. Signatures of all shapes and sizes appeared all over the page. Some were written upside down, and others crawled along the edges. I had succeeded in getting ninety-nine signatures. The line for one signature on the bottom of the document was still blank. The final, hundredth signature on that blank line was all I needed.

My target was the most elusive of all bureaucrats—a wily, cunning cretin who came to his office, placed his suit coat on the back of his chair, ordered the chai wallah to place a piping hot glass of tea on his desk every half hour, and promptly left the building for the day. He was the person needed to sign the document. The trick was to find where he was chewing qat that day and accost him when he was in the midst of a qat-induced stupor.

Once I found him, he refused to sign the document. He just sat in the mufraj with his face distorted by the extended cheek filled with qat, and green spittle oozing from the corner of his slightly opened mouth.

"But I have all the signatures required, sir," I implored.

"I can't see if Mohammed Abu Walashay signed."

"He did, sir. It's right here."

"Well, why are you importing your household effects now? You only have six months to clear customs when you come to Yemen."

"Well, I didn't have any household effects when I first came to Yemen."

"You should have sent your household effects in the first six months."

"Please stop saying 'household effects.' It's getting annoying. This is stuff for my new baby."

"You should have sent all that stuff when you first came to Yemen."

"But I didn't have a baby when I came to Yemen."

"You should have expected that your wife would be pregnant and shipped the Pampers nine months ago."

"Are you questioning the will of Allah?"

"Of course not. How can you ask such a thing!"

"Allah determines when, and if, my son will be born—not your paperwork!" I exploded.

The room fell silent, and heads began nodding in agreement that Allah's will determined the birth of my son.

The one thing that had prepared me for victory on this day was that first disagreement with Nadia, who had never liked it when I spoke lovingly of our unborn baby. She had admonished me to not be presumptuous. The will of Allah would determine our future. In this case, that included importing Pampers.

The petty tyrant was vanquished. He signed the paper.

One hundred signatures had been required to import one hundred packages of Pampers (and things of lesser import that Nadia wanted). It may have been the intoxicating whiff of qat in the air, but I thought I heard the ghosts of the Ottoman Empire clucking their disapproval.

A WELCOMING MOSQUE

My new friend from Syria, Ali, invited us to his house. Nadia wanted to meet his wife and to see their baby. Over dinner, I told Ali about my experience at the mosque. I shared that I wasn't keen to pray with AK-47s in my face. He shared with me the best place for Friday prayers: the mosque at the university. The sheik and his bodyguards never prayed there, so there were very few guns lying about. We agreed to meet there the following Friday.

Ali was friendly with the imam at the mosque, so I was not surprised that day when he got up from the floor and stepped to the front of the mosque, where he whispered something to the imam. To my horror, the imam then announced, "We have an American brother here with us today. Could Azzedine please come up and address the congregation?"

I protested, but he insisted. So I made my way to the front of the crowd.

I often wonder how I find myself in these situations. In way over my head, I was not prepared to address the congregation. I quickly greeted everyone and headed back to sit down.

Ali stopped me and said that it was now time for people to ask me questions. I didn't want to answer any questions, but they came fast and furious.

"Do you see any differences between our mosque and your mosque?" one man asked.

"Umm, everyone here seems to wear flowers in their turbans," I replied.

"We want to smell good!" came the laughing retort. "What else?"

"In Morocco, when you enter the mosque, you always say: 'Peace be with you,' and everyone responds. But here when I greet everyone, no one responds."

A young man jumped up. "By God," he shouted, "I thought you were Syrian!"

Ali was insulted. How was being Syrian a reason not to follow polite Muslim protocol and return a greeting? He began shouting back at the offender. The AK-47s I had faced at my local mosque seemed less dangerous than the brawl that was unfolding. Whilst more men joined the debate, I quietly slipped out the side door and never returned to that mosque.

In Morocco I had neighbors who brought me to the mosque in their neighborhood, so I learned, as a child learns, to follow the example of my elders. I learned where to leave my shoes, how to hold them so they don't touch other people. Some people held them high above their heads, and others held them lower to the ground, all in an effort not to sully the clothes of another.

In some mosques, people were quite strict about making sure that your feet touched as you stood shoulder to shoulder to pray. There were many small differences in how people sat, how they moved through the mosque—and in Yemen, I knew none of them.

I was at home in Morocco. I felt as if I had grown up in Morocco, and it was rare that I would have any problems going to a new mosque. The only time I was ever questioned was when I would go to the mosques on a tourist path through the old city of Fez. Non-Muslims were not allowed in mosques in Morocco, and sometimes someone would challenge me as I entered. Once I greeted them in Arabic, an apology was offered and I was welcomed.

Even on my first visit to a small mosque in Saudi Arabia, I was surrounded by friendly people wanting to know: Where was I from? And how did I find my way to their mosque? I kept looking for a welcoming mosque in Sana'a, but I never found one.

WHAT DOES IT MEAN TO BE "SYRIAN"?

One day, Nadia phoned me in a panic. Someone was in the house. She was, therefore, hiding in the bedroom. I jumped in the car, rushed home, and found our guard, Abdullah, ironing clothes in the parlor.

I helped Nadia calm down and told Abdullah that he should not be in the house when I am not home. The thought of being caught in the house, and seeing a woman not completely covered in the traditional Islamic dress that women wore, had him shaking. He admitted that he never would have entered the house if a Yemeni woman had been inside.

The style at the time was to wear the *sharshaf,* a voluminous pleated skirt that reached the ground. Above the skirt was a garment that resembled a cape. On their heads, women wore a number of veils that could be lowered to increase privacy and modesty. Some women also wore black gloves, completing the outfit that sheathed them from sight.

Because my Peace Corps job took me to schools around the country, I met with various ministry officials, mostly men, as well as principals of schools, some of whom were women. I found it difficult to speak to women if they had all three veils in full coverage mode. I had no facial expressions to go on, so I didn't know if I was making any sense or if she had simply fallen asleep.

Even though Nadia did not wear a sharshaf in Yemen, she did wear traditional Moroccan clothing and covered her hair whenever she went outside. She was conservative in all respects, except for the all-black body covering, so Abdullah's coming into the house uninvited was a brazen move. I was quite angry. Abdullah's explanation: he thought that we were Syrian so it would be OK.

I made a mental note to research what the word "Syrian" meant in the Yemeni dialect. First my experience at the mosque, and now this—it seemed to mean something much more than simply a person from Syria.

Perhaps it was akin to the way we would say, in Morocco, that all foreigners were from Nazareth in the Holy Land. Perhaps referring to someone being Syrian in Yemen just meant they were a foreigner, someone from anywhere outside of Yemen. In any case, I told Abdullah I did not want him in the house with Nadia alone, and he complied.

He did, however, continue his habit of sneaking up on us at night and tapping on the window as he looked in. In a somewhat creepy voice, he would ask if we needed anything from the market. I always said no, and he walked away with a disappointed look on his face. I realized later in life that Abdullah was actually asking to have some time off. He simply wanted to go outside the walls of the villa where we lived. Years later, I felt bad that I had never caught on.

Abdullah must have thought that Syrians were really dumb.

BECOMING EBBI

Abdullah was a simple man and never asked for much. He did, however, chew a lot of qat every day, and I was never able to convince him that he could not take care of his family if he spent more than he earned on qat. I was saddened by the hold qat had on him and so many others in Yemen. So much of the productive agricultural land that once produced beautiful fruit was turned over to qat production. With malnutrition being such a problem across the country, it was hard not to become angry when looking at the enormous amount of water, energy, and money spent on a tree that contributed to the scourge.

Abdullah often told Nadia that he missed his five boys who lived with their mother up in the mountains and asked if he could walk around the garden with Aziz. Aziz was still a newborn, so Abdullah had to wait for that walk, but they eventually became great friends. When Aziz began to babble and say his first words, Abdullah told him that he should call his father "Ebbi," the more formal Arabic for "my father." The name stuck, and all my children and their friends, our other family members, and my close friends call me Ebbi to this day.

There was an advantage to our little family growing together in a land far, far away. It was not my country, and it was not Nadia's country, so we had to learn to live together in a place that was new to both of us. I never really knew if I was adjusting to married life or to life in Yemen.

We seemed to be the only newlyweds among our Peace Corps and embassy friends. We didn't have anyone who lived nearby to help us understand all the changes that all three of us were going through. One couple with whom we were friendly had no children, but they did have a pet sheep. Bo Sheep lived with them in the house and got shampooed with Woolite every week. But they were not much help with children.

It wasn't easy on Nadia. As when many husbands ask their wives that age-old question, "What's the matter?" the answer always came back, "Nothing." My insisting that something clearly was wrong never helped the situation.

When I would see her crying, I assumed *I* had done something wrong, and I wanted to find out what it was. "Why are you crying?"

"I'm not."

"But you are, I can see the tears."

"It's nothing."

"But then why are you crying?"

"I just feel like crying."

Of course, that made no sense to me. But sometimes she was crying when she held the baby and said that she wished her mother could see her with a baby. That was something I could understand, so we would sit quietly together at night, thinking about it, until Abdullah tapped on the window and broke the mood.

Nadia wanted to show her female friends the new baby, so she invited a number of them over to get caught up. They wanted to hear the story of Nadia going to America to have the baby, and then began talking about being pregnant and giving birth in general. They regaled one another with stories of their pregnancies—stories that had a particular focus on morning sickness. Having had no experience with morning sickness myself, and not having witnessed it in Nadia, I proudly said, "Nadia, you were so lucky! You never had morning sickness."

"Oh, I did," she replied. "I was really sick all the time."

"But why didn't you tell me?"

"Well, I didn't know you very well."

At that moment, I thought I must have won the prize for most clueless husband alive. Looking for a silver lining, I also thought repeating that story was the perfect way to respond when people asked me what it was like to marry someone you did not know.

Here she was married and pregnant, but she felt as though she did not know me very well. And she didn't. Nor I her. Yet I'm not sure that all couples know each other as well as they think they do when they marry. I do know that the time I spent with her, building a new life and family in a new country—and becoming Ebbi—was nothing short of magical.

ZEES IS ZEE BEANCIL

Across the country, in the smallest of villages, teachers from Egypt were instructing Yemeni children. The invading army of teachers from Egypt was just one part of the financial aid that Egypt provided Yemen, which included the aforementioned driving instructors who schooled Yemeni drivers in navigating their way through the country with maximum chaos.

As part of my job visiting Peace Corps volunteers teaching English, I was asked to evaluate the Egyptian teachers. For the Americans, English was their first language, so the evaluation was more about the methodology of teaching and how well they managed the classroom. The Egyptians, meanwhile, were not native speakers of English, and seemed to be placed in cities, towns, or small villages—some atop mountains and some on the border between Yemen and Saudi Arabia—according to their level of English proficiency.

The drive up these mountains often took the entire day, which meant I stayed overnight in the village, typically a place with no hotel, as a guest of the local sheik. Since medieval times, Yemeni villages have been situated on the top of mountains as a defense against invaders from other tribes or villages. The source of water for the villagers came from rain collected in vast pools hewn straight into the rock. Peeking into the pools as we drove by often exposed stagnant, murky water covered in green algae. The results of drinking such water were much clearer than the water itself, and health issues abounded.

Even so, the ingenuity of the people who climbed these mountains, carved the pools into solid rock, and built towering homes atop the peaks was incredible. I made the climb not on the back of a camel or horse, as the founders of many of these villages had, but in a comfortable Toyota Land Cruiser. Sometimes it was hard to believe that navigating the path up the mountain would be possible, in a Land Cruiser or any other vehicle.

One day, when my Yemeni travel companions guided me along a path that led straight into a rock face, I thought they were testing their theory that all "Syrians" were dumb. When I laughed and asked where the real path was, they said to just put the vehicle into low gear and climb the rock. I called their bluff and inched forward, waiting for them to call off the prank, but they never did, and we slowly, unbelievably, climbed twenty feet up the rock face and continued on our way.

The village we sought that day was high in the mountains and sat like a saddle perched on the only flat spot for miles around. There were two teachers of English, one Egyptian and one a Peace Corps volunteer, in a tiny school stuffed with as many children as could make the daily trek. A room built for twenty held as many as fifty pupils crammed into about ten desks, each made for two. Each desk held five smiling faces, screaming out what they believed were English words.

As was the case in Mauritania, my assignment was to report back to the Ministry of Education on the quality of English language instruction in small villages. The Yemeni ministry had high expectations. I avoided pointing out to the government officials that teaching fifty pupils in a mountaintop village smaller than the size of a typical school auditorium was not a sought-after position for most teachers. It definitely was not a selling point to attract the most qualified teachers in Egypt. Still, I could not deny the enthusiasm of both the teachers and the pupils.

Once inside the classroom, I listened patiently to the thunderous repetition of four words over and over. The teacher screamed out the incomprehensible words, and the students repeated them with gusto. There was no instruction other than a fifth word: "Repeat!" And repeat they did, shouting with glee during the entire forty-five-minute class.

"Zees is zee beancil!" the pupils repeated.

The teacher was delighted with his success.

I didn't have the heart to tell him that he had not exactly changed the trajectory of the students' academic careers. The students believed that they could now go out into the world speaking fluent English, informing anyone who would listen that "Zees is zee beancil." As I pondered what I could possibly report back to the ministry in Sana'a, I took a photo with the pupils, including the teacher holding up the pencil in question, and declared the session a complete success.

"Zees is zee beancil" would become one of those phrases that stuck with me throughout my life and aptly captured any absurd situation. "Zees is zee beancil" sounds so much more interesting than "It is what it is."

INCOMPREHENSIBLE WOMEN

The American Peace Corps volunteer teaching English in the village fared better with pronunciation but was bombarded with questions around her marital status. Villagers expressed their sheer disbelief that her father could allow her to be out in the world, alone in a foreign place, with no one to protect her. In order to squelch the swirling rumors that a single woman living alone atop the mountain was either a witch or a jezebel seeking new markets, she was placed under the protection of the local sheik.

She was not the only foreigner in the village. An Egyptian doctor was also placed in this tiny village. There was no available housing for the new teacher, so she made the local pharmacy, basically a small room, her home for two years. She never left the village and preferred to spend time talking to the men rather than the women. Thus she was deemed utterly eccentric and was accused of all sorts of nefarious fantasies.

Worse, she was suspected of not really speaking English. The village children held a small parliament and declared that she did not sound at all like the Egyptian teacher of English they had known for years, so therefore she must be a witch.

The Egyptian doctor advised me not to be too concerned with the linguistic expertise of the children or, in fact, any of the female villagers. He was a native speaker of Arabic, but he had a great deal of difficulty understanding the women of the village. He believed they had become so isolated from the men over centuries that they had developed their own dialect among themselves. When women came to him with medical problems, he often just made a best guess as to what they were talking about. For example, he took a woman complaining of heavy snowfall on the mountain peaks to mean that she was a young lactating mother who was worried about leakage of breast milk.

I thought back on my own experience, at Harvard, when I was enlisted to interpret for a visiting Yemeni scholar with hemorrhoid problems. Perhaps I should have been more poetic, coming up with more euphemistic descriptions in Arabic along the lines of "His irrigation system is showing signs of strain." A lost opportunity to be sure, but in the end, I believe I served him well.

I was not as eloquent as I had hoped when speaking Arabic in Yemen, so I was a little relieved to learn that despite being a native Arabic speaker, the Egyptian doctor had trouble understanding the Arabic spoken in the village. Learning a language, even one that you think you already speak, requires patience and a healthy dose of humility. Like a student repeating, "Zees is zee beancil," I repeated the new words I learned with the best Yemeni accent I could muster.

As time went on and I absorbed more words and accents, my mixing of expressions and vocabulary only added to the confusion people experienced in trying to figure out who I really was and from where I came.

WAR BREWING

In the summer of 1990, with tensions rising across the Middle East, the American embassy started to brainstorm how to respond if the violence spread to Yemen. American diplomats were based in the capital city, so wartime evacuation plans focused on leaving the country via the international airport at Sana'a.

Peace Corps volunteers, however, were spread out across the entire country, some in very remote areas. Our evacuation plans had two phases: first, to get volunteers to Sana'a, and second, to arrange for flights out of the country. All this was taking place long before the days of mobile phones, so volunteers relied on sending letters or calling the Peace Corps country office from their local post office. Sometimes a person in the village, usually the sheik, had a phone, and the volunteer would ask to use it in emergencies.

I thought it best to talk to the volunteers in person. I wanted to check on their mental health and find out if they had any immediate concerns. So I set out across the country to visit all the volunteers and discuss contingency plans in the event that they had to leave their village quickly. I also wanted to avoid discussing evacuation plans over the phone or through a third party.

It was not always clear where the loyalties of local officials or tribal leaders lay. We came up with a protocol to surreptitiously contact volunteers through a series of messengers. The goal was to avoid alerting anyone that the embassy had ordered an evacuation from the country. We thought of ways to pass on a message that had some urgency to it. One such coded message was that a family member had passed away and the family wanted the Peace Corps volunteer to come home for the funeral.

This didn't seem like such a great idea, however, when I learned that one volunteer, working up on the northern border with Saudi Arabia, had already used that same excuse to slip out of the village a number of times. The sheik, becoming suspicious, phoned me to ask how many people in the volunteer's family were on the verge of dying every month.

The other fly in the ointment of our plan was that a number of volunteers had devised their own plan to live together even though they were not married. The local sheik had phoned me a number of times to ask why volunteers suddenly got married without their parents' permission. The young, fraudulent, betrothed volunteers would fly off to Cyprus on vacation, have a great time absent any real wedding, miraculously return as a married couple, and then enjoy living in sin for the rest of their tenure in the village.

As part of their cross-cultural training, I had given newly arrived volunteers a briefing on social norms, dating, marriage, and how sex outside of marriage was viewed in Yemen, a very conservative society. I tried my best to get the point across that although they might not agree with religious and social restrictions regarding men and women interacting, they needed to be aware of them. They also needed to be aware of the impact that flouting those norms might have on their ability to work in a small village.

When I gave this briefing, two young men in the back of the room were snickering. When I asked why, they told the room that they needn't worry because they were gay and planned on living together. They quieted when I pointed out that in Yemen, gay men had been known to be thrown to their death from a tower.

The problem with faux marriages arose when the newlyweds decided that marriage was not for them and broke up. The men typically went on their merry way with little consequence. The women, unfairly, suffered a reputational loss—now divorced and once again living alone in the village.

Other happily "married" couples also used the excuse that one of them had to go to Sana'a because of a death in the family and left their husband or wife alone in the village. From the sheik's point of view, there seemed to be a tsunami of deaths in so many families in America. He phoned again, wondering if war had broken out in that faraway land, not just in Kuwait.

BABIES AND ANGELS

Along the Yemeni border with Saudi Arabia, there were always skirmishes, related more to tribal issues than to larger national problems. In 1989, North Yemen and South Yemen existed side by side as separate countries. Saudi Arabia was concerned that a unified Yemen would mean that the population of Yemen outnumbered that of Saudi Arabia. A large population of armed tribesmen in Yemen posed a threat to the Saudi monarchy.

Around the same time, Iraq was threatening to invade Kuwait. Saudi Arabia was firmly aligned with the Kuwaiti monarchy, but also provided economic and humanitarian assistance to Yemen. The Saudi government had built a very modern hospital in North Yemen, near the border. The Peace Corps had volunteers working in the local school and in the Saudi hospital. I wanted to talk to the volunteers directly about the impending invasion, so I made the ten-hour journey, bouncing violently along a riverbed and arriving somewhat black-and-blue at the border with Saudi Arabia.

Upon arrival, the local sheik invited me to chew qat with him at his home, a beautiful, multistory, traditional Yemeni home with a mufraj at the very top of the house. A delightful man, he welcomed me warmly, told me he was very happy to have the volunteers in the village, and introduced me to his sons. I couldn't focus on meeting his sons, however, because a toddler was crawling across the rug toward an open window.

When no one appeared ready to stop the little one as he inched closer to the floor-to-ceiling open window, I politely pointed out the impending danger. The sheik just smiled and said not to worry—the baby had fallen out of the window last week and was fine. An angel had caught him as he plummeted to the ground, the sheik said nonchalantly, so clearly the child was protected by Allah.

The baby was now just inches from the open window. To me, at least, time seemed to slow. I wondered: *Should I grab the baby myself?* This may have been interpreted as an affront to the sheik and to his belief that Allah protected the child. At the same time, I could hardly let the baby fall out the window.

"Sir," I said, "I'm afraid the baby will fall again."

"Not to worry," the sheik insisted. "An angel caught the baby before, and he had no injuries."

"But . . . angels will only catch each child once in their lifetime."

"What?" the sheik asked. "Are you sure?"

"My father told me that," I replied, "and I think it is true."

The sheik jumped up, grabbed the little boy, and shut the window. If I accomplished nothing else on that visit, I felt as though I had saved a life.

Babies in danger seemed to become a theme of the visit. I visited the Saudi hospital and found that a small baby had just been left by his mother on the hospital steps. Still outside, doctors and nurses were caring for the baby, and I asked what was happening. Would they try to find the mother and reunite her with the child? Sadly, they told me, the woman who had given birth to the little boy was not married. There would be a scandal if it was ever found out she gave birth out of wedlock. The baby was now effectively an orphan.

A scandal of this type, in this part of the world, was far more serious than, for example, being shamed on social media. The threat of physical harm to the mother was real, and thus, the baby suffered the consequences.

I had a notion to adopt the baby, so I phoned Nadia to ask her what she thought of my idea. Suffice to say, I did not bring the baby home.

WHO DOESN'T LOVE A GOOD BATTLE?

With emergency plans in place for the Peace Corps volunteers in North Yemen, I headed back from the sheik's home near the Saudi Arabian border to Sana'a. A meeting with the US ambassador was called to discuss civil unrest in the Middle East and its impact on US citizens living in Yemen. Embassy officials were concerned by the number of young men returning to Yemen from Afghanistan after fighting with the mujahideen to expel Russian forces.

One of the US embassy's assistance projects was to teach English at the Yemen–America Language Institute. We had Peace Corps volunteers there, so I was in regular contact with teachers and students. I met with a group of young Yemeni students in their twenties who told me they had gone to Afghanistan to fight. They loved their time with the mujahideen, really enjoyed battle, and hoped to go to war soon. They were well armed and had little to do in their day-to-day lives.

Meanwhile, there was increasing talk among politicians about unification of North Yemen and South Yemen. All those concerns were communicated to officials in Washington but went unanswered. Indeed, in May 1990, North Yemen and South Yemen announced they were now one unified country.

Those of us living in Yemen were not shocked by the news, but the bureaucrats in Washington were furious. Why had they not been informed by the embassy that unification was imminent? The long trail of cables back to Washington, telling them exactly what was expected to happen, proved this complaint groundless. Furthermore, it exposed a weakness in the system. Some low-level analyst, sitting in a dark room in a basement somewhere in Washington, had made the unfortunate decision that our warnings merited no further attention from the higher-ups. The news from the US embassy in Yemen had choked on the dust of bureaucracy.

A second major global event took place that year when Iraq invaded Kuwait in August. At that time, the Yemeni school system was filled with teachers from Egypt but also from other countries, and Yemeni hospitals were staffed with foreign doctors and nurses mostly paid for by the Kuwaiti government. All along the roadsides, billboards informed drivers that the Kuwaiti government had financed the road improvements and built the hospitals. There were no signs lauding financial assistance from the Iraqi government.

If you were to ask people on the street which countries helped Yemen the most in its time of need, rarely (if ever) would anyone mention Iraq. Yet when Iraq invaded Kuwait, the Yemeni government declared its support for Iraq. Not surprisingly, Kuwaiti financial assistance abruptly ceased.

This further damaged the Yemeni health care system and the people it served, who were already struggling. When I asked Yemeni officials why the government would support Iraq over Kuwait, the country that had provided them with so much critical assistance, they answered that they felt they had to support Iraq, as it had been the first country to send them military advisors in 1962. My only response was to ask: "But what have they done for you lately?" Sadly, the absurdity of war prevailed and there was little logic in the reasons given me for supporting Iraq and not Kuwait.

SECURITY RISKS AND THE AMBASSADOR'S TOILET

The northern part of Yemen was always awash with arms regardless of any active conflicts, and the news that Yemen supported Iraq, while America supported Kuwait, threatened the security of Western foreign nationals in the country. In a show of excellent timing, the American government was also in the process of building a brand-new embassy complex in Sana'a.

Although I was invited to tour the new embassy building, I didn't get the news right away. The guy handling the mail at the embassy was still angry about being forced to deliver mail to Nadia, the "maid" I had brought from Morocco, and continued to find creative ways to punish me. Not delivering a message from the ambassador was one of these ways. I finally got the message through friends, though, and showed up at the designated time to begin the tour along with other staff.

I did not receive a warm welcome at the embassy building site, however. After quite a bit of shoe shuffling and hemming and hawing, the ambassador's deputy told me that I couldn't continue on the tour because of security concerns. Being married to Nadia put me into a new risk category, and I might see something that exceeded my top-secret US security clearance. Being married to an Arab (who was rumored to be a maid) now made me a national security risk.

As I left the tour of the unfinished skeleton of a building, a rat ran across the floor of what would become the mail room, and I wondered if that was some kind of cosmic metaphor.

The US ambassador may or may not have been aware of any rat problem, but he was not at all happy about leaving his office compound near the old city—a series of beautiful, traditional Yemeni homes that had been converted over time to form the American embassy. He was further upset when his personal residence was hit by a rocket-propelled grenade. Luckily for the ambassador, he was not home at the time. The only victim was his toilet, which did not survive the attack.

More concerning from my perspective was the provenance of the grenade, which had been launched from the home of a Peace Corps volunteer.

I spent a great deal of time with the FBI, the CIA, and various other officials in an effort to determine the level of the volunteer's involvement in the attack. As in most spy novels, the culprit was love, sex, the promise of marriage, or some combination thereof.

I had worked hard (although often in vain) to convince the young volunteers that their personal freedoms were not the same in Yemen as they were in the United States. We were living in a very different culture, and freedom to do whatever you pleased was (to put it mildly) not an accepted principle, even in Yemen's large cities. Still, the decision to fly off to Cyprus for a fake marriage, for example, showed the extent to which volunteers were willing to be very imaginative in circumventing cultural norms.

In this case, one foreign woman was less willing to play along with the charade, and brazenly (in the eyes of the neighborhood wags) had announced that she and her Yemeni boyfriend were living together. Who could have imagined that a love triangle would involve an American woman, a Yemeni man, and a mini missile? Well, that is what happened.

It had never occurred to the hapless woman that her boyfriend had ulterior motives in convincing her to rent an apartment overlooking the American ambassador's residence. She had been duped. The boyfriend was arrested, and she left the country. And in the end, I'm pleased to share, the ambassador's toilet was replaced.

LOVE, LUST, AND ESPIONAGE

As political tensions increased due to the war, female volunteers began coming into the office to tell me that harassment was increasing on the streets. One woman working in a health clinic asked me whether I could beat up a man who was bothering her. I said I would need a bit more information before I pummeled a stranger, so she shared that the offending male was not a random person on the street but the local baker, her friend.

I didn't want to get into the cultural interpretations of male and female "friends" in this part of the world, but I asked her again for more details. She had gone to the public oven to buy bread. The baker asked her if she wanted to go into the back room and watch his dough rise. She thought that would be fun. He agreed they would have a great time and then proceeded to show her his rising "loaf of bread." Because he was a friend, she didn't want to go to the police. She just wanted me to beat him up, but not a lot—just a little. I declined.

Another incident occurred when a Peace Corps volunteer came to me saying that men were banging on her door late at night, demanding to come in. Her Yemeni boyfriend had told all his friends that his girlfriend liked to party, and she was now in serious danger of attack.

She was not alone. Other Western women were experiencing harassment and physical abuse whenever they went out in public. The diplomatic community began to pressure the embassy to put in place emergency evacuation plans.

To get a better sense of the volunteers' safety, I began another round of visits to the most remote villages. On one trip back to the Saudi border, I came upon a group of men unloading crates from a pickup truck. One of the wooden crates, with "Iraq" written on the top, had broken open, exposing the weapons inside. Saudi Arabia had joined the Americans in backing Kuwait when Iraq invaded. Yemen, siding with Iraq, was helping to sow discord inside Saudi Arabia.

Weapons were not unusual in Yemen. In the countryside, everyone seemed to be armed. But this was the first time I had seen any evidence that Iraq was supplying weapons. I didn't want to be accused of collecting and passing on sensitive intelligence, but I also felt that I had to alert the American embassy. After all, the Peace Corps volunteers were in possible danger.

I spoke with a contact at the embassy and advised that the volunteers in the region should leave. I had intended to speak to just one person in confidence, but the meeting was joined by others, who welcomed any updates I could provide on the security situation. I was still smarting from being stopped in the middle of the new embassy tour. Didn't the US government still consider me to be a "security risk"? But the embassy needed to know that violence was imminent, even if it meant the cretin in the mail room (the man, not the rat) was protected along with the Peace Corps volunteers.

The embassy staff held on to some suspicions about Peace Corps volunteers because of the attack on the ambassador's toilet, and that was fair enough. But it meant I had to spend many hours with the FBI and CIA (again!) explaining what type of training we gave to the volunteers. The training did not include counterespionage techniques or how to avoid being recruited by nefarious types. In the case of the rocket-launched grenade being fired from a volunteer's house, it had not been about ideology, religion, or fanaticism, but about the most fundamental, widely available tool of espionage: love.

In general, embassy officials did not like the fact that volunteers were spread out across the country, as it made keeping track of American citizens all the more difficult. They also did not like the fact that the Peace Corps, administratively, did not report to the US Department of State and, therefore, to the ambassador. After being established in 1961 by an executive order within the Department of State, the Peace Corps then became part of another agency in 1971. In 1981, it was shifted to an independent executive branch agency, and from then on, the director of the Peace Corps was appointed by the president of the United States. There were still hard feelings among some in the diplomatic corps that the Peace Corps was autonomous. The targeting of the ambassador's toilet proved, to some, that our volunteers were out of control.

Whatever bad feelings remained, it was hard to ignore that American citizens living all across Yemen would need to be protected. Evacuation plans were complicated by the need to contact the volunteers without giving out too many details. The ambassador was concerned that someone inside the embassy was leaking information.

A meeting was called, to be held under a large tree in the garden of the old embassy. According to the ambassador, this was the only place believed to be devoid of bugs. *The tree looks healthy enough to me,* I thought. Then I realized he didn't mean insects.

The ambassador was fuming that we were forced to meet outdoors, and blamed it on some people at an embassy party who had drunk too much and began loudly speculating about who was working for the CIA. One drunkard insinuated that someone at the embassy was a spy, whilst presenting themselves as working for yet another organization. Out of the corner of my eye, I saw the mailroom clerk smirking as he stared at me. The ambassador made it clear that any further loose lips would result in immediate termination and being declared persona non grata.

BOMBS, WATER TANKS, AND A LOVE OF TENNIS

Atop every house in the city of Sana'a sat a water tank made of rolled metal sheets. Water was pumped up into the tank, which was then slowly emptied as we used that water throughout the day. The hot sun beat down on the metal during the day, but at night, the metal would cool, producing a loud boom. Nadia was initially frightened by the sound and would scream out that we were under attack. For a while, my explanation about the water tank cooling calmed her. She got jumpy again, though, once she became pregnant with our second child.

As the security situation grew tenuous, the sound of gunfire got louder and louder each night. I explained that it was just fireworks. I brushed off one particularly loud boom as the water tank, and Nadia and Aziz went back to sleep. I found out the next morning that it actually was a bomb that had gone off nearby.

The severity of the situation became undeniable one morning when we woke to see a neighbor's house split in two. A jeep with large antiaircraft guns sat out front. It had been responsible for the assault. Suddenly, my mosque experience—praying with the sheik while staring down the barrels of his bodyguards' AK-47s—didn't seem so bad after all.

Amid the stress of the deteriorating security situation, the ambassador announced that all nonessential personnel were to leave the country. Nadia and little Aziz were sent back to my father's house in Providence, fully expecting that they would return to Yemen. Once all the Peace Corps volunteers had been evacuated safely, I began discussions with Washington about my next assignment. It was not safe for my family to return to Yemen, and I had no intention of living there without them.

The ambassador told me that he did not see the conflict in the region being resolved quickly, so it was unlikely that normal operations would begin anytime soon. Bureaucratic arguments began around the shipment of my household effects. Incredibly, even in wartime, my nemesis in the mail room would not let go of this issue. I knew the curse of Fatouma was not real, but I had to wonder whether it was somehow evolving from a jilted lover's enchantment to a voodoo household hex.

No one else at the embassy seemed to have any problems being evacuated from Yemen, but the administrative gremlins were working hard to prevent me from leaving. At every turn, a bureaucrat emerged from under a rock to deny the shipment of my household items, as if to insist that I did not really want to leave the country. Nor did the gremlins think I should be issued a plane ticket home. Furthermore, they explained, I had originally arrived in Yemen with no household effects, so why should I be entitled to ship anything to my next assignment?

What saved me in the end was the ambassador's love of tennis. He had heard that I enjoyed tennis too, so he would call me away from work to play tennis on the clay courts at the residence. Between missing shots and screaming, "Baby girl!" (his version of a swear word), I caught him up on all the news around town, including my travails with the cretin. He cleared the path for me, approving the shipment of our household effects, and we have been friends ever since.

EVIL KNIVES AND A SHEEP COMPANION

While packing up the house—something Nadia would never have allowed me to do if she had been around—I began to find mysterious clues to my wife's approach to child-rearing. The most notable discovery: knives under the mattress of Aziz's crib.

I phoned Nadia and explained what I had found, and how disturbing it was. There was silence on the other end of the phone. "Nadia, please tell me what is going on," I begged her. "Were you planning to stab me in my sleep?"

"Don't be ridiculous," she exclaimed. "The knives are there so Aziz can protect himself."

"But Aziz is a baby! How could he wield a knife against an intruder?"

"That's silly."

"I know! How could Aziz possibly use the knives?"

"Aziz won't use the knives," she explained. "The knives will use themselves."

"The knives are . . . alive?"

"No! The knives will ward off the evil spirits that will try to invade Aziz's soul." She seemed to be implying that everyone knew about this protective charm but me.

On the off chance that the knives had actually captured evil spirits, I threw them away and continued packing. Before leaving Yemen, however, I had one more important problem to solve.

My friends with the pet sheep were leaving too and could not ship their pet home with them, so they asked me to take care of her. I could tell immediately that the sheep was lonely. She had spent her entire life living inside a well-appointed home, being bathed in Woolite every week and watching movies with her human family. She needed a new companion, so I bought a ram. I figured the two of them could live happily ever after as a couple.

The problem was, while the ram was delighted to have found a female who smelled like Woolite, the ewe was not at all happy with her new beau. Having spent her entire life among people, not other sheep, she began losing her mind. The courtship went so badly that I found her up a tree, trying to escape the affections of a ram with very large horns. I sold the ram right away.

Then I asked Abdullah to take care of the sheep, and it was one of my best decisions ever. As I left the house for the very last time, I saw

Abdullah sipping tea in his room with the sheep sitting next to him, looking happy as a clam.

GILLIGAN'S ISLAND

For the next few months I lived alone in Washington, DC, waiting for reassignment, while Nadia stayed with my father, waiting for the new baby. Not knowing when work or the baby would arrive made it difficult to make travel plans, so we lived out of suitcases. A number of opportunities came up, but I wanted to make sure that we were not going back into a war zone.

I made a quick trip to the Comoros Islands, off the coast of Africa, and was offered the position of country director. It was a beautiful island with an active volcano and white, sandy beaches. I had a good chat with the current director about living there with a family. The biggest danger was not the smoking volcano looming over his house, he explained, but the jackfruit that fell in the garden, which were large enough to crush a child's skull.

I turned down the assignment.

My concerns were not only about fatal fruit, but also about my career. How would I ever find my next job whilst sitting on what amounted to Gilligan's Island? I got the impression that living on a faraway tropical island meant I would be forgotten when new job opportunities came up.

Peace Corps assignments at that level were typically two-and-a-half-year contracts; the idea was to avoid staff becoming entrenched bureaucrats. Having gotten a taste of bureaucracy in Yemen, I thought the Peace Corps' practice had merit. Moving around so much did, however, make it difficult to build a career when you had a family to look after.

So I returned to Washington, DC, and took on special assignments as they came up. When September arrived, and the projected birth date of our new baby approached, I was given a new assignment at last.

Romania

My Second Baby—and Others Less Fortunate

Going to Bed Hungry Like the Rest of the Country

But You Must Know Dracula!

Unwanted and Unloved

MY SECOND BABY—AND OTHERS LESS FORTUNATE

After the dissolution of the Soviet Union had begun several years earlier, the Peace Corps was invited into a number of countries in Eastern Europe. My job was to design projects that would help the transition from communism to more open societies. My first visit was to Romania.

Travelling through Eastern Europe in those days exposed many of the myths of Soviet power. It was hard to believe that the Soviet Union could have invaded Western Europe. There was little petrol for tanks to drive across town, let alone across Europe. The power grids were collapsing, and many people were left without heat or electricity. The lack of power had a domino effect, and food was in short supply. Long lines of hungry people formed all across Eastern Europe.

"Fiscal reform shock" seemed to be the name of the game for privatization in Eastern Europe. Part of the plan was to move quickly, not gradually, from a communist society to a market-driven economy. As the social safety nets were removed in each country, civil unrest grew. And I had a front-seat view.

In Romania, the communist leader Nicolae Ceaușescu was overthrown and executed during the 1989 revolution. His government was considered one of the most repressive in Eastern Europe, and his cult of personality provided cover for the dire straits that most Romanian people faced every day. After his execution, one of the most distressing discoveries was the existence of orphanages filled with babies suffering from AIDS. After the incredible media coverage of the plight of these babies, there was a huge public outcry to do something to help them. My assignment in Romania was to design a project that would assist the orphanages—these homes of the unwanted.

My boss told me that we were to leave on assignment the very day Nadia was due to give birth. Because I had not been present at the birth of Aziz, I was all the more eager to be at the birth of our second child, so I requested a change in the date of travel to Romania. Even though our assignment was literally to take care of babies, my boss (a man who was not married and had no children) was not sympathetic to my plea.

Nadia had been in the hospital in Providence for less than an hour when she gave birth to Aziz. Now, just two days before I was scheduled to leave for Romania, she phoned to tell me that she was in labor and heading to the hospital—and then gave birth to our daughter, Amira, after just twenty minutes. I missed the birth of our second child! And not because of an unalterable work obligation this time, but because when it came to giving birth, my wife was insanely efficient.

I made a quick trip to see Nadia and Amira, and then left for Romania with my boss. There was no electricity in the city, and our high-rise hotel could do little but offer flashlights so we could get to our rooms. As I lay in bed thinking of my newborn and how I had missed the birth of my children, I noticed small pockmarks in the ceiling. Surrounding the pocks was a strange, colorful light. The colors reminded me of light shining through a prism. I didn't know where the rainbow light was coming from until I looked over at the window and, seeing small holes in the glass, realized that bullets had been fired from the open square below, piercing the glass and leaving the pockmarks in the ceiling above my bed.

Living with civil unrest was becoming a habit in my life.

GOING TO BED HUNGRY LIKE THE REST OF THE COUNTRY

My boss had chosen me to accompany him on the trip to Romania because I spoke French. While French was not the country's official language, all of the officials with whom we met were delighted to speak it openly. Our first meeting was over lunch, but the only meal on the menu was pork. I explained that I was Muslim and did not eat pork, so I was offered fried cheese. This was the first indication that we were woefully unprepared for our Romanian expedition.

No one had told us to carry dry foods with us from the States, in the event that the hotel restaurants had no food. Nor had we brought flashlights with us, so we struggled to make our way to hotel rooms in the windowless corridors, in complete darkness. As we inched along walls, we felt for the numbers on the doors of each room until we felt the right room.

I went to bed hungry most nights, declining the pork dinner and developing a block, mental and otherwise, when it came to fried cheese.

BUT YOU MUST KNOW DRACULA!

One of the Romanian officials who accompanied us on the trip was an odd fellow with translucent skin. Having lived under Ceaușescu for so many years, he was understandably humorless. But when he told me that he was from Transylvania, I thought we might have a laugh about the legends of Dracula. He stared blankly and said he knew nothing of Dracula.

I pressed on: "You must know who Dracula is."

"I don't."

"You don't know the story of Dracula and his castle in Transylvania?"

"I don't know anything about Dracula."

A doctor from the Netherlands had joined us and began to show interest in the Dracula discussion. "You must know Dracula and the other vampires," the doctor added helpfully. "You are from Transylvania!"

"I don't know Dracula, and please stop talking about vampires."

"Ah, so you do know Dracula."

"I know about Vlad the Impaler and the good work he did to kill Muslims during Ottoman times."

I gave him the benefit of the doubt, assuming he did not realize he was speaking to a Muslim at that very moment.

"Well, I have a business idea," offered the Dutch doctor. "You could rent out Dracula's castle on Halloween. People from the West would pay a fortune to sleep in Dracula's bed."

"I don't know what Halloween is."

"I think you are hiding something. Are you *related* to Dracula? Are you his great-grandson?"

The conversation was getting heated, so I suggested we all just have the ice cream offered by the waiter. Also, it was the only dessert available.

The vanilla ice cream arrived, and it was clear the waiter had done his best to make it fancier by drizzling ruby red raspberry sauce over the top of the little ball of very white ice cream.

The Dutch doctor pounced. "My God, the waiter has been bitten by a vampire and is bleeding all over the ice cream!"

"I am leaving if you keep making jokes about vampires!"

"All right, all right, sorry. I won't talk about vampires anymore . . . but you definitely have a werewolf problem in Transylvania!"

Needless to say, the Dutch doctor was not invited to any more social events.

UNWANTED AND UNLOVED

The next morning we went to a large, bleak building, where a Romanian colleague began the visit by telling us that many of the children in the orphanage were not "orphans" at all but had been abandoned by their parents in the hopes that the government could provide for them. Ceaușescu had taken advantage of his "infallible" power to ban the use of birth control as a way to increase the population. With the collapse of the Soviet Union, however, any financial assistance dried up and the country was impoverished. Even condoms were not available.

The prophylactic would have not only prevented unwanted pregnancies but also slowed the spread of the deadly AIDS virus in the late 1980s. But by now, the orphanages were filled with unwanted babies born with AIDS.

That first orphanage we visited was a massive, Soviet-inspired, cement-block building with no architectural charm. Brutalism seemed cute in comparison. The entire building exuded a sense of hopelessness. Inside, it was far worse.

There was no heat in the building, and the children looked cold and malnourished. Large rooms were filled with metal cribs that held wailing babies. A nurse explained that on cold mornings, they often found the babies' tiny fingers frozen to the metal slats of the crib; they had to heat water to pour over the little hands to free them.

When I picked up a baby, I was confused by the weight of the child, who seemed so heavy and felt more like a lump of soft clay than a squirming baby. My boss also picked up a child and asked why the child felt so heavy. These children were dead weight and did not know how to be held. The nurse told us that no one would touch them because of their illness, so they spent their days lying inert in the crib. They had not developed any muscle tone and had no natural inclination to reach out to anyone. They did not understand how to cling to another person or cuddle in our arms.

The vision of so many babies lying there, untouched, unloved, haunts me to this day. At the time, I could not erase the image in my mind of my own newborn daughter being swaddled in blankets and love. I did not consider myself wealthy in any financial sense, but it was abundantly clear that I was able to provide my young family with so much more than these babies were afforded.

Bulgaria

NOT SEEING CLEARLY

In December 1990, after the communist government of Bulgaria collapsed, I took an assignment to establish English language education and small business development programs there. In January 1991, I travelled to Sofia, the Bulgarian capital, to find an office and a place to live for our growing family.

Leaving the airport in Sofia, I could not see beyond the hood of the car. "Is it usual to have fog this thick?" I asked the taxi driver.

He responded that Sofia never had any fog.

Pointing to the thick fog, I said, "That's odd, because we are in the thickest fog I've ever seen."

He laughed and told me that what enveloped us was air pollution—a daily occurrence in the winter. As I learned too late, temperature inversions in Bulgaria were a common occurrence. Across Eastern Europe, in fact, air quality was always a problem because of the absence of any pollution controls on cars and factories.

A popular Bulgarian joke at the time was that the Trabant—a tiny, laminated cardboard car produced in East Germany—was the longest car in the world at three kilometers from the tip of the hood to the tail end of the exhaust plume.

It became immediately clear to me that the country was suffering shortages of most food items and there was not yet an open market for rental space. There was no private enterprise. What may have looked like a private business was actually a state-owned enterprise formerly controlled by the government. The country was basically bankrupt, so everyone got by as best they could. The stores were empty, and lines for petrol stretched for miles.

How do I get myself into these situations? I thought again. I had not done my homework, and the Comoros Islands with their murderous jackfruit suddenly looked more enticing.

JUST MAKE IT THROUGH THE WINTER

One of the first business ideas that Bulgarian entrepreneurs came up with was a hustle known as "petrol providers." The hustle was to charge people a fee to sit in their car at a petrol station and to push a car with an empty tank ever forward, over a matter of days, until you finally reached the pump. It was not unusual to see four men walking by, carrying one of those Trabant cars home. They had left the chassis with a petrol provider in the long line at the petrol station so they would not have to wait and brought the rest of the car home so that nothing would be stolen from it.

That first winter, it was clear to me that Bulgaria was no place to bring a young family with no family ties or office support. Instead, Nadia and the kids went to Morocco to stay with Nadia's father—or "Baba Sidi" to his grandchildren. Our plan was for everyone to be together again when spring arrived and I had figured out the lay of the land in Sofia. I felt bad that the Bulgarian adventure was off to such a rocky start. But while I could probably find a way to scrounge for food at the hotel, it would not be possible for the entire family to make do like that.

I didn't speak Bulgarian, so I signed up for lessons. At the very least, I wanted to be able to say good morning to people in the local language. I met an older gentleman who said he would be happy to tutor me. In return, I would tutor him in English. The bartering system was used quite a bit, actually, because no one seemed to have any money.

The issue of having cash was an immediate problem. Although the official exchange rate was 2.8 Bulgarian leva to the US dollar, the exchange rate among the money changers in the street was 28 leva to the dollar. Everyone pretended to use the official rate, but hardly anyone did. The first (and last) time I went to the bank to change a hundred-dollar bill, I was turned away by the surly bank teller, who said my money was not clean enough. I spent a good half hour explaining that it didn't matter if the bill was dirty, torn, or mangled—it would still be accepted by a US bank—but he was not buying it.

I needed cash to buy what little was available to buy, so I turned to the money changers instead. But even having cash did not help all that much, because the store shelves were empty everywhere I went. What were people eating?

As I found out, Bulgarian families were great at canning and pickling vegetables and storing supplies of food to survive the winter. The embassy staff clued me in to their practice of ordering from Peter Justesen, a food supply company in Denmark that shipped goods around the world to the diplomatic community. The embassy relied on Peter Justesen for pretty much everything they needed. When the duty-free provider didn't have what they needed, they would drive two or three hours to Greece and go shopping.

My tutor, Kosta, taught me much more than the Bulgarian language. Like many Bulgarians under communist rule, he and his family lived in a small apartment, about 150 square feet. Also like many Bulgarians, he was highly educated and had played a part in the revolution to overthrow the government.

Over time, I learned that Kosta's family had been very wealthy before the communist regime took over. They had lost everything, including a large manufacturing plant, but Kosta remained a positive person, having survived the despised communist government. One of the most important things he taught me was how to can pickles and peppers, our food basics to get through the winter. I got the sense that he believed my canning expertise was lacking and that what I had canned would rot before the first snowfall. Luckily, that first year, he made sure that my colleagues and I had a choice of something to eat from his own supply.

Kosta also introduced me to the family who eventually rented me the lower floor of their home. As springtime grew closer, I was eager to move out of the Sheraton Hotel in downtown Sofia, the place where the previous government had insisted all foreigners stay. The only food available there was a very expensive hamburger, and I felt as though I was continually watched.

Asking a guest what their room number was would reveal which ones were suspected of being involved in espionage. It was fairly easy to see the pattern: foreigners were in rooms 101, 201, 301, 401, all the way up to the top floor. The hotel had given them rooms one above the other, which made it easier to monitor them.

I narrowly escaped death in that hotel after embassy officials in the room above me, after a heavy night of drinking, decided that they were going to find the bug placed in their room by the Bulgarian security agency. Under the carpet, in the center of the room, they found a small metal plate. Believing they had located the bug, they unscrewed the brass plate, only to hear the chandelier come crashing down in the room below—mine. Not all spies are infinitely clever.

OUR FIVE-YEAR-OLD INTERPRETER

Our new landlady spoke no English, French, or Arabic, so we communicated with her via her adult daughter and through our own version of sign language. Her grown children had produced no grandchildren yet, so she was delighted to have Aziz and Amira in the house and quickly scooped them up and took them upstairs to her floor. Bulgarian grandparents were obsessed with grandchildren and spent every possible moment with them. Our landlady was a great help to Nadia, but when we realized that Amira's first language was becoming Bulgarian—which neither of us spoke—we grew concerned.

I had a friend in Yemen whose wife was German. He spoke no German, but his wife spoke only German to their child. He had spent so little time with his daughter that they got to a point where she would speak to him in German, and he couldn't understand a word she said. I didn't want to wind up in a similar situation.

Aziz was a little older, and we thought it would be good for him to have some playmates, so we registered him in the local preschool. He soon came home speaking Bulgarian too, and the landlady, Aziz, and Amira would babble in Bulgarian together as Nadia and I listened, not understanding a word, wondering what we had done. I loved learning new languages, but I also wanted to be able to speak to my own children.

Aziz became our little interpreter. He gave us information about what was available in the local store and what time Nadia should run down to find bread or meat. Even as food supplies began to appear in some shops, there were still long lines for most everything. The lines for bread stretched by our house, so Aziz also would tell Nadia when the line moved.

One cold day, our five-year-old interpreter taught Nadia a secret that would serve us well for the next two years. She had bundled up Amira and taken both children to the store, where she dutifully stood in the line waiting her turn to purchase the food. The woman standing in front of them said something, and Aziz translated: *If you have a baby with you, you can go to the front of the line.* This was welcome news! From then on, Nadia took Amira with her whenever she went shopping and went straight to the front of the line. All the grandparents standing in the line nodded in approval.

One day, Amira was sound asleep and it was cold outside, so Nadia left her with the landlady—but still went straight to the front of the line. When the butcher gave her a quizzical look, she said, in the only Bulgarian she had learned, "*Baby spee*": *The baby is asleep.* That seemed reasonable to everyone in the line, and no one objected to Nadia's jumping the queue. For the next two years, Nadia left Amira at home when she went shopping and simply said, "Baby spee," whenever people challenged her. Finally, the ruse was up when Nadia announced, "Baby spee," and the butcher replied, "Madame, that baby has been sleeping for two years."

THE COMMUNIST THERMOSTAT AND SIDEWALK CAFÉS

In the warmer months, we kept our windows and curtains open during the day. Our home, like all homes in Bulgaria, had central heating—that is, the heat was centrally controlled by the government. The massive pipes that fed all the buildings hot steam were turned on and off by the government according to the season. It was turned on for a certain date, no matter if the temperature was still warm, and then turned off on a specific date, no matter if it was still freezing cold outside. The only way to control the heat inside the house was to open the windows.

Most people in the neighborhood opened the windows but kept the curtains drawn. When I asked why, I was told it was to avoid people spying on one another. Sadly, one in four people were believed to be informers for the Bulgarian version of the KGB. In a family of four, like ours, that meant one member of the household was likely to be an informer. Most people in our neighborhood assumed it was Nadia who was the informer in our household. I, on the other hand, suspected Amira, whether she was asleep or not.

The upheaval was total, pervasive at all levels of society, as people fled the country or stayed put and tried to build a new life. There had been a serious brain drain as so many people with expertise left government service, often taking government funds along with them, to form their own private businesses. Across the remnants of the Soviet Union and its satellites in Eastern Europe, clever bureaucrats transferred existing debt to the collapsing government accounts and moved all the profits to their newly formed private enterprise. I found myself in the odd situation of explaining to a bank teller in Bulgaria that all the funds I needed for our official work would be transferred into a private account via electronic fund transfer. The teller told me he didn't know how to effect such a transfer.

It wasn't only the debt that was left behind in the wake of the government's collapse. It was also the people who didn't know how to manage in the new private sector. They sat in their office chairs, pondering how the world had changed. They remained in their jobs with salaries that met the needs of a loyal communist system employee but were not enough to pay for a cup of coffee in an entrepreneur's new sidewalk café.

As a free-enterprise system began to emerge, these small sidewalk cafés popped up all over the city, consisting of two plastic lawn chairs and someone making you a cup of coffee. The café was usually on the literal sidewalk or in an empty parking space in the street. I saw this as progress, but it was rare to hear anyone congratulate the new small-business owner. Some people were saddened that the communists had become capitalists.

I guess they just couldn't get used to the idea right away. Neighbors would steal the plastic café chairs to use in their own plastic chair café. When I asked why this would happen, I learned there was a dark side to Bulgarian humor, as in this expression: "I would burn my house down if I thought it would burn your house down with it."

Apparently, the Bulgarian culture and ruthless capitalism go hand in hand.

CABBAGES, RAKIA, AND FUR COATS

I wasn't just adjusting to the culture shock of living in a crumbling economy. I was adjusting, like everyone else, to living in a wave of change. Having spent so many years in very conservative countries in the Islamic world, I often misinterpreted what I was seeing on the streets in Bulgaria.

One day whilst waiting in a car outside the embassy, I watched women in very mismatched fur coats, short skirts, high heels, and too much caked-on makeup leaning against the wall of the building, smoking cigarettes. I asked my colleague how it was possible that the embassy allowed prostitution, a very lucrative business anywhere, to take place right outside the embassy door.

"What are you talking about?" he asked.

"The prostitutes working outside the embassy."

"When did you see prostitutes outside the embassy?"

"Right now."

"Where?"

"Right there! Can't you see them leaning against the building smoking cigarettes?"

"Those women right there?"

"Of course right there!"

"Those women are waiting in line to get visas to go to America."

After so many years in Yemen, working with women whose faces I never saw, I had clearly gotten the wrong impression here.

I suppose it was the rabbit fur coats that threw me off. In Sofia, there were only two items for sale in any abundance: cabbage and fake mink coats. A sign of relative wealth, fur coats seemed to be everywhere. To me, the mismatched pelts gave an impression very much the opposite of glamour and wealth, but I made it a point never to ask too many questions about style.

Despite my best efforts to avoid the topic, however, I was sometimes drawn into discussions around women's clothing. My work centered on promoting small-business development and entrepreneurship in a post-communist society. My first idea was to create a link to markets in Western Europe. Bulgarian factories produced a number of items that I thought would sell well in Germany at a much lower price than was offered in the well-stocked German shops. So I established a network of offices, called Multi-Link Centers, where entrepreneurs could go to get information about possible markets in Western Europe, and use the computers we provided to contact buyers.

Peace Corps volunteers with small-business experience worked at these centers, and we had a number of early successes. I met with the mayors of cities across the country and asked for free office space. The meetings often took place over lunch and rakia, a potent alcohol. Like in Romania, the only thing served at my lunch meetings seemed to be pork. Not eating pork and not drinking rakia put me in the category of being extremely eccentric, but the maître d' of the restaurant usually came to my rescue and had the chef prepare another slab of fried cheese. Great.

THE WORLD YOU KNEW IS GONE

I didn't have a budget to set up any of the business centers—our contribution was the staff—so I hustled any donations I could find. I reached out to the Open Society Foundation established by George Soros and bluntly asked him for free computers. I got a very positive response, and the centers had their first donated units of business equipment.

The following year, I met Soros personally when he was a member of a delegation from the United States that included the former college roommate of President George Bush, and Elaine Chao, the new Peace Corps director and wife of Senator Mitch McConnell. The delegation came to Bulgaria to open the newly established American University. Not wanting to miss an opportunity to circumvent protocol, I hit Soros up for some more free computers, which he again provided.

The American ambassador in Bulgaria was supportive of my entrepreneurial spirit, but others in the embassy were not. I wasn't following all the protocols they thought were in place. But the world they once knew in Bulgaria, I would often point out, was gone.

There was little to no administrative infrastructure to support private enterprise. It was difficult to hire employees because there were no contractual agreements for the private sector. Employment agreements were based on the communist system and basically took the entire salary in taxes paid back to the government. The communist system of state-supported social services, subsidized housing, and subsidized food had collapsed entirely. Young people entering the job market were not about to accept a job in which they paid their entire salary to a government that provided no services.

As I learned from my experience in Yemen, American bureaucrats could be just as difficult as communist-era petty tyrants. The US ambassador kept asking me how I was able to get things done in Bulgaria. How did I buy vehicles and furniture for the Peace Corps office, when they had to wait for everything to arrive from the States?

The answer was: the Peace Corps is a much nimbler organization than the US government, and we did not have to follow some of the more ridiculous government rules that made no sense. One of those rules was encapsulated in the Buy America Act. For example, the embassy had to buy American vehicles—vehicles that could not be serviced in Bulgaria. Meanwhile, I bought Volkswagens directly from Germany that were easily serviced locally. The ambassador asked if he could borrow a car from time to time, and I happily agreed.

YOU CAN STILL GET INTO HARVARD FROM THE DINING ROOM TABLE

One American official was especially incensed that I had found a private house to rent. When he asked what protocols I had followed to find the house, I told him I had just asked around. He then focused his ire-filled gaze on the furniture I had bought for our house—specifically, the desk I had bought so my children could do their homework in a home library.

This official complained that his teenage children were being forced to do their homework at the dining room table. He asked the ambassador if he thought it acceptable that a lowly Peace Corps executive should have better accommodations than a diplomat. The ambassador intervened only to say we had more important things to discuss.

The bureaucrat would not back down, however, and only became more and more irritable. How could his son ever get into a good school by doing his homework at the dining room table? The ambassador looked at me for support. I explained that I had grown up doing my homework at the kitchen table, and I graduated from Harvard, so the dining room seemed like a step up to me. I was not sympathetic to his plight.

When he didn't get his way with the homework debacle, the official said he opposed the establishment of the Multi-Link Centers. He did not understand why they had to be so business-focused and sound so technical. After failing to block their establishment altogether, he then stated his objection to the name. From a marketing point of view, he felt strongly that they should be called Daffodil Centers. Perhaps he had a master's degree in flower arranging.

I didn't take his suggestion.

TRADING COMPUTERS FOR CHEESE

In 1992, I set out to market the business centers and travelled the country promoting their services. When visiting a technical college, I met a man who wanted to sell cheese. For the time being, however, he was a teacher of computer programming and invited me to see his class.

The students were furiously typing away and never looked up for the entire time I sat chatting with the future cheese merchant. I asked one student what he was working on, and he told me he was programming.

"Wonderful! What are you programming?"

"A program."

"Great! What does the program do?"

"It's just code."

There was an awkward silence in the room, so I let the question drop. It turns out that Bulgaria had established itself as the world's most prodigious source of computer viruses. The Soviet Union then sent these viruses around the globe in an effort to disrupt democracies. The students were writing code that would help them move ahead in the security apparatus.

I decided to focus on the cheese.

Bulgaria produces a type of cheese much like feta, and Bulgarians claim the origin of this Sirene cheese much as they claim the origin of the Cyrillic alphabet that most people associate with the Russian language. Bulgarians swore that two Byzantine monks, Cyril and Methodius, were sons of Bulgaria, and disputed the Slavic ties of these religious heroes to Macedonia. The two monks are credited with creating the written Cyrillic alphabet, which was needed so the Bible could be written in a local language as opposed to Greek or Latin.

Heated arguments over rakia, raki, Sirene cheese, feta cheese, Turkish coffee, Greek coffee, Bulgarian coffee, and anything else hailing from the region occupied hours of time. The one thing Bulgarians seemed to agree on was that the Turks were monsters and had ruined their lives.

I often pointed out that, while it was true that the Turks had ruled Ottoman Bulgaria for five hundred years, they had been thrown out of Bulgaria back in 1878. The fact that no one arguing around the table had been alive at the time made no difference to their passion in despising the Turks. Even though they had all suffered through the communist regime, it was still the Turks they hated.

Grudges die slowly in Bulgaria.

My cheesemonger friend came to my office one day to announce he had just completed a huge deal to sell the famous Bulgarian (not Greek!) cheese to a German supermarket. He wanted to know where he could send my commission: 200,000 dollars. I admit there was a moment when I thought about sending him my bank account details, but sadly, I had to explain that I could not accept any payment for helping to broker the deal.

He found it odd that government officials couldn't accept a commission, but he was also 200,000 dollars richer, so he immediately told me of another deal he was working on and needed my help with. He wanted to sell brassieres.

THE POLITICS OF A WOMAN'S DELICATES

I explained to my Bulgarian cheesemonger friend that bras were really not my specialty, but he insisted that I inspect the bra factory with him. I reluctantly agreed, and before I knew it, I had embarked on a new chapter of small-business development.

The factory manager greeted me warmly and offered rakia, which I forcibly declined. It was ten in the morning. He confessed to not knowing how we could possibly make a deal without imbibing the rakia.

I understood the significance and suggested we drink tea whilst discussing business. My interpreter said then that the manager was muttering something about Turks drinking tea when doing business, about hoping I wasn't some sort of crazed Muslim. No tea was offered.

When the bulk of the sample bras arrived, I secretly wished I *was* a heavy drinker. These brassieres had the largest cups I had ever seen. This was no "small business"—this was a job for a tentmaker.

"What do you think?" asked the cheesemonger.

"I'm sorry," I explained, "I don't have any experience with bras."

"I thought you said you were married!"

"I am married, but I've never seen anything like this."

"Do you think they will sell well, like the cheese in Germany?"

I turned to the factory manager. "What else do you make?"

"We don't make anything else," he replied. "The Soviet system was to assign manufacturing quotas, so we made bras."

"Why don't you make something else, like shoes?"

"No one wants to wear Bulgarian shoes. They were the downfall of the Soviet army."

He had a point. "OK," I conceded, "but I don't think there is a market for these bras."

"You just said that you have no experience with women."

"I didn't say I have no experience with *women*. I said I don't have any experience with a bra that looks like two circus tents connected by a transatlantic cable."

The factory closed the following month. No one wanted Bulgarian shoes *or* bras that could be used as hammocks. But the factory owner must have taken to heart my mumbling about tents and hammocks, because he opened up a successful sporting goods store the following year using the warehouse full of industrial-strength bras. So the meeting wasn't a total failure.

THE BOBBLEHEAD MEETINGS

Meetings with Bulgarian staff often ended with everyone, including me, more confused than when the meeting had started. I never realized that there were so many muscles in the human neck or that the head could swivel in so many directions.

I had experienced the type of noncommittal head bobbing that the Indian staff members used at the Taj Sheba hotel in Sana'a. Were they signaling that they agreed? Disagreed? Simply wanted to avoid saying anything? It took a highly trained eye to figure out if they were saying yes or no. But things were far worse in Bulgaria.

No one had warned me that nodding your head "yes" meant "no," and shaking your head "no" meant "yes." Every meeting would start with me announcing the agenda and asking if there were any items to add. Everyone nodded their heads, so I asked for suggestions. There were none. Rather than agreeing that they had items to add to the agenda, they were saying "no."

Until I got the signals right, it was exhausting to carry on a conversation. I never knew if they were agreeing with me or wanted an argument. It became comical: as they tried to adapt their nodding/shaking heads to my practice, I tried to adapt mine to theirs. Most meetings ended early, with nothing agreed upon. Finally, we came up with an entirely new system: A smile meant yes. Closing your eyes meant no.

The whole system broke down, however, when I told them I was taking the family to Istanbul for a vacation. Somehow vampires and Vlad the Impaler worked their way into the conversation, and I was reminded of my time in Romania. Vlad the Impaler, a real-life historical figure thought to be the inspiration for Dracula, had impaled hundreds of Turkish heads on spikes and was a great hero in Romania—and apparently, in Bulgaria as well.

Dracula was a hero. Clearly the world was topsy-turvy. I shook my head and no longer cared if they knew what I was saying.

HOLIDAY IN TURKEY

The drive from Sofia to Istanbul took eight hours. The exodus of Turkish families, working in Germany but driving back to Turkey for summer holidays, had begun. Large families stuffed themselves into small cars along with a year's worth of supplies for the two-month vacation, piled high on the rooftop. Once everyone had set out, the roadways were crammed. Everyone was in a festive mood, sharing food and tea at all the rest stops. The border with Turkey was a grand affair with hundreds of cars waiting to pass through customs, but it was all very organized.

It was completely different from what we had experienced on the Bulgarian border with Greece. Travelling to Thessaloniki in northern Greece to buy food and clothes for the kids seemed like taking a country back road in comparison. All cars coming from Greece were forced to drive through a pool of murky water in order to rid the tires of any possible germs being brought back into Bulgaria. As far as I could tell, it was a leftover feature of the defense system to prevent democracy from spreading from its birthplace into communist Bulgaria.

The border guards on the Turkish border were very friendly, but they were confused by Aziz and Amira. Nadia had gone off to the ladies' room, so I stood waiting with the kids. One guard was giving me a suspicious look and made his way over to ask who the children were.

"These are my children," I replied.

"Who is the boy?"

"He is my son, Aziz."

"He can't be your son."

"He *is* my son. Why?"

"He is a Mediterranean boy. You look like something else."

"What do I look like?"

"You have blue eyes and gray hair, and he has dark eyes, dark skin, and brown hair."

"Allah has willed it."

That was the end of that conversation, but I was again struck by the need of so many people to assign others an identity that made sense to them. I had grown accustomed to the blue-eyed confusion, but the gray hair was a new one. My hair had begun to turn gray when I was sixteen, and I never thought too much about it. Now that I had children, it seemed to be an issue. Strangers wondered how old I was and marveled at my vigor to have such young children.

It seemed I could not win. I was either a virile old man or a lying young man. Still, Istanbul was a delightful change of pace from Sofia. Everywhere we went, people picked up the children, pinched their cheeks, and generously held them while we scarfed down more baklava.

SHOPPING IN BULGARIA

Back in Sofia, the embassy staff was still angry that I had betrayed Bulgaria by travelling to Turkey and were even angrier that we had a great time there. Once they heard our stories about the great shopping with full stores and restaurants in Istanbul, they turned their ire back on the former communist government, and all was well.

We were still dealing with shortages of pretty much everything, and we relied on the generosity of Kosta and our landlady to provide pickled veggies and Sirene cheese. Aziz often came up from the cellar smelling like cabbage. I followed him down there one day to find him taking the cover off a wooden barrel that was filled with bubbling water, long vines from the grapes growing in the garden, and cabbages in the murky depths. Aziz would drink the pickling water, which is why he smelled of cabbage coming and going to the bathroom for the rest of the day.

Prior to the collapse of the Bulgarian government, there were well-stocked stores in the country, though they were reserved for diplomats. Those stores still existed, but they were as empty as all the other shops. Even so, I made a habit of checking in every day to see if there was anything to buy.

The common wisdom was, if you saw a line of people waiting to buy something, you just got into the queue. You waited patiently despite the fact that you didn't know what you were waiting to buy. One day, there was great commotion around a large bin filled with one-kilo bags of flour. This was a huge leap forward in the economy, and when it came to my turn, I grabbed two bags of flour and headed home to tell Nadia the good news. We were now able to make bread!

We gave one bag to our landlady to repay her kindness to us. Nadia kept the other, and I headed back to the office. Shortly after I arrived at my desk, the phone rang. Nadia was laughing hysterically, although I detected a worried tone to her voice. My dream of having homemade bread was dashed. The bags were not filled with flour; they were filled with lye. Both Nadia's and the landlady's hands were burning—but not badly enough to stop them from seeing the humor in it.

Perhaps not surprisingly, though, Nadia never let me go shopping again.

THE BLACK SEA IS ANGRY

The summer months brought relief from the air pollution and the most extreme shortages. We had enough petrol in the car to begin taking short trips around the countryside, so we visited the Rhodope Mountains whilst listening to the haunting sounds of traditional Bulgarian singers on the radio. Travelling to the southern parts of the country exposed us to the world of Islamic Bulgaria. I thought of the animosity my Bulgarian staff felt toward the Turks, but also realized they had never travelled to these small Muslim villages with beautiful mosques and great food. I felt hope that once they did visit, they would begin to appreciate the diversity of their country.

We spent weekends in Varna, a seaside resort town on the Black Sea. I had always thought the name of this inland sea was related to the color of the water, but it actually refers to the personality of the sea: often unexpectedly angry, with storms that blew in without warning.

Walking into the sea on our first trip to the beach in Varna, I held little Aziz in my arms as the waves grew higher. I saw one particularly high wave coming toward the shore, and I held him tighter in my arms and turned my back to the wave so that it would hit me and not Aziz. The wave crashed on my shoulders, but Aziz slipped through my arms and was lost in the surf.

I bent over and put my arms low in the water, expecting that when the surf receded, I would feel Aziz in the foamy water and grab hold of him. I began shouting in Arabic for help, but no one understood.

As I looked to my left, I saw a tiny hand in the white foam heading out to sea. He was beyond my reach. Thankfully, a woman nearby grabbed his hand and pulled him up, where he gasped for air. I thought he would be scarred for life, but he just let out a laugh and screamed, "Let's do it again!"

I brought Aziz back to the warm sand, where he played whilst I trembled for two hours before calming down.

The following year I was more cautious around the angry Black Sea. I kept a close eye on Amira and didn't let her go into the water. She was right at the shoreline when she tripped and fell and lay there unmoving.

When I ran to pick her up, her lips were blue and her eyes had rolled back in her head.

I held her upside down, and water poured from her mouth as she began to breathe properly. A beachgoer sitting next to us, a doctor, said she was OK but suggested we take her to the medical tent just to be sure. His wife, sitting with Nadia, was sobbing quietly. I tried to calm her, saying Amira was OK. The doctor explained that their own child had fallen, face first, into a small puddle in their garden and drowned. She was five years old.

The Black Sea is indeed an angry master, but even a small puddle can be a murderer.

FREEDOM IN CHAOS

As the economy began to improve, more and more Western consultants and embassy officials poured into Bulgaria. The people whose experience had been shaped by living and working under the communist regimes struggled to adjust to this influx of new ideas and activity. No regulations governed private enterprise, because until now there had been no private enterprise. Labor and tax laws were stuck in the communist era, but Bulgarian young people, entrepreneurial in their outlook, had very different expectations.

Economists around the world argued over the pace of change. American officials who had worked under the communist regime expected that change could take place only at the pace that the new Bulgarian government could (or was willing to) adjust. As with many other societies faced with a cumbersome bureaucracy, however, Bulgarians moved forward without waiting for everything to be just right, and the supposed experts were left behind.

Every week the country team, made up of the directors of each US government agency working in Bulgaria (including mine, the Peace Corps), met with the US ambassador. The ambassador was growing frustrated and wanted more and more information from each director on the team.

The CIA station chief would only say that he had nothing to report.

"Even if there was something to report," the ambassador mumbled, "I suspect that I would not be informed."

The station chief nodded in agreement.

The defense attaché constantly asked why I was even in the meeting and questioned whether I had the proper security clearances. I assured him I did. He most likely didn't appreciate my making jokes about fictional secret agent Maxwell Smart and the cone of silence, but that's what it felt like. We were required to have the meetings in a secure box that looked like a walk-in freezer, with blowers going full blast in an attempt to keep our conversations secure from the Bulgarian secret police.

In a particularly tense exchange, the defense attaché asked me if I knew how Hitler had died, then proceeded to tell me to take my brief-case out of the cone of silence. He told me that there could be a bomb in any briefcase left unattended. I wanted to say that I had no intention of being a suicide bomber but, instead, I pointed out that Hitler did not die in a conference room bombing. In any case, I removed my briefcase from the room and left it just outside the door.

The bureaucrat who had advised us to implement Daffodil Centers continued to complain that he could not hire people, buy cars for the office, purchase furniture, or find housing outside of the brutalist apartment buildings. At one meeting, he demanded to know how I was accomplishing all those things. My secret, of course, was to accept the current reality and not wait for the government to catch up.

For the bureaucrats, the lack of government regulation was a hindrance. I saw it as an opportunity.

When the ambassador finally ended the meeting, the station chief shook my hand. The defense attaché kicked my briefcase on the way out.

MR. DIPLOMATIC POTATO HEAD

In the spring of 1992, our sojourn in Bulgaria came to an end. Bulgaria had shaped our little family in unexpected ways. Nadia was no longer a maid but a gypsy, the target of racist comments and uninviting glares.

Aziz was called the "little capitalist" at preschool and still has a scar on his face from an angry communist toddler. Amira was a native Bulgarian speaker. And I had narrowly avoided embarking on a new career as a fashion designer specializing in brassieres.

We had skied at Mount Vitosha for two dollars a day, and Aziz and Amira have loved skiing ever since. Aziz had reached through a tiger's cage at the Sofia Zoo, squeezed the sleeping tiger's tail, and fell forever in love with tigers. Nadia learned that pouring boiling water on the stairs during a snowstorm would only result in solid ice–covered stairs.

We learned to can vegetables to get us through the winter. We were grateful for the kindness shown to us by people who were experiencing massive changes in their personal and professional lives. Our landlady brought us into her family, and we shared many a wonderful meal of bread, cheese, thick red peppers, and potatoes that we had helped plant and harvest at the farm near the border with Yugoslavia, a country that was also breaking apart.

I had been called many things during my time in Bulgaria: diplomat, spy, Ottoman Turk. One of the most interesting of all was a name applied to my family. The story goes like this.

As many other Bulgarian families did at harvest time, we filled our station wagon with the potatoes we had helped plant in the countryside and headed back to Sofia. What our landlady did not tell us was that pretty much every other Bulgarian would do the same exact thing at the same exact time of year. The two-hour ride to the border of Yugoslavia had taken, predictably, two hours. The return trip to Sofia became a ten-hour traffic jam. There was nothing else to do but look at all the other cars filled with potatoes. When fellow travellers saw the diplomatic license plates on our car, however, they began shouting out good-natured gibes to our family. In my heart, I'm proud that we will forever be known as the "diplomatic potato family of Sofia."

Finally, I left Bulgaria knowing that Sirene cheese would soon be enjoyed all across Europe—and that I was correct in assuming no woman would want to wear a bra the size of a hammock.

Foggy Bottom
and the Stans

In September 1993, Prime Minister Yitzhak Rabin of Israel and Mahmoud Abbas of the Palestine Liberation Organization signed an agreement at the White House in Washington, DC, with President Bill Clinton looking on. I stood outside the White House that day, the signing of the Oslo Accords, hoping to witness the moment. I believed it would be remembered as an historic event and a harbinger of peace. While the bells of peace rang in one part of the Middle East, I was managing another evacuation of Americans from war-torn Yemen.

Bill Clinton took his time filling senior government positions, so I was appointed by him to keep the seat warm for the eventual Peace Corps director for Europe and the Middle East. Whilst the brassiere business in Bulgaria had not exactly been a total success, economies in Eastern Europe were making good progress. International focus began to shift to the Russian Far East as well as to the region known as "the Stans," a nickname for the countries that ended with the same suffix: Kazakhstan, Turkmenistan, Uzbekistan, and Kyrgyzstan, to name a few. Technically, those countries were not in Europe or the Middle East, but my office was tasked with expanding Peace Corps programs also in countries formerly within the communist sphere of influence.

I learned too late that people from those countries hated the term "the Stans" and insisted that government officials stop using it. As a result, conversations involving the region took much longer, especially when everyone realized that too many bureaucrats used the nickname because no one could remember which country was which.

CAN EYEBALLS FREEZE?

The internet, at that time, was mainly a tool used by universities. There was little to no connectivity for anyone else. US embassies had the private, secure system of sending cables back and forth with Washington. They also had the diplomatic pouch to send messages, but that archaic method took weeks, and delivery of the pouch could be interrupted by cretins like the fellow who refused to give me my mail in Yemen.

In the Washington office we had an IT expert, Manu, who maintained all our computer networks. I decided to send him to Vladivostok, Russia, to set up the internet in our new office there. When he began the project, we didn't expect that he would be setting up the internet for the entire city, but that is basically what happened. Once small-business owners found out that they could easily communicate with contacts in Western Europe via the internet, they sought him out.

Manu was well suited to the work but not to the cold. He phoned me one day to ask if it was possible for eyeballs to freeze. He was not known for his sense of humor, so I asked him to explain the situation. He was outside in Vladivostok and told me that he could not close his eyes because they were frozen open. He wanted to know if he should go to the hospital nearby. I suggested that he first go inside and get out of the -50 degrees Celsius weather. He hadn't thought of that solution, so it was hard for me not to wonder if I had made a major mistake sending him there.

Seemingly run-of-the-mill negotiations in the former Soviet Union could turn dangerous rather easily. While negotiating a rent increase in our office space in Ukraine, the landlord put a pistol on the desk and asked if the new price was reasonable. I remained calm, which seemed to unnerve him a bit. He had expected fear. I immediately agreed that the price was reasonable but asked if we could also agree that we should continue our good relationship.

Manu, on the other hand, lacked such tact and had a habit of blurting out whatever was on his mind. We cut his trip short and he returned to Washington, but his fame lived on as the man who set up the internet in the Russian Far East.

CASH IS KING

I made regular trips to Foggy Bottom, the oddly named area of Washington where the US State Department is located. As I interacted more and more with State Department officials, the "foggy" moniker began to make more sense. Massive sums of foreign assistance money were flowing into the former Soviet Union, and a deputy secretary of state was serving as the ambassador-at-large, overseeing all that money. The scuttlebutt around town was that he was also an unofficial, and unwilling, spy for the Russians. Given my background, real and imagined, it was a pleasure working with someone suspected of being a secret agent, even if it was for the KGB instead of the CIA.

The main purpose of our meetings was to determine how we could move the money faster. The banking system was not to be trusted, and as I had learned while living in Bulgaria, no one wanted to change money at the official rate at the bank. Credit card use was not common, and most everyone we dealt with wanted US dollars and not rubles. Cash was king.

The bureaucratic gremlins working in the bowels of the building were not happy that we found ways to work in countries struggling with collapsed economies and banking systems. One of those ways was to carry large sums of cash. It was dangerous, to be sure, but in order to pay for all that was required to set up new offices, you simply had to pay in cash.

There were so many problems to solve to get even the simplest of things done. I became known as the fixer. No one asked too many questions about whether I had correctly filled out the utterly unimportant, fictitious Form 29-A. My reputation far outweighed my ability to solve every last problem. It bordered on the comical when the Peace Corps director, Carol Bellamy, in frustration at an organization-wide meeting, shouted, "Azzedine, when are you going to solve Russia?"

DROP THE VOLUNTEERS FROM THE SKY

The countries that seemed to move the fastest toward recovery were Poland and the Czech Republic, so our programs worked pretty well there. Russia, meanwhile, was problematic from the very beginning.

There were many times when I stayed at the office late into the night, figuring out how to overcome every hurdle the Russian government threw at us. One night, as the newly assigned Peace Corps volunteers for Russia sat on the airport tarmac in New York City, waiting to take off, we got word that the Russians had canceled their visas. There was no reason given. It was a blatant move simply to make things difficult, even though the Russian government had requested Peace Corps volunteers.

As always, I found it best to keep a good sense of humor. I suggested that we could parachute the volunteers in, vehicles and all. The vehicles were cleared by customs, so technically it was the vehicles arriving in Russia, not the volunteers sitting in them. When the proposal was taken seriously, I realized that it was too late at night to suggest absurd solutions, no matter how creative.

HAVE YOU SEEN THIS MAN?

With all the pressure in Washington to hasten US assistance to countries in the former Soviet Union, I was sent to the Stans to negotiate the establishment of Peace Corps operations there.

When I landed in Alma-Ata—now Almaty, Kazakhstan—I was to be met by an embassy official who would take me to Kyrgyzstan, a beautiful country known as the Switzerland of Central Asia. The country is also known for some of the longest poems in the world, something I saw firsthand when I encountered a Kyrgyz doctoral student at Harvard. When we met in the laundry room, she had been a doctoral student for nearly ten years and was presently studying ten lines of a five-thousand-word poem. As we folded laundry, I asked why she was still working on her dissertation after so many years.

"I just couldn't come up with the doctoral question," she explained.

"Why not come up with the answer first, and the question will reveal itself?" I joked.

She got her doctorate the following year and returned to Kyrgyzstan with her thousand-word question.

Now I stood waiting for two hours outside the Almaty airport, which had closed for the night. The embassy official never showed up. Another waiting American, who told me he was a military advisor, suggested we leave for the Kyrgyz capital, Bishkek, on our own. We paid a guy wearing a long black trench coat and driving a nondescript black car with no license plates to take us to Bishkek. I sensed that he was not a taxi driver. We arrived without having disclosed any sensitive information, and I checked into a hotel that had no electricity or working phones.

Back in Washington, faxes were flying around the city with urgent messages to security officials. They believed that I was missing and may have been abducted by a former KGB agent. In point of fact, I was already meeting with Kyrgyz officials and doing my best to avoid drinking warm mare's milk in each of the many yurts I visited. I didn't have the advantage of that large wooden bowl at the camel bar in Mauritania, where I could hide my face and avoid partaking of the treasured drink. So I sipped the fermented mare's milk and smiled the best I could.

Three days later I met, as scheduled, with the American ambassador. When I explained that the embassy official had never showed up at the airport, he was livid. But he insisted that the embassy had sent someone and wanted to know how I had made my way to Bishkek on my own. In his eyes, my story about meeting an American military advisor and paying a private car to take us didn't hold water.

"There are no military advisors at the embassy," he insisted, glaring at me. "To spread such misinformation puts all our lives in danger." We agreed only that I had taken a taxi, and I knew enough to let the matter drop.

A BIRD'S-EYE VIEW OF THE CARGO HOLD

Travelling through Central Asia by air provided a first-row seat to the dissolution of the famed Russian airline Aeroflot. Governments, newly independent of the dissolving Soviet Union, seized any Aeroflot planes that were left on the ground. Now the property of the Newly Independent States, or NIS—a short-form term far less cool than "the Stans," if you ask me—these planes weren't much to brag about. It's fair to say that the best planes were already on the ground in Russia.

On my flight from Bishkek to Almaty, through the floor beneath my seat, I had a bird's-eye view of the cargo hold. I tried to enjoy the ambiance, convincing myself that despite the dripping water coming through the ceiling, the fuselage was not breaking apart in midair. I focused instead on the young man a few rows in front of me having an episodic nervous breakdown, screaming that we were all going to die.

Upon landing in Almaty, we were informed that there would be an hour-long delay while awaiting our luggage, because the conveyor belts had no electricity. My next flight, into Turkmenistan, included an upgrade: the flight attendant asked for volunteers to push the luggage truck from the plane to the terminal. By the time I left Ashgabat a week later, passengers were climbing into the cargo hold to load and unload our own luggage.

Travelling the Silk Road has never been easy.

LOST IN TRANSLATION

Not everyone I met in the NIS was happy that the Soviet Union had collapsed. Statues of Lenin still sat atop intricate Islamic-tiled pedestals. Years and years of anti-Western propaganda had convinced many that anyone working for the US government must be a spy. Dealing with all the suspicion was tedious. And in many places, it wasn't just that I was most likely a spy: I was also Muslim.

Once, when asked why I was not eating during the day, I explained that it was Ramadan and so I was fasting. Upon realizing I was a follower of Islam, one particularly disagreeable chap offered to take me to see a beautiful mosque. I thought it was a nice gesture until we arrived at the former mosque. It was now used to hold pigs before they went to slaughter. Our relationship deteriorated from there.

There were other, small ways to irritate the foreigners who presumed to know anything about the country, the culture, or the language. Some of these incidents were quite comical, and sometimes we even deserved what we got.

While visiting the new office in Tashkent (the capital of Uzbekistan), for example, the Peace Corps director and I hired a driver to take us around the country, visiting possible volunteer placements. After a very long day driving through a desolate landscape, the director decided we were lost. He insisted that the driver had taken a wrong turn and we were headed farther into the desert. The driver said nothing, further agitating the director. The longer he remained silent, the angrier the director became.

My colleague turned to me for support, but I, too, remained silent. When he insisted that I give my opinion, I said calmly that I did not know the road well and was on my first trip to Uzbekistan. Shouting at the driver about the road sign he had read a few miles back, the director insisted that Tashkent was in the other direction.

I had studied Russian a little at university in Switzerland, so I was able to read the Cyrillic alphabet but otherwise didn't know what most words meant. Still, I had seen the road sign, and it didn't look like the word "Tashkent."

The director screamed for the driver to pull into the next gas station. He ran inside to ask directions, while the driver calmly lit a cigarette and said in perfect English: "That sign back there—it says, 'Tires sold and repaired.'"

We both laughed quietly. When the director got back in the car, we rode in silence the rest of the way to Tashkent.

A TRADITION OF DISPLACEMENT

There was so much that was new to me, and the layers of culture often conflicted. It was difficult to discern, for example, what was part of Uzbek culture and what was derived from Soviet influence. The Soviet Union had spanned eleven time zones and comprised many people, cultures, and languages. The communist-era dictator, Joseph Stalin, moved groups of people from one region to another, updating the centuries-old strategy of mass displacement of ethnic and cultural groups to uproot some three and a half million people between 1930 and 1950. The first deportations sent people from Poland and Ukraine to Kazakhstan, among other lands, far from their homes.

The more people I observed in the Stans, the more I wanted to learn about the Soviet policy of deportations. Others from among my colleagues were not so curious about this unfortunate history, and it cost them.

Manu, the famed Peace Corps internet guru, phoned me again for advice—this time from Kazakhstan. It wasn't about his eyes freezing open this time. It was about love.

He had met a "traditional Kazakh girl" and wanted to know what he must do to marry a Muslim girl. She was from a very traditional family, Manu explained, and her father demanded that he convert to Islam in order to marry her.

Despite my own arranged marriage, I cautioned him to move slowly.

Manu challenged my advice, saying that he was just as brave as I was. Come hell or high water, he was going to make this Kazakh girl his wife.

I reminded him that I had chosen to marry someone from a culture I knew and loved. When Nadia and I were wed, I had already lived in Morocco for seven years, spoke the same language, and shared the same religion. In my case, unlike his, there were fewer unknowns.

Manu agreed and got off the phone. Then he asked the girl to marry him.

When Nadia and I arrived at his mother's house in Maryland for the small family ceremony, the mood resembled more of a funeral than a wedding. Manu's family sat in silence as his mother sobbed. The bride was nowhere to be seen.

Manu made a last-ditch attempt to blame the whole situation on his mother. "You told me to bring back a girl!" he shouted.

"I meant bring back a maid for your filthy apartment!" shrieked his mum.

The door to the bedroom opened, and in walked the traditional Kazakh girl, dressed in a micro-mini spandex skirt, skyscraper stiletto heels, and enough makeup to cover the entire surface area of Kazakhstan. She made her entrance while screaming curses at Manu's mother in Russian.

Natasha may have been born in Kazakhstan, but only because Stalin had forcibly moved her family there from Mother Russia decades earlier. And she was not "traditional" by any stretch of the imagination.

The marriage lasted two months, and no green card was given as part of the dowry.

THE MALTESE AFFAIR

During this period as the Peace Corps' interim director for Europe and the Middle East, more and more of my time was taken up by crisis management. In 1992, the two Libyan citizens accused of carrying out the bombing of Pan Am Flight 103 over Lockerbie, Scotland, in December 1988 were cleared of wrongdoing by the Maltese minister of home affairs, who declared that there was no evidence that his country was involved in any way. The American government, which suspected a connection between Malta and the masterminds behind the tragedy, was not happy with that conclusion.

I was called to a meeting in a secure, soundproof Washington bunker to discuss how the United States should respond. The purpose of the meeting was announced loud and clear: How should we punish Malta? The meeting's chairperson asked that we go around the table and offer our suggestions. Each person represented a different branch of the US government, yet I found it odd that a representative of the Peace Corps would be asked to attend. Even so, I listened as each agency representative proposed a punishment.

One suggestion from a defense attaché caught my attention. He proposed that we shift the type of military aid we provide to the government of Malta and pointed out that a shipment of military jeeps to Malta had been approved already.

The chair asked whether perhaps we could cancel the jeep shipment and prevent them from going to Malta.

"No," came the reply, "something better." The United States should ship the jeeps to Malta, the attaché explained, but remove the engines before the vehicles were delivered.

I burst out laughing, thinking it was a joke. It wasn't.

Next it was my turn to provide a suggestion on how best to punish Malta. The glaring attaché added that if I could not take the meeting seriously, I should leave the cone of silence in disgrace. The best punishment I could offer was to remove one of the two Peace Corps volunteers teaching English in Valletta, the capital city. Perhaps their absence would bring Malta to its knees.

The attaché, for one, considered my proposal seriously. Was he actually entertaining such a ludicrous suggestion? It was ridiculous to think that removing a teacher of English would have any effect on diplomatic relations between the two countries. I wondered how many high- or low-level meetings like this were taking place throughout the entire bureaucratic system.

I soon found out.

EVACUATION REDUX

In 1994, war broke out in Yemen once again. Unification of North and South Yemen had not lasted very long. The US State Department ordered the evacuation from Yemen of all American citizens. I was instructed to report to the command center in Foggy Bottom for the midnight to eight a.m. shift on the evacuation task force—the busiest time slot because of the time difference between Yemen and Washington. It was daytime in Yemen, and the fighting raged mostly during those hours.

The logic behind handing me the assignment was that, having already gone through civil unrest in Yemen, I would be able to assist in planning and executing the evacuation. My previous experience in Yemen, however, had involved *being* evacuated from a war-torn area. My involvement this time around would be from the bureaucrat's point of view.

The first crisis management meeting I attended was held in a stadium-style room with row upon row of officials from every agency who had personnel stationed in Yemen. Assembled in the room were some of the best minds Washington had to offer—and some of the worst. The military officers, in uniform, offered up their assessment of the situation and proposed how to resolve it rapidly. I thought it would be a quick night.

"We have a few hundred citizens who need to get to safety, people. Let's come up with ideas to get them home," encouraged the leader of the task force.

The first suggestion, to my horror, came from the cretin who had denied me Nadia's mail at the embassy in Sana'a. He had been evacuated from Yemen during the Iraqi invasion of Kuwait and was now making people's lives miserable from the basement of the State Department. He began his monologue by saying, "Let's not forget everyone's household effects and all the paperwork required to clear customs."

Not a great start, but I figured he would be shot down immediately. Sadly, far too many people around the room were nodding their agreement.

The cretin continued: "And I will immediately take decisive action to bring everyone to safety by sending an email to three airlines to request the lowest bids. As we all know, three bids are standard government operating procedure for any procurement of services and goods, and—"

"Thank you, thank you, very helpful," interjected the leader. Surveying the room, he spotted a heavily decorated military figure. "General, what can you offer up?"

The look of disdain on the general's face betrayed his true thoughts. I was almost certain the words "Belay that order!" were about to slip out, but he composed himself and said, "Within twenty-four hours of the order to evacuate, I will have these American citizens on a military transport plane leaving Yemen and heading to safety."

"That's wonderful!" beamed the leader. "All right then, we will take that suggestion under consideration. And in the meantime, let's go with the idea to get three bids from commercial airlines."

I stared at the task force leader in disbelief. Wasn't he aware that no American carriers flew to Yemen?

"Of course," he continued, "we will need to get a congressional waiver from the Fly America Act, which requires all American government employees to fly with American airline companies. Move out!"

A SLOW BOAT TO CHINA

On the second night of evacuation discussions, the nerve center was divided into two groups: those who had access to information and those who were excluded. A hierarchy of idiocy was organized along the lines of security clearances and levels of bureaucratic lunacy.

The cretin continued to push his approach to airlifting people to safety via the lowest possible price and mountains of paperwork. Anytime there was a critical piece of information to share, the snobs with the highest level of security clearance would retire to the top-secret room to giggle that they had information no one else had. They could, therefore, remain in total control and strangle any good idea in its crib.

At the back of the room, reserved for the peons, sat a man working feverishly on his computer, not paying a bit of attention to the glorious leader blathering on at the front of the room. I watched him for an hour as he sat silently, never trying to convince the feckless of anything. He got up only once, to procure a cup of bad coffee.

Meanwhile, I was on the phone with the Peace Corps country director, hunkered down in Yemen, who told me over the sound of gunfire that she had gathered all the volunteers from around the country in Sana'a, save for fifty-three people trapped in the port city of Hodeida, on the Red Sea. After a few failed attempts to get the task force leader to share any information about the situation in Hodeida, I introduced myself to the mysterious man at the back of the room.

He had an intense look about him but engaged in conversation easily enough. He ignored my questions about his work but asked why I was on the task force. I shared my challenge: fifty-three Peace Corps volunteers stuck in Hodeida, with no way to get to Sana'a for a flight out of the country. His response was simple and delivered with a smile: "I will help you."

He told me not to pay too much attention to the people who wouldn't tell me anything, because he had everything I needed, right there on his terminal. He shared that he was part of a military intelligence unit and also had people trapped in Hodeida. Cutting through all the nonsense, he asked, "What's your goal? Getting your people to Sana'a or getting them out of Yemen?"

I glanced over at the cretin and his sycophants, celebrating the arrival of a single bid from an airline. "We need to get them to safety," I replied. "That's my goal, and I'll follow your lead."

His first idea was to get them out to a tanker that was passing through the Red Sea. "It's moving slowly from the Suez Canal, passing Hodeida. They have agreed to take your people on board."

"That's great. When will it pass Hodeida?"

"Early tomorrow morning."

"Do we need to get approval from the task force?"

"I don't."

"Right, let's do it. Where is the ship heading?"

"To China."

"You mean, literally put them on a slow boat to China?"

We put that idea aside and considered other options.

The Yemen Hunt Oil Company had tugboats in the port and was in the process of getting its people out of Hodeida. The idea was to make the short trip over to Djibouti, the famed city that serves as the base of operations for the US military at Camp Lemonnier. Considering the options laid out before me, the decision between working with the legion of bureaucrats or this lone problem solver was a no-brainer. No thanks to the cretin and his lowest possible bid, we got all the people trapped in Hodeida to safety. The focus and determination of the military mind is admirable indeed.

I had already developed a dislike of bureaucracy, but to judge following the rules more important than saving peoples' lives? That really got to me. For far too many people in that evacuation command center, the focus on process—no matter how ridiculous—was more critical than achieving the best possible outcome.

I decided then, once and for all, that working for a large government bureaucracy was not for me. Fate must have agreed with me, because it soon put another opportunity in my path.

PLAYGROUND ARREST

There are times when otherwise insignificant events somehow twist your plans, and you are left with the impression that your entire life could, in fact, be maktub. In 1993, I had walked down to the White House to witness, from afar, the signing of the Oslo Accords. There was great excitement in the air. For a fleeting moment, the prospect of peace in the Middle East seemed real. I took the train home that day feeling hopeful.

Outside our home, I found our Iranian neighbor waiting for me. He apologized for being the bearer of bad news. Then he told me that the police would soon be coming to my house to investigate reports of child negligence. His friend at the police station had given him a heads-up: they received reports that we had let our children play outside.

Instead of being neighborly and speaking to us directly, the complaining neighbors had approached my Iranian friend and said, "We know you are a foreigner, and the Downes family are foreigners. So perhaps you could explain to them that children should not be allowed to play outside in the yard." They had called the police, too, and said they were concerned that children playing outside would be kidnapped.

When the police arrived, we had a nice cup of tea together. Then they suggested we find new neighbors. So the following year, when I was offered a new job out of the country, I took it.

We had grown accustomed to being foreigners in every country where we lived. Why break the habit now? Nadia and I packed up the children and our household effects, and once again travelled back in time.

Jerusalem

BACK TO THE FUTURE

I arrived in Jerusalem in 1994—the Islamic year 1414—and settled our young, growing family in East Jerusalem. The medieval Kingdom of Jerusalem had fallen to Saladin in a siege many centuries earlier, in the year 1187 (Islamic year 582), but to some residents of the city, that might as well have been yesterday. We dropped into this city with its pulsating history: Nadia, Aziz, Amira, and our youngest son, Charif.

Charif and I had a special bond, as his was the only birth that I had witnessed. Given Nadia's history of giving birth only moments after arriving at the hospital, her doctor told us to head to the hospital the moment she felt any contractions. We lived along the Beltway outside Washington, DC, so I asked Nadia to not start any contractions at rush hour. But to get me back for missing the births of our first two children, she announced that she was in labor at seven thirty in the morning: the peak hour for traffic.

The fifteen-minute weekend drive took us two hours that day, but Nadia didn't give birth in the car, so we were off to a good start. Dressed in my suit and tie, I held her hand as the serious contractions began. Instead of congratulating Nadia on her amazing calmness, the doctor commended *my* composure and congratulated me for really paying attention during the Lamaze courses. I had no idea what he was talking about and said so.

As he began to berate me for being a clueless husband, Charif arrived. I nearly passed out when I heard the doctor say: "Oh baby, don't do that!" The umbilical cord was wrapped around little Charif's neck, and he was in distress. It all worked out fine, but that's how I knew from the start that Charif was a survivor. He would do well in his new home, tumultuous Jerusalem.

The Old City has changed hands many times over the centuries. Millennia of memories and countless grudges over past injustices linger, just like the enduring cobblestone streets. Every rock, every mound of dirt, every street corner, and every conversation somehow linked to a moment in time, some recent and some ancient. The Oslo Accords were to bring in a lasting peace between the Palestinians and Israel. But neutrality was an illusion.

As in Fez, in Jerusalem it was possible to move through time. Passing between the years 1187 and 1994 was as easy as passing through the Damascus Gate of the Old City. Families who had lived and worked in the same place for generations spoke of events long past as if they happened yesterday.

Even the simple task of buying coffee was steeped in history. The smell of coffee being ground and mixed with spices in a tiny shop along Saladin Street drew me in immediately. Patrons shouted out orders by their family names, and the coffee master knew the exact mix of spices to add to the coffee—just like the public bakeries in Morocco.

My family name had no history in this shop, so on my first attempt at a purchase, I was offered the generic version sold to tourists. The denizens of Jerusalem immediately began the process of placing me in the proper context. Who was I exactly? What was I doing there? What was my family background? Could I be trusted?

Weeks later, on my second attempt to purchase freshly ground coffee, I moved from being a tourist to something unknown—which was a step up, in my book.

IN 1492 . . .

Many people think of the year 1492 as the year Columbus arrived in America. Muslims also mark it as the year that King Ferdinand II of Aragon and Queen Isabella I of Castile conquered the eight-hundred-year-old Muslim Kingdom of Granada. Whilst many converted to Catholicism to escape the horrors of the Spanish Inquisition, most Jews and Muslims fled Andalusia—present-day southern Spain—and settled in Morocco. As the traditions of Andalusia continued in the medina of Fez, there was a blurring of what was Muslim and what was Jewish.

When modern Israel was formed in 1948, Jews from across the Middle East were expelled in response, their land and wealth confiscated.

Moroccan monarchs had a much more welcoming view of the Jewish community than most leaders in the Middle East, but although no forced expulsions took place, many Moroccan Jews voluntarily emigrated to Israel. The Moroccan Jewish community became the largest ethnic group in Israel. It remained so until the arrival of the Russian Jewish community after the collapse of the Soviet Union.

When Nadia told people in our newly adopted city that she was from Morocco, they commented that they thought everyone in Morocco spoke French and was Jewish, not Muslim. As if relaying yesterday's nightly news, they recounted the story of the Jews being expelled from Spain in 1492 and settling in Fez. The more we tried to explain about modern-day Morocco, the more confusing the conversation became.

The politics of modern-day Israel clouded any discussion of how best to place us politically. Were we pro-Palestinian, neutral, or pro-Israeli? Once we mentioned Andalusia and the Kingdom of Granada in 1492, we were properly placed in Muslim history, and casual conversations were based more on curiosity than politics. That didn't stop acquaintances from making assumptions about who we were, exactly.

In Arabic, the word for Morocco, Al-Maghreb, refers to the West. As Islam spread across North Africa, Morocco was the point of its farthest western expansion. The exact geographical position of the country and the language spoken there, however, seemed to be confusing to our new neighbors in Jerusalem. Some people referred to it as Andalusia, and others insisted that Marrakech was the name of the country rather than just one of its cities.

The confusion had applied to Americans as well. When explaining that we had family in Morocco, we got a barrage of questions ranging from "Where is that?" to "What a tragedy, about Princess Grace!" (referring to Monaco). I usually cleared things up by saying: "No, you know Rick's Café in the movie *Casablanca*? That Morocco."

People in the Middle East often view the world as though they're travelling through, and stuck in, an ancient time period. Despite being accustomed to seeing the world through this lens myself, I was surprised that many I met in Jerusalem were still talking about Andalusia or the Arab West. Like dealing with the Moroccan belief that all foreigners were from Nazareth, however, it was just easier to let people believe what they wanted to believe and get on with life.

Once, while we were in a shop buying shoes for the children, the shopkeeper asked where we were from. I asked him to take a guess. He looked at Nadia, the children, and then me, sizing us up.

"You are a son of Jerusalem—though you have been gone a long time, by the sound of your accent—and your wife is from Andalusia," he proclaimed confidently. "Once you are back home for a while, you will sound more normal."

WHEN EAST MEETS WEST

Living in Jerusalem was akin to living in many different worlds at once. Just as passing through Damascus Gate into the Old City was like passing from modern times into ancient times, East Jerusalem was a world apart from West Jerusalem. Palestinians lived in East Jerusalem, and Israeli Jews lived in West Jerusalem. Where the city began and ended was a constant political battle. Borders were clearly marked at military checkpoints, but many invisible borders existed too. Not knowing about them caused offense and could even lead to physical harm.

The yellow Israeli plates on your car indicated where you lived, but not your political affiliations or sympathies. One way to navigate through the city safely was to keep the Palestinian headscarf, the keffiyeh, in your car. You would make sure it was clearly visible on the dashboard as you passed through some neighborhoods, and then take it down again in others. Knowing when you crossed an invisible border took a trained eye and local knowledge. There was no handbook to guide you; sometimes it was a rock hitting your car that indicated it was time to change the keffiyeh.

Crossing from Jerusalem into the West Bank or Gaza required a whole other level of diplomatic skill, patience, and willingness to suffer indignities.

WHAT HAVE I GOTTEN MYSELF INTO?

On my first trip to Gaza, I had that same sinking feeling I had upon leaving the airport on my first day in Bulgaria, enveloped in air pollution so thick that I could not see beyond the hood of the car: *How do I get myself into these situations?* It was the first and last time I was able to drive through the checkpoint between Israel and the Gaza Strip.

Gaza is a tiny strip of land on the Mediterranean Sea, sitting between Israel and Egypt. As part of the peace process that stemmed from the Oslo Accords, Israel withdrew from Gaza, which was hailed as a great step forward, toward the ultimate goal: Palestinian governance of Gaza.

In reality, though (as many colleagues told me), life was better when the Israelis patrolled inside Gaza. Withdrawing from Gaza, and closing every entrance and exit, turned Gaza into a large prison of over a million people in a mile-wide area. Israel controls the northern border, and Egypt controls the southern border, and neither country allows free travel. Israel patrols the sea around Gaza, too, so there is no way for anyone to leave or arrive in Gaza without first passing through either Israeli or Egyptian security.

Palestinian liberty and freedom under the peace accords was an illusion.

Atop high towers at the border sat Israeli soldiers with weapons trained on the cars stopped for inspection and questioning. The morning I first drove there, a caged procession of Palestinian workers waited to pass into Israel for the day's work. When a soldier began shouting through a loudspeaker in Hebrew, it wasn't clear to whom he was speaking. But my car was quickly surrounded by Israeli soldiers who were also shouting frantically in Hebrew, which I did not understand.

I stopped, waiting for some clarity, as a small, remote-controlled robot, which looked like a toy car, made its way past my car and rolled toward the empty car in front of me. There was neither a driver nor passengers in the car, and it wasn't clear why the vehicle was there. Suspecting a car bomb, the soldiers directed the robot into place beneath the car and exploded it. There was no bomb in the car.

Staring at the smoldering debris from the crippled robot, I discovered that the question from Bulgaria had become a little more ominous now: *What have I gotten myself into?*

All future visits to Gaza required that I park the car in a sandy lot, walk across no-man's land, pass through two security checkpoints (one Israeli and one Palestinian), and then walk into Gaza, where a staff member would pick me up and drive me into Gaza City.

The news often reports on a travel ban, called a "lockdown," between Israel and the West Bank either being put in place or being lifted. The truth was, a travel ban was always in effect for most people. Still, travelling from Jerusalem into the West Bank was much easier when there wasn't a total lockdown. The drive from Jerusalem to the Palestinian city of Ramallah, for instance, was not that far, and Ramallah could be reached after passing through only a small checkpoint manned by young Israeli soldiers. The soldiers stood by a makeshift barrier of metal barrels, looking fairly relaxed—in the early days, anyway.

There was an enormous amount of new construction in the burgeoning suburbs of Ramallah as Palestinians from around the world returned in the hopes that the Oslo Accords had signaled an end to violence and even the formation of a Palestinian country. That dream was shattered by the assassination of Prime Minister Yitzhak Rabin in November 1995 by a young, far-right Israeli zealot.

Travel anywhere in the country became increasingly difficult.

FEARING THE ORDINARY

Part of my new job was to serve as the country director of a nonprofit organization working to improve cooperation, training, and development in Jerusalem, Gaza, and the West Bank. I hired young staff members who had recently moved to Ramallah from the United States—Palestinian Americans holding US passports. Some had been born in the United States and had lived there their entire lives. Others had moved to America with their parents as young children and were now returning. Initially, they were able to drive to our office in Jerusalem with no problem. As violence increased, the checkpoints became a source of anxiety and frustration.

In our first year living in Jerusalem, a bus bomb exploded near the French Hill intersection directly below our house and cracked the window in the bathroom as I was taking a shower before work. It was impossible to convince Nadia and the children that the shaking of the house was just the water tank on the roof, as I had been able to do in Yemen. The sound of wailing sirens, and the voices of those who had survived the blast, told the real story of the carnage.

The bus bombings continued throughout the year, and I began to understand the true meaning of terrorism: it makes you fear doing the ordinary.

You begin to change small things about the way you live. For instance, whenever driving, I took special notice as I approached a bus, calculating when the bus would arrive at the traffic light. I would either slow down or speed up, so that I was never driving alongside the bus or arriving at a red light at the same time as the bus. The possibility that the bus could explode was real, and my strategy was to reduce the risk of being too close to the blast.

Logic and emotion were in constant conflict, but the goal of both was to prevent me and my family from being killed in a bus bombing. Walking by the American Colony Hotel in East Jerusalem, I thought of the violence that had taken place in the city throughout history, and how unrealistic it was of me to expect peace just because a signed document like the Oslo Accords said there would be.

So many people had suffered loss of loved ones through violence, and clearly there could be no logic to the emotional reaction that followed a violent death. The region, populated by people with long memories and grudges, had always been a tinderbox. In Jerusalem, violence unfolded before my eyes on a daily basis.

BOILING VATS OF OIL AGAIN

On one beautiful, sunny day, Nadia and I were sitting with the children outside the Damascus Gate, enjoying the warmth against the cool stones of the ancient Old City walls. The gate sits at the start of the road from Jerusalem to Damascus, Syria. In Arabic, it is called the Gate of the Column, a name that dates back to Roman times, and it is indeed a portal in time and space.

There was no inkling that violence was in the air that day, only a great deal of laughter, with tourists, shoppers, and kids running around. Israeli soldiers on horseback were making their normal rounds. Then, just as an older Palestinian woman crossed the street, one horse broke into a quick trot. The horse knocked her down.

Within moments a full-scale riot of rampaging teenagers was underway. Israeli military vehicles appeared almost immediately, and as the crowd pulsated, one could feel the crush of humanity engulfing all in its path. I grabbed our youngest, Charif, in my arms, and we pulled Aziz and Amira along with us as we ran through the Damascus Gate into the Old City.

Not knowing what was happening outside the walls, people in the crowded street began to stampede. A boiling vat of oil used to cook falafel turned over and spilled down the sides of the sloping cobblestone street. Shopkeepers barricaded their shops, slamming closed the metal doors normally shuttered only at night. Women with children were crushing into the shops to hide. Nadia and I saw an opening and pushed toward the shopkeeper just as he shuttered the doors. He allowed Nadia and the children to enter but stopped me and said I was on my own.

"Go inside with the little ones!" I shouted to Nadia. "I will find you later in the day." I had no choice but to run with the stampede through the narrow alleyways until the crowd dissipated.

Riots are like a cancer cell destroying one part of the city's body whilst other parts of the body carry on seemingly unaware; so it was that day. The farther I got from the Damascus Gate, the more normal life appeared. Shopkeepers sat sipping tea. Tourists bargained for trinkets.

Israeli soldiers, with their fingers on the trigger, walked calmly through the streets surrounding the Dome of the Rock. Even the air seemed to shift, and calm returned as quickly as it had been shattered.

I made my way back to the Damascus Gate, where Nadia and the children were enjoying falafel from the righted vat of boiling oil that, only moments ago, had evoked scenes of the Crusaders pouring oil over the ramparts to repel Saladin's siege.

STATIONS OF THE CROSS AND THE CHURCH OF THE HOLY SEPULCHRE

And yet Jerusalem is a magical place. It inspires awe and, for some, religious epiphany. The mental health phenomenon called the Jerusalem Syndrome is well documented: visiting tourists who arguably have no history of mental illness experience religious delusions, believing they are characters mentioned in the Bible. Whilst this doesn't happen to everyone stepping foot into Jerusalem, it is easy to feel overwhelmed by the powerful, often competing versions of religious history there.

The tourism trade for Christian pilgrims, centuries old, encourages people to follow the footsteps of Jesus Christ on the Via Dolorosa. The tour guide is often a man dressed as Jesus carrying, or pulling on rollers, a cross as he traces the steps of Jesus en route to his crucifixion. My father—who thoroughly enjoyed sitting in the empty hills of Galilee where the Sermon on the Mount took place, and who shook in anticipation of his walk along the Via Dolorosa—was heartbroken to see all the shops selling tourist items along the way. He abandoned his walk at the seventh "Station of the Cross" T-shirt shop and walked away in tears.

I have always been one to question what doesn't make sense to me. Although I have strived to pose my questions in nonthreatening ways, sometimes I have failed. As a child in grammar school we learned, from the imposing Sister Superior, that in 1965 the Vatican Council determined that Protestants could now go to heaven. There was, however, a fence in heaven, with Catholics on one side and Protestants on the other.

I raised my hand and said I didn't think that was fair; you either got in or you didn't. I spent the rest of the day in detention for questioning the Pope, whom I had never even met! I was reminded of my early distaste for dividing lines in holy places during my many visits to the Church of the Holy Sepulchre.

In a world where so many people spend their lives in opposition to others, some believe that the simplicity of the message *Love one another* will overcome religious divisions. History, sadly, tells us otherwise. Visiting the Church of the Holy Sepulchre reinforced the notion that some faiths, uniquely, own the "true" message.

The famed church is located in the Christian Quarter of the Old City, which also contains the Muslim Quarter, the Jewish Quarter, and the Armenian Quarter—which in itself tells you how the organization of the human mind (and real estate) permeates every step you take. I pity the tourist who is only given an hour to visit the church, who is rushed by locals trying to make a living by selling sweets next to a rock with a sign that says "Jesus sat here" before being marched back to a bus headed for Nazareth.

My approach to travel and tourism typically involved visiting a place before I did any real research about it. It seemed more wondrous to be astonished at every turn. This approach also led to being shunted to the side so paying tour groups could ask if they were standing in the exact spot where Jesus is believed to have turned left. I enjoyed eavesdropping on the tourists, who all had the guidebook to the church in their hands. But I was also astounded and dismayed by the vapid questions and stock answers I heard.

The interior of the church mirrors the divisions in the quarters of the Old City except that all the competing faiths are Christian. Over the centuries, there have been so many arguments over control of the church that responsibility for the key to the massive front door was given to a *Muslim* family, the Nuseibeh family, by Saladin in 1192.

I became friendly with the current key holder, from whom I learned much of the oral history of the church. No short visit to the church can begin to unravel what you are seeing or reveal the history behind every chair, icon, or stone. We visited often, and I found explaining the history of the church to little Aziz was helpful for him to navigate his own journey in Jerusalem.

Children are amazed by the smallest things and have an incredible ability to ignore the majesty of a place. So it was with Aziz, when he spotted a secret stone staircase that led to a secret cave, where he was convinced that Richard the Lionheart was being held captive before he could return to England to support Robin Hood. (I may have fostered his belief in that version of history, but I will never admit it.)

As the two of us walked back down the stone stairs alone, we saw a woman washing only the top five stairs. I asked why she stopped at five, and she told me that she was cleaning the Greek Orthodox steps. The next five were Armenian Orthodox steps, and they could clean their own.

I asked where the Ethiopian stairs were.

She scoffed and said, "They are up on the roof, and no one knows what is going on up there."

Like the sudden eruption of violence at the Damascus Gate, violence inside the church has been known to erupt following the simple act of moving a chair into the shade. The chair in question was moved to a place not agreed to in the status quo of 1853, and this event resulted in eleven monks being injured during the melee that ensued.

Tradition holds that many of the most significant moments in Christianity took place within the confines of the present-day Church of the Holy Sepulchre. Accepting that tradition as though it is historically accurate has made it much easier for pilgrims to visit the defining moments in Christianity in under an hour. I had always imagined that visiting the holiest of holy places would inspire a quiet inner reflection on one's life. Instead, a frenetic energy crackled inside the church as pilgrims bustled from one chapel to the next.

Like in Mecca, many people came knowing that this would be the first and last time in their life that they were in the presence of profound holiness. It would also be an opportunity to buy a plastic bottle of water and pour it over a beautifully carved marble slab, purported to be the slab of marble that just happened to be nearby when Mary Magdalene washed the body of Christ. By pouring the bottle of water on the marble, soaking it up with a sponge, and squeezing it back into the bottle, the pilgrim could return home with water that had "washed the body of Christ."

The sight evoked in me a sense of sadness, not reverence. Like the scene of pilgrims in Mecca—pushing and shoving to touch the black rock of the Kaaba, causing stampedes that killed thousands—it gave me a sense of overwhelming loss that spoiled the moment. I felt no baraka emanating from the jostling pilgrims as they fought to get more water than their tour bus companions. Jesus wept.

BENDING THE RULER

Aziz had started preschool in Bulgaria because I thought it would be a good idea to help him learn Bulgarian. Indeed, he arrived not speaking a word of the language but was serving as my interpreter within a few months. In Jerusalem, he announced that he would no longer speak Bulgarian because he now spoke a "big" language. Kids are like sponges.

Amira was facing her first school years in Jerusalem, and was bouncing around the house in anticipation, as was her way. The challenge was in choosing the right school for her.

Over the years, I had watched many families put their children in the international school system or in schools where the language of instruction was the mother tongue of the parents. I wanted the children to experience living in Jerusalem, so the local schools seemed to be the best option. That way, they could make friends in the neighborhood, speak Arabic, and grow up in ways that did not isolate them in an expat bubble.

Few choices fit the bill.

Amira was enrolled in Rosary Sisters School, run by Catholic nuns, and came to describe herself as *Bint Ourdia* ("a Rosary Sisters' flower") in a very Jerusalem-accented Arabic. Her school was well run and kept the girls safe whenever violence broke out across the city.

We enrolled Aziz in Saint George's School (*Madrasat al-Mutran* in Arabic), an Anglican school established in 1899. While the religious affiliation of the all-boys school was Christian, it was mostly attended by Muslims—another example of how everything in Jerusalem melded in unexpected ways.

When it came to learning and political activism, Aziz's school had a very different approach from Amira's. Aziz faced his first ethical dilemma because of his English teacher, who turned against him when he refused to hand over his ruler. The teacher had broken her own ruler, and now wanted his ruler so she could continue whacking his best friend, Majid. She saw Aziz's refusal as a challenge to her authority and failed him in English.

I still had bad memories of my own youth and blamed my balding head on the nun who taught my first-grade class. She would lift up my hair and whack my head with a ruler. It was a technique that left no marks on our bodies but inflicted pain nonetheless. Apparently, Aziz had told his teacher in Arabic that no one could understand her English and that his father would come down and teach the class.

I met with her, witnessed her broken English, and told her that she was not to strike my son for any reason.

SMALL VICTORIES AND BLUNDERS

East Jerusalem is small enough to get around on foot most times. His school was not far away, so I taught Aziz how to walk from there to my office. I did not want him to get lost if he got separated from his mates on the schoolyard. On the way home from school, the boys would stop to have piping hot falafel stuffed into the traditional Jerusalem sesame-seed-covered bread. It was a childhood delight to walk with your friends down a street where everyone knew you, waved hello, asked after your father, and kept you in line. The falafel merchant would prove to be a great friend.

Amira had a school bus that picked her up and dropped her off every day. Like the school itself, Amira's school bus was reliable almost all of the time. We had arranged for a small van to pick up Aziz, too, along with other boys in the neighborhood, and deliver them all to their homes. Aziz's van was also reliable. Aziz himself, on the other hand, had too many friends to distract him from getting on the van that was supposed to take him home.

His math teacher lived next to my office, though, so Aziz sometimes walked over to the office with her. After having a snack one day, he announced that he was going to spend time with his friend Mary in the garden. Curious about Mary, I spied on him as he played in the garden and sat quietly in an olive tree. Mary, it turns out, was the olive tree. The two of them—a young boy and a centuries-old olive tree—had a great friendship only they could understand. I made a mental note to make sure that Aziz had plenty of time exploring nature.

Both schools required uniforms, but only Amira's school was strict about the dress code. Amira wore a pale blue get-up that looked like a cross between an apron and a miniskirt. Every morning, the nuns would inspect the cleanliness of the pupils' nails and the kempt appearance of their hair. The curriculum focused on reading, writing, and arithmetic, and in no way included sex education—although Amira did inadvertently give an anatomy lesson to the girls of the Rosary Sisters.

The bus came early that fateful morning. In a groggy fog, Nadia hurriedly dressed Amira in her uniform and pulled pink tights over her legs instead of the regulation blue tights before putting her on the bus. When the girls presented themselves for inspection, Amira was cited for noncompliance and forced to remove the pink tights and go about her school day bare-legged.

Unfazed, Amira joined the girls at recess, climbed the monkey bars, and began her usual routine of hanging upside down. But Nadia had not only put the wrong color tights on Amira, but also failed to put any underwear on her. All was exposed. With the full moon rising, the nuns promptly restored the pink tights to complete the school day.

Aziz's school was not strict about the dress code. It was hard for the boys to look neat and tidy when brawling. And although recess is normally a time for play and an escape from schoolwork, Aziz spent his recess organizing the fights that took place every day after school. When he first told me how much he was looking forward to the fights, I thought he meant the usual roughhousing in which boys regularly engage. It turned out he meant actual fistfights.

There didn't seem to be any organized recreation, so the boys, in an entrepreneurial spirit, had come up with their favorite game: king of the schoolyard. Aziz, now six years old, had worked his way up the ranks and was fighting boys in the seventh grade. None of the teachers thought to intervene, and the boys—both winners and losers—seemed to remain schoolyard friends as they left the battlefield together. I like to think that Aziz shared his victories with Mary in the garden, and she told him of her own experiences living through the ages.

THE WESTERN WALL

In Jerusalem, history slapped you in the face every day. Like most parents, I asked at the dinner table what the children had done that day at school. One day Aziz said, "We went to some old building, and the teacher was talking about something." Asked to divulge more about the old building, he said it was a strange place with "some dead guy hanging on the wall."

I decided it was best to take him back to the Church of the Holy Sepulchre for an educational tour. Aziz's only comment: "So that's what the teacher was talking about."

Not all my attempts to use the city for a history lesson worked out so well. When Aziz came home in a heated mood one day and asked me pointedly why the Jews wanted to take our land, it was clear that some of the teachers were feeding him a level of animosity that can only be actively inflicted.

"No one is trying to take 'our' land," I said patiently. "Battles over lands such as this have been going on for centuries." I also explained that many of our Palestinian friends had gotten along quite well with their Jewish neighbors before 1948, but the wars had made enemies of friends.

It was exhausting to live in a place where history was so alive. I knew that no peace agreement, however historical, was going to change the minds of local teachers who influenced children on a daily basis, and perhaps just reflected the minds of the parents. I had arrived in Jerusalem in the hope that peace could be achieved through negotiations. I soon realized that change could only take place one person at a time.

I decided to take Aziz to the Western Wall (also known as the Wailing Wall) while explaining the origins of the Temple, the Dome of the Rock, and the attachments that people in Jerusalem—indeed, around the world—had to these places. Before we reached the Wall, we were stopped by an Israeli soldier who asked for our destination and identification.

I carried with me my Virginia driver's license. Despite the neighbors calling the police on us, we still owned the townhouse in Springfield, and that address appeared on the license. The soldier took a look at it and told us to wait while he made a call on his mobile phone. Whilst I could not understand everything he said, I understood two phrases: "Azzedine Qassam" and "Springfield, Virginia."

Azzedine Qassam was the leader of the military wing of Hamas and was said to have some connection to someone in Springfield, Virginia. The combination of Azzedine and Springfield was enough to deny us entrance to the plaza adjacent to the Western Wall, and the soldier told us to leave.

"See, Ebbi," Aziz said as he turned to me, "the Jews want our land."

History lessons were always political. What Aziz didn't know was that the plaza was the site of the Moroccan Quarter established by Saladin's son in the early twelfth century but razed after the Six-Day War in 1967. So, although he is not Palestinian, Aziz—son of the Moroccan Nadia—had a point.

Aziz and I did eventually get to visit the plaza together, along with his Irish grandfather. During his visit to Jerusalem, my father wanted to go to the Wailing Wall and say a prayer. He had written a prayer on a small piece of paper and looked forward to placing it in a crack in the stone wall. Such notes are collected twice a year by a rabbi and buried in the Jewish cemetery on the Mount of Olives. Jews who pray at the wall can be seen rocking back and forth, their souls ignited like the flame of a candle flickering back and forth.

After we had lived there for a while, Aziz enjoyed giving his own Jerusalem etiquette lessons to anyone who would listen. So when my father approached the wall and stood silently praying, Aziz had advice for him.

"Grandpa, that's not how you do it," he said. "You have to dance." Imitating the motion of several Jews praying nearby, Aziz rocked wildly, screaming, "Like this, Grandpa, like this!"

Prayers of any type were forgotten as I scooped him up and made haste out of the plaza. Ah, the innocence of children.

THE TODDLER TERRORIST

Charif was a toddler with a cherubic face. As a two-year-old he had no political leanings but presented a threat just the same.

To experience all of Jerusalem, we would sometimes go to West Jerusalem to shop and eat out in the open cafés. At the entrance to every shopping mall sat armed guards who frisked you and checked any bag you might be carrying. In theory, all shoppers were stopped and searched. But in reality, Israeli settlers from the West Bank walked past the soldiers unimpeded; the automatic rifles stayed slung over soldiers.

On one visit, our cherubic toddler toddled past the guards along with a group of the settlers without being frisked, and the security guards shouted for us to stop the child! The settlers continued into the mall. Charif, along with Nadia, Aziz, Amira, and I, were barred entry to the mall on security grounds.

We argued for a while but made no progress. We had violated the security protocols and were now refused entry. It didn't matter that the only person in our group to commit the offense was a small child.

We returned to East Jerusalem and got *bouza*, the ice cream the kids loved, and I did my best to paper over the experience. Children are no fools, though, and the lesson was clear: we were not welcome there. I felt a smoldering anger at the injustice. Children describe the feeling best when they shout at their parents, "That's not fair!"

Injustice, and the feelings it evokes, is used to invoke passion. Passion is met with violence. The cycle of violence has no root in logic or politics, but its provocation is often strategic and deliberate. A perceived threat to our children causes otherwise tranquil parents to abandon reason.

Just as raw emotion drives violence, fatigue weakens any attempt to temper that violence. It is insidious in its path to martyrdom.

HOLIDAY IN JORDAN

Nadia and I decided that we needed a break from everyday life in Jeru salem. The Dead Sea has resorts in both Israel and Jordan, so we headed to an area in Jordan where I thought things would not be so tense. I was partially right.

There were moments of wonder, amusement, and recreation. Along the road from Jerusalem to the Dead Sea was a rest stop with a stone marking sea level. It was an odd sensation to think that the road curving ever downward was below sea level whilst still high in the mountains. Covering ourselves in the famed Dead Sea mud was great fun and a form of much-needed relaxation.

We also loved hiking in the mountains. I didn't give the children a history lesson on all the sites—Sodom and Gomorrah were a prime example—but we did hike all the way to the top of Masada. The tour guide, seeing little Aziz make the climb, said he was the youngest to ever hike up to the natural fortress. The significance of the massacre at Masada in the year 73 escaped Aziz, but he remembers that he made the climb whilst others took the gondola up.

Crossing over into Jordan was easy. The Allenby Bridge, near the famed city of Jericho, was the entry point. From the West Bank, we crossed the River Jordan and entered a land far less tense than the one we had left behind. It was a sense of relief not to see soldiers manning checkpoints. In Amman, it was a delight to go from hotels to restaurants without fear of being stopped and asked for identification.

Returning to Jerusalem was not so easy. We arrived at the border of Jordan and the West Bank and presented our passports to the Israeli border guard. As the queue behind us grew longer, nerves began to fray because of the wait. It didn't take long for the short respite from violence and tension to wear off.

No one likes to wait in line. Expressing frustration at waiting is not typically a political statement, but in this case, suspicions arose. *Why is the line so long? Who is causing a problem? Why are the border guards being so difficult? Has there been another bombing?*

We had been waiting for three hours when we reached the passport control counter. The border guard took our passports and didn't say much at first, but then he began asking questions. He stamped mine, Aziz's, and Amira's passports, but then turned his attention to Nadia and Charif.

We all travelled on US passports, which indicate the place you were born. I was glad of my decision to send Nadia back to the United States to have the babies. Years ago in Yemen, it was this moment I had imagined would be a problem. With the exception of Nadia, we all had been born in the United States.

The problem the soldier had with Nadia was that he did not believe she was Moroccan. Her US passport clearly stated that she had been born in Tangiers, Morocco. (She was, after all, the girl from Tangiers!)

It wasn't clear why he had a problem with Charif, beyond just wanting to be difficult, but he demanded to check the baby's passport multiple times. After the third time, he asked me to lift Charif up to the window, and I began to push back. "Charif is a baby," I said. "He hasn't changed since the last two times you asked me to lift him up so you could look into his eyes. Let's move on."

The Palestinian mothers standing behind me began quietly telling me to do whatever I was told and not to make any trouble. But all our documents were in order, so I asked why we were being detained. I also pointed to the front page in the passport, which reads: "The Secretary of State of the United States of America hereby requests all whom it may concern to permit the citizen/national of the United States named herein to pass without delay or hindrance and in case of need to give all lawful aid and protection." Charif and Nadia were American citizens, and I didn't see why we were being delayed and hindered.

The border guard told us to follow him, which we did, until he stopped in front of a heavy metal door, saying, "I am taking Nadia inside for further interrogation." He began to close the door behind him as he pushed Nadia forward into the room.

I stuck my foot in the door and said that I would accompany my wife.

He objected at first, saying he was the one who would decide who entered the interrogation room, but then relented.

Next, I insisted that our three young children would also accompany Nadia.

The border guard was taken aback by being challenged, but he really had no reason to detain us, so he disappeared into the darkened room beyond the metal door. Nadia and I waited silently whilst the children wailed. He returned with an Israeli from a Moroccan family and said that he wanted Nadia to speak with his colleague in Moroccan Arabic.

The Moroccan soldier got just one word out of his mouth before Nadia launched into a fiery history lesson of how all Moroccan Jews loved King Hassan, the only Arab who treated his Jewish subjects with respect. She went on to say his mother would be embarrassed by his behavior. "Is this how you repay the kindness of your king?" she screamed.

The hapless Moroccan soldier ran back into the room shouting, "By God, she is Moroccan! Let them go!"

THE MOST DANGEROUS PEOPLE IN THE WORLD

As violence increased in Jerusalem, it became more and more difficult to carry on with ordinary, day-to-day life. Even going to Friday prayers at the Al-Aqsa Mosque, the third-holiest site in Islam that sits on the

Temple Mount, required passing through a series of security checkpoints. At one point, all men under the age of fifty were turned away and denied the right to pray at the mosque.

The very presence of military checkpoints at the mosque caused drama. It made one feel that there was little real security reason to assume that all men under fifty years of age were potential terrorists.

Even driving was political. Residents of Jerusalem had yellow license plates on their cars whilst residents of the West Bank and Gaza had blue license plates. An extreme Israeli Knesset member proposed requiring Israeli citizens of Palestinian heritage to attach blue plates to their cars instead of yellow. He did not see the parallel to Jews being required to wear yellow stars on their clothing, but most everyone else in Israel— including Israeli Jews supporting the peace movement—did, and the proposal was shot down.

The Palestinian National Authority, the newly formed government outlined in the Oslo Accords, was based in Gaza, where I travelled often as part of my work to strengthen transparency, governance, and effectiveness of the various ministries. Moving in and out of Gaza had always been difficult, but every time there was an attack by Hamas against Israel, the lockdowns became more intense. Agricultural products on which entrepreneurs relied in their hopes of building a Palestinian state, like oranges and carnations, rotted in the trucks delayed at the border. Food supplies in Gaza became increasingly scarce, and United Nations agencies began to warn of malnutrition among children.

Our office director in Gaza, who had five children, asked me to bring frozen chickens to him the next time I came to Gaza. I agreed and soon became known as the Chicken Smuggler of Gaza. I am not sure why people felt the need to give me and my little family strange monikers like the Butcher of Harvard and the Diplomatic Potato Family of Bulgaria, but I gladly accepted this new one: the operation fed a hungry family in Gaza.

After a number of successful smuggling trips, I was apprehended with the contraband chickens. The Israeli soldier at the border found the five frozen chickens in my suitcase and said that the colonel wanted to speak with me. I was brought to a small room at the border checkpoint and met with the colonel, who began our conversation by asking my name. Looking at my passport, he acknowledged that Azzedine was clearly an Arabic name but did not know where the name Downes came from.

I explained that I was Irish and that Downes is our family name. He looked down at the five frozen chickens and said: "Arab and Irish? You are a combination of the two most dangerous people in the world."

It was hard not to laugh at that—and we both did.

LIVING WITH VIOLENCE

Scraping away all the politics and violence, most people around the world want the same things. Paramount among them is to feel safe and to provide safety for their children. How people suffering from violence achieve their dream of security differs widely, but I always try to keep in mind that no matter what uniform you're wearing, there is a level of fear that your life could end at any moment.

After living in Jerusalem for over a year, I still could not adjust to the daily threat of violence. Driving from Ramallah to Jerusalem after visiting family friends, we stopped at the checkpoint on the outskirts of Jerusalem. Young soldiers asked for our papers and began looking into the car at the passengers: Nadia, Aziz, and Amira, with Charif strapped in a car seat. The young, nervous soldier asked for the children's papers. I responded that as they were only young children, we didn't carry their passports with us. When the soldier opened the back door and pointed his gun at little Charif, I was out of the car in a second. Rage propelled me, and I pushed the soldier away from the car. There was neither calculation on my part nor consideration of the consequences.

As the soldier trained his gun on me, his comrades calmed him and allowed us to go on our way, but the damage was done. Witnessing the act of threatening a baby made me understand the senselessness of violence. Victims of terror either bend and submit or refuse to be bowed and rise up when the opportunity arises. There was no courage in my reaction, only instinct—and that moment could have led to my own death and even more ensuing violence.

Fear makes for bad decision-making. Violence is not always calculated; it bubbles up slowly over time. Irrational moments can strike unexpectedly, triggering explosive reactions. I came to Jerusalem with expectations of nurturing the seeds of peace, but I learned that living with constant violence wears the spirit down.

BRIDGE OVER TROUBLED SAND

The Palestinian National Authority is the government entity that was formed to oversee the West Bank and Gaza. Between the West Bank and Gaza sat Israel. How to physically connect the two geographical areas, and govern them as one future Palestinian state, was a constant topic of conversation.

There were all sorts of proposals. None of them ever came to fruition, but they included creative solutions—like building a bridge over land so that Palestinians could drive from Gaza to the West Bank without ever being able to enter Israel unless they jumped off the bridge.

My work focused on building planning capacity in the Palestinian Ministry of Finance, the Ministry of Justice, the Ministry of Planning, and the Civil Service Administration. The US government funded the work as part of the Oslo Accords, despite the political divisions in the US Congress over any type of foreign aid. Because foreign aid in the Middle East had many more complications than in other parts of the world, I was always walking a tightrope to keep all the warring factions from scuttling the work. In hopes of presenting a balanced evaluation of the project, my organization's headquarters asked me to appear before a congressional committee in Washington to update them on progress.

During what I thought was a straightforward briefing on Capitol Hill, I got a taste of what was to come when congressional aides began attacking me. It was clear that there were congressional offices in favor of the Oslo

Accords and those that opposed them. There were pro-Palestinian and pro-Israeli factions, both of whom used the presentation as an opportunity to promote their own political agenda.

The project I managed was funded by the US Agency for International Development (USAID). In my presentation to Congress, I did my best to present a balanced picture of progress and challenges. That balanced approach made me an enemy in the eyes of those who opposed any funding of the Palestinian Authority, and accusations of lobbying for the Palestinian Liberation Organization began spilling from the lips of the most vitriolic of bureaucrats.

I received a very mixed message: stop the project, but also get a higher profile for the work. Officials from USAID in Jerusalem complained that the US government was not getting enough credit for the work. I left Washington and returned to Jerusalem feeling beat up, but still focused on the task of promoting USAID and the project.

KOSHER CARROTS AND FOOD POISONING

The flight back to Jerusalem was raucous. We had been delayed for hours on the tarmac, making the very long ten-hour flight ahead even longer. It made things worse when the flight crew did not seem aware of, or supportive of, the cultural and dietary requirements of many of its passengers.

The first argument broke out as we were taking off, when a group of Israeli men wanted to pray, an activity which required them to stand up. The flight attendant came running down the aisle screaming for them to sit down, which they refused to do. It was too late for the pilot to abort takeoff, so into the air we went with a mini melee underway.

Once the prayers were finished, the carts carrying food began rolling down the aisles to first serve the kosher meals. Sitting in the rows behind me, where the prayers had taken place, were two very large Orthodox families who apparently were very hungry. But the man directly behind me refused his kosher meal, saying that he had ordered a kosher vegetarian meal instead.

The flight attendant told him there was no such thing as a kosher vegetarian meal and that what he was given was all he was getting. He informed her that he was a rabbi and that there certainly was such a thing as a kosher vegetarian meal, and he had ordered one.

Without hesitating, she replied, "Oh really, Rabbi? What do they do, slit the throat of a carrot?"

The argument over standing during prayers at takeoff looked like a lovefest in comparison to what unfolded next. The flight attendant ran for her life, and the pilot removed her from our section and put her in first class for the rest of the flight—which perhaps was her strategy all along.

Arriving back in Tel Aviv, I went through the usual questioning at the immigration desk, but it seemed that I had been put on the list for secondary questioning. Over the years, I learned to answer questions with short replies, not offering anything more or anything less. It was not my job to explain anything; it was simply my job to answer only what I had been asked.

I had learned the hard way that offering up explanations only led to more and more questions. Some of the questions were designed to make you angry: *Why did you marry an Arab? Why would you have children with an Arab woman? Did you get her pregnant, so you were forced to marry her?* Answering these types of questions was akin to having food poisoning: there wasn't much you could do except wait for the pain to pass.

From border guards to politicians to people on the streets, everyone assumed everyone else had a hidden agenda when it came to this part of the world. It made working in the region more difficult than it ought to have been.

The one thing that almost no one ever assumed was that a person was exactly who they said they were. Israelis assumed you were a Palestinian sympathizer, Palestinians assumed you were pro-Israeli, and Americans assumed it was unclear whether your sympathies lay with the embassy in Tel Aviv, the consulate in West Jerusalem, or the consulate in East Jerusalem. Congressional delegations were increasingly arriving on fact-finding missions, so more of my time was spent navigating the American politics of the Middle East.

I also had to tread carefully to protect my family.

WHAT'S A KIDNAPPING BETWEEN FRIENDS?

Early in 1997, the relative calm surrounding our home was broken. We lived in the section of the city called Sharafat, high on a hill and close to the checkpoint separating East Jerusalem from the West Bank. Our house was owned by a Palestinian family with whom we shared a wall separating our two gardens. Everyone else in the small neighborhood had known each other since birth, and we always felt safe.

That ended one day when Aziz came running into the house, saying that two men had tried to take him away in a car.

I ran out to the street and found his little friends standing with their parents. The neighbors helped to calm us down, but they were upset, and for good reason. It was about more than just our family's safety. The neighbors were also concerned about what we planned to do about the attempted kidnapping.

One mother sheepishly asked if we were going to the Israeli police to report the incident. I told them that my only immediate concern was to keep Aziz and the family safe. Making the wrong choice of how to provide security could put my family in more danger. I knew what happened to people accused of being collaborators with Israeli security forces. I also knew what could happen to our Palestinian neighbors, the parents of Aziz's schoolmates, if Israeli police discovered the two men had tried to kidnap Aziz and then targeted their relatives.

I decided to first go to the Orient House, the symbolic seat of the long-dreamed-of capital of a Palestinian state in East Jerusalem. I explained the situation and was asked to give the Palestinian authorities time to investigate. The situation in the neighborhood remained calm and there was a great deal of support for our family, particularly after I turned to Orient House for help and not to the Israeli police.

An undercover, and very unofficial, security detail patrolled the neighborhood, and the two culprits were found. They professed their innocence, saying that they had only wanted to give Aziz a ride. I was assured they would be dealt with, and I never asked any more questions.

YASSER ARAFAT, FROZEN BANANAS, AND THE ECSTASY OF BALDNESS

Shortly after the kidnapping incident, I received a message that President Arafat would like to meet with me to discuss the progress on reforming the Civil Service Administration, the office responsible for all government employees. In preparation for the meeting, I gathered the project staff in Gaza.

One consultant, an American named Joe, was a rather odd guy who seemed unaware of the constant danger he put himself in. At night, he would roam around areas of Gaza along the Israeli border and get lost. He spoke no Arabic and tried to speak Hebrew to young Palestinians who were most likely involved in attacks on Israel. He couldn't understand why what he was doing was dangerous. "After all," he would say, "a peace agreement had been signed."

Joe lived in a two-story villa owned by a Palestinian family who grew and sold bananas. The small, dotted bananas of Gaza were very sweet and were a sign of hope for the Palestinian economy. Mohammed, the owner of the villa, gave Joe a fresh bunch of bananas every morning. Joe told his landlord that he loved the bananas and ate the entire bunch every morning for breakfast. It seemed odd that anyone could eat that many bananas, but it wasn't until Mohammed saw a third freezer being delivered that he paid a visit to Joe's house.

When Joe answered the door, he told the landlord that he had guests and didn't want to disturb them.

Mohammed pointed out that no other people should be living with

Joe, but all the neighbors had seen people sitting by the windows every night. And then there was the issue of the bananas. No one could eat that many bananas every day, so clearly Joe had people living with him—and Mohammed wanted them out.

Mohammed pushed his way into the home, where he found blow-up dolls and cardboard cutouts of people scattered throughout the house. Opening one of the three large freezers in the middle of the living room, he found a hundred pounds of frozen bananas.

Joe had not wanted to tell Mohammed that he didn't like bananas at all and that he was accepting them to avoid insulting his landlord. He bought the blow-up dolls and placed them in visible spaces to give the impression that he had parties all the time, at which he served ... banana daiquiris, of course. He couldn't just throw the bananas away because Mohammed would have seen all the rotting bananas in the garbage bins. In the end, both the bananas and the blow-up dolls were thrown into the garbage, and Joe was forced to find a new place to live.

Joe had another strange habit: rubbing his bald head when he was lost in thought. He would sit quietly in our office meetings, eyes closed, not paying attention to anything being said, and slowly rub his head as if giving himself a massage. Then he would begin to moan, as if astroplaning to another dimension.

The moaning would grow so loud, it would disrupt our meetings. Once we stopped laughing, we had to bring Joe back from whatever state of euphoria he was experiencing. He seemed unaware that he was doing it, so it was awkward to address the issue directly with him. It was equally embarrassing to tell him that under no circumstances was he to start rubbing his head when we met with President Arafat.

The day of that meeting, we arrived at nine in the morning at Arafat's office in Gaza. At this point, Arafat was still able to move between Gaza and the West Bank, and he often chose to work in this office that sat on a beach overlooking the Mediterranean Sea. I was surprised by the informality of the presidential complex and the lack of security as we began walking across the soft sand parking lot adjacent to the president's office. As we got closer to the building, we were met with security guards who briefed us as we walked the final short distance to the front door.

Joe suddenly said he needed to go back to the car to get a newspaper. The security detail told him that if he left our group, he would not be allowed in to see the president. Joe laughed and said that he knew how meetings with government officials went—that we would be kept waiting for hours, so he had plenty of time. On the contrary, we were ushered into Arafat's office immediately upon arrival. The large doors were shut and locked. Joe was nowhere to be seen.

Arafat sat behind his desk and smiled as he welcomed us. He was a short man and looked bulky, but I realized the heft was the bulletproof vest that he wore under his jacket. He had a pistol in a holster on his hip and a bowl of candies on his desk. As we sat at a long table in front of his desk, he offered us one candy per person.

Arafat had spent many years in Tunis, and when he heard me speak, he started saying things in Tunisian dialect, which I didn't really understand. I explained that I was not Tunisian, but it didn't seem to make any difference. We each took another piece of candy.

Before the meeting went any further, there was a commotion in the reception hall outside of his office. The shouting became more frenetic, and Arafat's bodyguards drew their guns and stood in front of the office doors. Arafat asked me to hold the bowl of candy as he drew his pistol.

There was loud banging on the doors, and then we heard Joe shouting that he was supposed to be in the meeting. The doors opened and all guns were pointed at Joe.

"Don't kill him," I shouted. "He's with us!"

Joe stood there with the newspaper in his hand and—you guessed it!—began rubbing his head.

THE CURSE OF FATOUMA REARS ITS HEAD

There were quiet moments in Jerusalem when life seemed normal. At least, normal for us. Nadia was constantly on the lookout for signs that the curse of Fatouma was reasserting itself in attempts to disrupt our marriage. I had shared the story of Fatouma with Nadia, thinking she would find it funny. She did not.

Nadia was always a firm believer in the power of the evil eye and saw evidence of it everywhere. For her, the curse of Fatouma had no expiration date. Nadia believed that because I did not marry Fatouma, I would face constant threats to my marriage. In one woman named Helga, Nadia saw just such a threat.

Helga fancied herself a conservative Muslim woman who was eager to become a second wife. She covered her head in the Islamic fashion, but Nadia pointed out that whilst her head was covered, her behind was "swaying in the wind." It was impossible to counter Nadia's impression of Helga's swaying behind without actually commenting on Helga's behind. Like most unsuspecting husbands, I learned that wives set all sorts of traps. If I agreed with Nadia, it meant I was looking at Helga's behind; if I didn't agree, it meant I was defending Helga and was interested in a second wife. There was no winning this game.

Helga was also eager to serve as our family's tour guide around Jerusalem. One place she insisted on me seeing was the Dome of the Rock. I told her that I had already visited the site, making my way down the stairs to see the holy rock protected by plexiglass—a precaution so it was not worn down by pilgrims and tourists.

Helga asked if I was amazed that the rock was floating above the ground. When I told her that it was not floating, that it was firmly in the ground, she flew into a rage and said I could not be a true Muslim if I did not see the rock floating.

I invited Nadia to the office that day so she could see how angry Helga was with me, and that would end the debate over Helga's intentions of becoming my second wife. When Nadia arrived, she witnessed Helga's rage and I congratulated myself on the small victory. We sat in the garden having tea, and I thought all calm was restored.

But when Helga followed us into the garden and asked me to take off my sunglasses so she could see my beautiful blue eyes, Nadia exploded.

As Helga fled, it was clear that Fatouma and her curse were no match for Nadia.

CONFUSED . . . OR CONFUSING?

As Aziz and Amira spent more time at school, they spoke increasingly with the accents of little Palestinian children from Jerusalem. It was natural that they would sound like the other children as they learned new vocabulary, repeating words exactly as they heard them. As I spent more and more time speaking Arabic with my Palestinian colleagues, I learned new expressions, too, and repeated words just as I heard them.

As with politics, people wanted to place me in the appropriate box and assign my speech to a specific geographical place. The problem was, I spoke in what I described as a salad dialect: a mixture of all the expressions and accents of the places I had lived. I was always from somewhere else. It gave the more suspicious people I met the sense that I was hiding something.

When I travelled in Morocco, people thought I was from the Middle East. When I travelled in the Middle East, they thought I was from North Africa. Once, when I was giving a speech in Dubai, in the United Arab Emirates, I made a joke in Arabic that the mayor's Arabic was so much better than mine, I was going to finish the speech in English. Chatting with people afterward, two young men commented that they were amazed by how good my accent was. I thanked them, acknowledging that my Arabic is a mixture of many different places. They looked confused: they had meant to compliment me on how well I had learned English.

One colleague commented that I was a very confused person, with mixed-up language and mixed-up culture.

"I may be confusing, but I am not confused," I replied. I was simply childlike in my approach to language, repeating what I heard and making no attempt to synthesize dialects.

It wasn't just my Arabic that caused confusion. When learning Italian in my school days in Switzerland, I asked my professor how I was doing.

She said I was doing well but my Italian was heavily accented. I was surprised—normally my grammar is poor, but my accent is good.

"Oh no," she corrected me, "you speak Italian with a heavy *French* accent."

Going shopping in the marketplace of Tunis, in Tunisia, the tourist guides trying to lure me into their shops would call out (for some reason I still don't quite understand), "Hey, Saudi! Come in here and spend a lot of money!"

I found this ability to be a chameleon amusing most of the time, but it was less amusing when going through customs.

When I arrived in Syria, an immigration official asked for my passport. I presented an American passport, and he looked up and asked where I was from. I told him I was born in Boston, Massachusetts. He looked quizzical and asked where my father was from. I told him our family was Irish, but my father had been born in America. Then he asked where my grandfather had been born. I answered honestly that he had been born in Ireland.

The official grew angry and said that he knew I was originally Syrian. He wanted to know if it was my father or my grandfather who had Syrian nationality, and he wasn't letting me pass until I told him the truth.

I decided to give him what he wanted to hear. "You are right. My great-grandfather was Syrian."

He smiled and said, "I knew it." Then he gave my passport back, and off I went.

But when meeting one Syrian colleague for the first time, I said, "Hello," to which he replied, "My brother, you are from Lebanon?"

Exactly where I'm from was in question, and the whole world seemed to know it.

It wasn't just accents that people found confusing about me. At a diplomatic reception in Jerusalem, one fellow asked why I wasn't drinking alcohol. I told him I was Muslim and didn't drink.

"You don't look like a Muslim," he retorted. "You don't have that crazy look in your eye."

At social events, my not drinking alcohol could be a trigger for both Muslims and non-Muslims. I never made a point of announcing that I didn't drink alcohol; I simply didn't take part. Reactions were varied: sometimes angry, sometimes querulous.

There were entreaties from fellow Muslims that I found akin to whispers in my ear during Ramadan: "Just drink. Just eat. I won't tell, and no one will find out." People who persisted were convinced that I secretly wanted to do exactly what they were doing. I didn't.

Some Muslim colleagues who drank alcohol with me present would be embarrassed. Others would lash out, saying, "You think you are better than me?" But I wasn't making a statement about them—only doing what was right for me.

KIDNAPPED WHILST ASLEEP

As concerns grew that the Oslo Accords were not making progress, the number of US congressional delegations increased. Cracks in the Palestinian Authority appeared, as factions in Gaza and the West Bank struggled for power. I was meeting with members of one delegation one day when Nadia phoned to say that Amira had not arrived home from school.

Amira normally arrived home on the same school bus at the same time every day. That day, Nadia had waited at the bus stop outside our house, but Amira never got off the bus. The incident with Aziz was still fresh in our minds, and we feared Amira had been kidnapped.

Ambassador Robert Dillon, who was the current CEO of my nonprofit organization and who had previously served as US ambassador in Lebanon when the marine barracks was destroyed in a bomb blast, stayed with me the entire afternoon as we searched for Amira. I did my best to remain calm as we retraced Amira's steps back to the school. She had been at school all day and should have arrived home at the usual time.

Then we found Amira's school bus; nothing seemed out of the ordinary. The driver told us that the bus had stayed on its usual route and had not stopped anywhere new along the way.

I decided to drive the route in case Amira had gotten off at the wrong stop. Aziz had done that once before and wound up taking a ride around the entire city. His friends had waited patiently at the bus stop and brought him home whilst scolding him for being careless. Along the school bus route, however, we saw no sign of Amira.

I returned to the school and told the headmistress that it was time to contact the security forces at Orient House, as I had done when Aziz had been threatened. But first I wanted to search the school bus for any clues to her disappearance.

In the last seat of the school bus, we found Amira fast asleep. She woke up and merrily said that she was hungry.

FACING THE FIRING SQUAD

Two days later I got a call from the US embassy in Tel Aviv. It was seven o'clock in the evening, and I didn't normally get calls from the embassy at night, so I thought it odd. The call was short: "Put on a suit, drive to Tel Aviv right now, and be prepared to be fired. I will try to peel the ambassador off the ceiling before you arrive."

I wasn't given any more information and had no inkling what had happened. I was scheduled to be in Gaza the following day for the launch of the first joint conference, with Palestinians and Israelis attending, to promote a peaceful future of government cooperation. I had already packed a bag for the conference, so I took a quick shower, put on the suit, and drove to Tel Aviv, arriving around nine o'clock that night.

USAID had been complaining for months that as the funders of our work, they had not received enough public acknowledgement. They wanted the USAID logo prominently displayed on documents and public announcements of all the training programs, meetings, and conferences they had funded. The Palestinian Authority had resisted the publicity because they were walking a fine line between those who wanted to move forward in a Western form of democracy and the more hard-line elements who wanted an Islamic state. The U.S. was seen to be more pro-Israeli than pro-Palestinian, and the logo represented a perceived, uneven support.

Eventually, I convinced the Palestinian Authority that the logo should be included on the agenda of the upcoming conference. The theme of the conference was envisioning the future in 2030, and the sessions were designed to advance the Oslo Accords. It was to be the first conference where Palestinian and Israeli employees of various government agencies would work together. The mere fact that it was taking place at all was an achievement and a sign that the peace process might have a chance to survive.

Palestinian leaders from Gaza and the West Bank were on the agenda to give remarks at the official opening of the conference. After Nabil Shaath, minister of planning (who later became prime minister of the Palestinian Authority), and Hanan Ashrawi (longtime leader of the Palestinian movement) gave their remarks, President Arafat was to give the keynote speech. International press was covering the event, and there was a great deal of excitement among all those involved in the planning. I assumed that the US government would be thrilled by the fact that Israeli officials would attend, too.

I was wrong.

I sat alone in the lobby of the American embassy for a while, waiting for the director of USAID. The ambassador was too furious to meet. In fact, the director said, he had never seen the ambassador so angry.

"You, personally, will be responsible for the cessation of financial aid to the Palestinian people," he said. "The policy of the United States government is to recognize the state of Israel. There is no Palestinian country or Palestinian state. The Palestinian Authority administers the areas of Gaza and the West Bank, nothing more. You knew that Senator Jesse Helms was a firm supporter of Israel when you met with his staff recently. You were supposed to understand that nothing can jeopardize that support. You are responsible for destroying the Oslo Accords. Your career is over."

Considering all the violence I had witnessed over the years, the prospect of my career being over paled in comparison to my life being ended by a bomb. So I remained calm and asked, specifically, what the issue was that had the ambassador so angry.

The director pulled out a copy of the conference agenda and pointed to two things: the title of the conference and the USAID logo. In my ignorance, he insisted, I had recognized Palestine as a country by titling the conference "Palestine Vision 2030." And I had added insult to injury by affixing the USAID logo on the conference agenda.

After sitting quietly for a minute, I asked if he spoke Arabic.

He admitted he did not.

I agreed that, if true, it would be a huge diplomatic blunder. But then I pointed out that in Arabic, the title did not say "Palestine"; it said "Palestinian," which was in keeping with the Oslo Accords' use of the words "Palestinian Authority."

It was the director's turn to be silent. He picked up the phone and asked if any of his Israeli staff spoke Arabic. We sat, not speaking, waiting for the Arabic speaker to arrive. When he did, and the director asked him to read the title of the conference, he confirmed that it read "Palestinian" and not "Palestine."

The director phoned the ambassador and told him that the international crisis had been averted.

No apology was given.

AT LEAST ARAFAT THOUGHT IT WAS A GOOD IDEA

Despite that tempest in a teacup, the ambassador still wanted the USAID logo taken off the conference agenda. It was now going on ten thirty at night, and the conference was scheduled to start the next day. It made little sense to me that USAID had complained for months about the Palestinian Authority refusing to include the logo—and yet now that I had succeeded in convincing them, I had to somehow remove the logo from hundreds of documents in just a few hours.

I left Tel Aviv, drove to Gaza, and arrived at midnight. There was no time to reprint the agenda, which we planned to distribute in the morning. The only option we came up with was to black out hundreds of logos with magic markers.

After we woke up the only guy with the keys to the government office building, we started making calls to wake up as many ministry staff members as could, asking them to come to the ministry. By two o'clock in the morning, we had an army of people with black magic markers, busy at work masking the offending logo.

When the minister arrived at three in the morning, I explained the events of the evening before adding that it was unclear whether I would be around much longer, given the threat to fire me. My meeting in Tel Aviv had ended with the director informing me that the embassy was sending two Arabic-speaking Israelis to the conference to monitor everything being said in public, and then a decision about my career would be made.

In the morning, the conference hall was packed. I sat in the front row with two of the scheduled speakers, Nabil Shaath and Hanan Ashrawi, thinking about the long night and the days ahead. I gave my short remarks to the assembly, wishing everyone success in the meeting and hoping for peace in the future.

It was hard to concentrate. I had been up all night, and as the shock of the evening wore off, I was angry. I thought back on my time in Israel so far: all the competing agendas, the politics, the violence, the attempted kidnapping, the bus bombings, and the idiocy of bureaucracy.

Then I heard Yasser Arafat wrapping up his speech, saying that he wanted to recognize someone who had shown great courage in organizing this conference but may lose his job for showing that courage. He never mentioned my name but I felt vindicated enough to stay for the rest of the conference.

The two Israelis from the embassy reported to the ambassador that the conference speakers never mentioned any formation of Palestine and that the working sessions were a great example of Israelis and Palestinians working together.

The ambassador was furious that we had removed the USAID logo.

LEAVING JERUSALEM

The Temple Mount, the site of the holiest of holies and the Dome of the Rock, is where humans will meet on Judgment Day, according to Islamic belief. There is great emotion surrounding anything and everything associated with this place. When going to Friday prayers at the Al-Aqsa Mosque, I had always hoped that the sanctity of the Temple Mount would overcome any sectarian divisions, but I never found that to be true.

Whenever Israeli security forces suspected that violence was brewing, they would institute restrictions on who could enter the Al-Aqsa Mosque. Sometimes the restrictions were based on your age, like when they assumed that Friday prayers were a potential source of violence and continued to prevent anyone under the age of fifty from attending, even if there was no violence in the air. But this was always subjective. I know this because sometimes I looked old enough to be granted entry and other times was told that no one under the age of fifty could enter.

When I was allowed to attend Friday prayers, I once made the mistake of sitting in an area of the Temple Mount that, unofficially, was reserved for certain Muslims who believed they were the only true Muslims. They somehow missed the memo where it was pointed out that all Muslims were brothers, so I was kicked out of the small space outlined in rocks, which were later used as projectiles to pelt people praying at the Wailing Wall below.

For many, getting used to violence means you've simply become numb to it. For some, the violence awakens them from the numbness of everyday life. For others, the numbness allows them to remain calm in the face of violence. I fall into the latter category. It wasn't that I no longer cared; it just took more and more energy to trigger a fight-or-flight response.

In the year 1996, the Israeli government opened the entrance to a tunnel in the Old City's Muslim Quarter, and a massive riot ensued. Fifty-four Palestinians and fourteen Israelis were killed in the mayhem. Outside my office, Israeli security forces on horseback were pushing people back toward the center of the city.

Nadia, holding Charif in her arms, phoned me to say she was hiding in the small pharmacy around the corner from my office. Amira's school phoned to say the school was locked down and they would not send the girls home until parents came to collect their daughters. We had not heard from Aziz's school.

There is no rational thought in a mob. The mob is a pulsating organism of humanity seeking the path of least resistance. Navigating through it with purpose signals you out to security forces, so I was stopped on my way to find Nadia and Charif. As a policeman on horseback used his mount to push me back, I shouted over the firing of teargas that I needed to find my wife and young son, who were right around the corner. As he pushed the horse into me, I ran.

A policeman on foot grabbed me and told me to go home. At this point there was no possibility of persuading him, so I broke away and continued to run toward the pharmacy.

In front of the pharmacy door sat an overturned car ablaze. I ran between the flames and the storefront and banged on the glass door. I could see Nadia and Charif inside. They ran to me, and the shopkeeper opened the door for them, and we ran toward Aziz's school.

But before we got there, walking happily through the crowd came Aziz, smiling, with not a care in the world. The school had dismissed the boys, telling them the Jews were trying to take their land and they needed to join the resistance.

We left Jerusalem and returned to Morocco.

Going Home to Morocco and America

YOUR CHILDREN ARE FOREIGNERS

Upon our return to Morocco, we decided to register Aziz and Amira in the Rabat American School in the hopes that the children would be better looked after as they learned. Although Aziz had not been frightened by walking through the riot in Jerusalem, any more than when he had nearly drowned in the Black Sea, it had left me scarred. He had an amazing quality of facing danger but seeing only adventure.

"Ebbi, why are you upset?" he asked. "I know the way to your office. You showed me." But the lack of school security in Jerusalem stayed fresh in my mind. Releasing him in the middle of a riot seemed unforgivable.

When we got home that day, our Palestinian neighbors asked if we were going to donate blood at the hospital, but no one ever asked about the children or shared our horror that the boys had been sent out into the riot.

As part of the registration process at the Rabat American School, Aziz and Amira took a placement test. The headmaster of the school asked that we go over the results of the test in person, because he had a number of concerns. His major concern was that Aziz was not a native English speaker. My reaction was a mix of amusement and embarrassment, and I questioned whether that was actually the case. I explained that both children had studied at local schools in Jerusalem and that the language of instruction was Arabic.

It was true that Nadia and I spoke Arabic to one another, and that Aziz had studied in Arabic, but it was also true that I spoke to Aziz in English, although I couldn't really estimate how often I did that. But the headmaster also pointed out that Aziz and Amira did not speak Moroccan Arabic, and that they might have trouble being understood by their Moroccan schoolmates. Amira also had a very confused English accent, he pointed out, but she did well on the placement test—which, to me, looked like no more than pictures of animals.

The two children were admitted to the school despite these linguistic challenges, but the problem of language was not the most significant challenge for Aziz. The first teacher-parent conference came two days after the start of school.

Aziz was beating up boys at recess.

When it came time for recess, he would walk up to the tallest kid he could find and land a few punches. He was utterly confused when a teacher broke up the fight and brought them to the headmaster's office. Asked why he hit another boy, he said with a smile, "It's recess time."

In Jerusalem, the only activity in the schoolyard was fighting, so Aziz thought that's what all kids did. The headmaster told him that he was in trouble and that his father was coming to the school for a meeting. Aziz burst out laughing, thinking it was a prank.

I had to explain to him that no one was allowed to fight. In Morocco, he would be taking swimming lessons and playing soccer instead. He said he would miss the challenge of pugilism, but he liked other sports so he would leave his fighting behind.

Meanwhile, Amira loved her new school, but a teacher-parent conference was also arranged for her, after only four days. Amira thought that kids sleeping at school was the greatest invention ever devised. When the teacher told the kids it was nap time, Amira settled in for a sound four-hour siesta. The teacher had a hard time waking her up, and when they did, she would sometimes cry, saying that she had forgotten her language.

"What is your language?" her teacher asked.

"Bulgarian," Amira told her, adding that she was very sad about forgetting her country, too.

At the parent-teacher conference we had to explain that Amira had lived there as a baby and did speak Bulgarian at the time. The teacher seemed suspicious, and she checked on the passport copies we had filed with Amira's application to the school. Eventually Amira reaffirmed her identity: she had left Bulgaria behind and was really a Jerusalem girl. I'm not sure the teacher was reassured by this.

Charif was too young for the Rabat American School but wanted to go to school nonetheless, so we enrolled him in a Moroccan preschool. He cut his own hair on the first day of school and wore a blue bucket hat for three months to cover the damage. He refused to spend any more time on homework than it took for him to arrive home on the school bus.

His preschool teacher declared that he would never amount to anything if he didn't get serious about studying. We weren't too worried. He was only four at the time.

THE SQUASH INCIDENT

King Hassan of Morocco fell ill in 1996, and there was a sense that his days were numbered. We lived in a neighborhood in Rabat that was exploding outward, with every empty space filled with new buildings and villas. Word on the street was that anyone working near the king was profiteering in his waning days. Government salaries were not generous, yet the number of villas being built by government functionaries belied the size of their paycheck.

Rabat had always been populated with people filled with a great sense of themselves, but the atmosphere in the city now reeked of the bonfire of the vanities. When the king was well, it was easy to know who was truly powerful and who was a sycophant. As the power structures began to crack, many pretenders emerged and made life miserable for people lower down on the power ladder.

Nadia's father still had many friends inside the palace from his days working for King Hassan's brother, so he kept up with the news. Like his brother Youssef before him, Nadia's youngest brother went to school with a young prince, who had developed a liking for Cherry Coke. That sweet drink was not available in Morocco, but I found it being sold at the commissary at the American embassy, so I would always pick up an extra case and send it to the young prince via Nadia's brother.

From time to time, a car from the palace would be parked outside our house, and it was whispered around the neighborhood that we had palace connections. Whilst it was true that we knew a guy who knew a guy, it was not something we ever profited from—that is, until the squash incident.

In our neighborhood, and across Rabat, everyone was measured by their social status, using a gauge that could be either obvious or obscure.

Your status could be measured by proximity to the king, but also by the amount of dust on your shoes. Did you know that Morocco arguably has the highest number of shoeshine boys per capita in the world?

As was our custom, Nadia prepared couscous every Friday. A short walk from our house were a greengrocer and a butcher, with all the ingredients Nadia needed for a massive couscous lunch. At first, Nadia made the mistake of walking to the shops. But walking instead of driving meant that she must be on the lowest level of the social totem pole and was thus deserving of the privilege of being treated with disdain at the market.

One of the more obvious signs of influence, if not true wealth, was the type of car in which you were ferried around by your driver—and another was how little you were forced to get out of it. It was not unusual to see someone drive their Mercedes as close as possible to the colorful piles of vegetables; to block every car in the parking lot, whether coming or going; to leave the car running and jump out, shouting their order to the greengrocer, who then filled the order while ignoring everyone waiting in the queue.

But Nadia and I were regulars at the market, so the butcher, the greengrocer, and the olive merchant knew us by name—even though, living so close, we often walked there. We always exchanged polite greetings, asked after one another's health, and shook our heads at the ignorance of the stuffed suits who disrupted the atmosphere of mutual respect in the marketplace.

One Friday morning, Nadia went to the market to buy what she needed. When she asked one of the boys for a kilo of orange squash, he told her there wasn't any available. The greengrocer's shop was a collage of colors, and nothing was prepackaged. Vegetables were carefully arranged in pyramids, one piece atop the other. Shoppers told the greengrocer the type of vegetable and the desired quantity, by weight. The orange squash was often a massive affair, three or four feet long, so the greengrocer would cut it with a knife worthy of a warrior.

But our friend the greengrocer was not there that morning, and the boy manning the shop told Nadia that she had come too late—most people had already bought their couscous squash, and he refused to cut open a massive, untouched squash for her. She left with the other vegetables and walked home.

When Nadia's sister arrived, she offered to head back to the greengrocer's shop together, and when they arrived, they found the large squash cut open wide, exposing Nadia's lack of social standing.

Our friend the greengrocer apologized for the boy's lack of respect for a regular customer and offered to cut as much squash as Nadia liked. Nadia's sister, however, was having none of it. She began screaming that Nadia should never have been treated with such disdain, and that the gaping hole in the squash was a glaring example of what was wrong with Morocco today. By the time I got home, news of the squash incident had spread throughout the city.

Even without the squash, the couscous was delicious. In any case, I was the only one who liked the squash anyway, so I thought surely the slight would soon fade. I was very wrong.

Nadia's sister phoned her youngest brother, who then asked his schoolmate—the prince—for assistance in rectifying the squash incident. The palace snapped into action, and a plan was devised to restore Nadia's reputation.

Meanwhile, Nadia's sister had returned to the greengrocer with the certainty of a fortune teller, predicting the wrath that was to rain down on the entire market. According to her, the situation had become so grave that it was no longer the slashing of the squash that was at issue, but an insult to the king that would result in the entire marketplace being razed to the ground. When a motorcade of Range Rovers with the royal number plates arrived, Nadia's sister was taken seriously at last.

The five Range Rovers had to do no more than take a one-minute detour from their scheduled route, stop at the greengrocer's shop, nod to Nadia's sister (who nodded back), and drive off in a roar. The message had been received. The palace was involved in the squash incident.

The following morning, the greengrocer arrived at our doorstep with the very wealthy owner of the entire market in tow, carrying a massive bouquet of the most beautiful lilies the flower market had to offer. He apologized profusely and asked me to intervene with the palace.

Unaware that the squash incident had taken on a life of its own, I assured the market owner that the palace had no intention of razing his buildings and that the lilies were more than enough as an apology. He went on to say that he had no idea who we were and how powerful our family was. And that's when I became angry.

The whole situation had seemed rather humorous, but now I saw it clearly: had Nadia arrived in a chauffeur-driven car, treated everyone with disdain, and jumped the queue, the squash would have been cut without hesitation.

"Do we not come to your shop every day, offer greetings of peace, ask after your health, wait our turn patiently, and offer thanks and peace as we leave you?" I said to the greengrocer. "Yet the people who treat you so badly are the ones treated with respect. Why?"

"Because we are afraid," the owner whispered.

The foundation of our relationships in the market was built on squash and respect from that day forward.

THE MISPLACED SALUTE

It wasn't only squash that built our reputation in the city of Rabat. A flat tire played an important role, too, in building respect among the police force.

I had bought a minivan from an American colleague who had brought it overseas in his household effects—a futuristic vehicle called the Pontiac Trans Sport, which resembled a spaceship, with an incredibly long nose and a massive windshield. It was the only one in the entire city, perhaps even the entire country. This car would have been recognizable even before the flat tire incident, but on that fateful day, we reached the greatest heights of palace influence yet.

As I struggled to change the tire that day, a traffic cop came over and offered to help. I thanked him but said it was no problem and he needn't bother. He insisted that he could do it much faster, and remembering how I had once hit myself in the face with a tire iron, that seemed a reasonable supposition.

I handed him the tire iron, and he fixed the tire quickly so I thanked him for the help. His blue uniform had faded to a hue of purple from years in the sun, and his shoes were worn thin. I gave him a tip of 100 dirhams, around ten dollars, and thanked him again. Ten dollars was not much for me, but the tip clearly made him happy because he gave me a crisp salute as we drove off.

As time went on, we saw that policeman quite often, as his post was directing traffic at the large intersection near Charif's school. He saluted every time we drove by, which was a bit embarrassing, but I always waved back and exchanged greetings if we were stopped at the red light. The intersection was along the route where a number of princes lived, so there was constant traffic to and from the palace through the neighborhood.

One morning, as I entered the intersection, my friend the policeman saw me and turned toward the van, clicked his heels, and snapped a salute. At that same moment, the prince entered the intersection going in the opposite direction. Normally, in the presence of a prince, a traffic cop would stop all traffic, stand at attention, and salute as the prince drove by.

The policeman did not see the prince, however, and remained at attention toward me, with a big smile on his face. As the prince and I passed one another, in slow motion, a look of surprised amusement crossed the prince's face, and a look of horror appeared on the face of the policeman.

The prince just raised his hand in a gesture that meant, *What the hell is happening?* and laughed. My friend the policeman crumpled, thinking of the consequences of not acknowledging the prince. I pulled over and assured him there was nothing to worry about. The prince apparently found the situation funny, and just to be sure—as a peace offering—I sent over another case of Cherry Coke.

All was forgiven. For the first time in many years, life was calm.

It was time for a change.

TRAVELLING THROUGH TIME

Living in Yemen, Bulgaria, and Jerusalem we had experienced great joy and incredible violence. Leaving Morocco and moving to the United States seemed as though it would begin a new, less intense period of our lives. The rhythm of everyday, predictable life was disrupted on September 11, 2001. The lens through which people saw the world, and our family, clouded. When the US government began putting in place security measures designed to thwart future acts of terror, the net of fear was thrown wide. The simplistic assumption was that all Muslims are terrorists until proven otherwise.

There was a proposal that electric meter readers working for the utility companies should spy on Muslim families and report any suspicious activity. My father thought it was a great idea and only fell silent when I asked him if he thought it was a good idea to have meter readers spy on *my* family. When a colleague expressed her desire to have all Muslims rounded up and deported, I asked her if she meant me, Nadia, Aziz, Amira, and Charif. The image of what a Muslim should look like was always a source of interesting conversations, but now the events of September 11 made it easier for people to say what they really thought.

At the gym one day, a man asked me if I had heard the news about the crazy Muslims. He went on to tell me that the Pakistanis "had the bomb" and, like all the crazy Muslims, were going to kill us if they could. He was easy enough to ignore. But there were other people, other times when I had to intervene to keep conversations from going way off track.

After we moved to the United States, Nadia was speaking more English, but her use of the language was not always accurate. One day, in a grocery store on Cape Cod, I heard her telling an astonished couple that she loved terrorists and that terrorists were very important to the local economy. As the couple ran off screaming, I shouted, "Tourists! She meant tourists!"

I was asked to give presentations to the local schools about Islam, in an effort to calm fears about the Muslims among us. I tried to make it fun by bringing Moroccan clothes to school and letting the kids dress up. It went well for a while, until too many parents complained that my presentations were indoctrinating young minds.

During that same month of September 2001, a local parade took place as it always had, and our family was asked to march in the parade to show what "normal" Muslims looked like. I was hesitant but eventually agreed.

The staging area for the parade was at the end of our street. One float had the theme of "God Loves America," and the young kids from Charif's class sat on it, waving American flags as they listened to the country song "Proud to Be an American." Just before the parade was to begin, the kids began complaining that they had to go to the bathroom. I offered to take the whole bunch of them up to our house so they could use the facilities before the long parade began.

When one little boy came through the front door, he looked up and stared at the Arabic calligraphy hanging on our walls. I instantly regretted bringing the kids inside.

"Your house is really weird," he said. "This is America."

"Well," I said, "America is made up of many different kinds of people—"

"I know," he interrupted, "but are you guys Puerto Rican?"

"Absolutely we are!" I replied. "Why don't you hit the bathroom so we can get going to the parade?"

We marched in the parade that day to the country music, and all was going well until the soundtrack changed to "Johnny Get Your Gun." As Nadia walked along, waving her little American flag, she said she was too scared to carry on, and we dropped out of the parade.

A SIMPLE TIME TRAVELLER

I began this part of my life journey in Morocco in the year 1402 and ended it centuries later in the year 2001. It was not hard to live that long, as you know by now. It was just two different calendars, two different worlds, coinciding in time.

Travelling back and forth through time was sometimes as easy as walking through the gates of the old cities of Fez, Sana'a, Jerusalem, or

Damascus. Time travel alternately changes you in subtle and dramatic ways, and those changes—also known as "growth"—can make it difficult for people you know and new people you meet to accurately place you in time and space. Floating between worlds appears to be an affront to those you have left frozen in another time and place. I have never understood why anyone would want to remain unchanged through time, and I resist their insistence that I remain tethered to the time and place where we first met.

The absurdity of many of the situations in which I have found myself on this journey has given me many hours of laughter. Other moments unlocked a profound sadness. And both of those are as it should be.

At a family gathering, I once found my Aunt Mary crying, and when I asked her why, she said, "I look at your children, whom I love so much, and I weep that they will burn in eternal hellfire." As my father was singing Irish songs in the background, it didn't seem an appropriate time for theological discussions, but her words never left me. It wasn't that I had any concerns about hellfire that distressed me; it was the fact that she believed my children would burn for all eternity. Despite her love for me and my children, she remained tethered to a belief she had learned as a child. Her experience of loving my Muslim children did not change her belief system. She remained exactly the person she had always been. Yet I was more curious than upset. I realized in that moment that our shared bond had not changed her vision of who I, and my children, *should* be.

Our lives are not linear; they are circular, but not repetitive. Connections to the past are often more than a coincidence. Nadia's sister married a boy from Saudi Arabia who was great friends with a student whom I had taught English in Switzerland in 1979. One new job brought me back to Yemen after many years, and Aziz, then grown and a university student, accompanied me to a meeting with the prime minister.

As the years went on, the confusion over who I was—that vague thought that perhaps I was a spy, an outsider, a time traveller—continued unabated. I almost always found it comical, like when I sat with the Yemeni prime minister, the sun shining through the windows and bouncing off my bald head so badly that the television cameras turned to focus on Aziz, a handsome young man with a full head of hair. It wasn't clear who Aziz was either, but the prime minister's staff, fearing a security breach, came up with the explanation that he was my personal bodyguard. Aziz appeared on the evening news. I did not.

During the televised meeting in which I did not appear, I presented the prime minister with a gift of a traditional Yemeni dagger. The handle was made of beautiful agate instead of rhino horn, the use of which was driving rhinos to extinction in the wild. The gift was meant to encourage a new fashion in daggers that did not involve killing endangered species. The gift was unexpected, so my action did not fit the mold of what was expected to happen at such a meeting. The prime minister was confused: Why was his non-Yemeni visitor presenting him with a Yemeni gift? Shouldn't *he* instead be presenting something to his guest?

A staff member was sent off quickly to find a Yemeni dagger so the prime minister could present me with a gift in return. I laughed at the juxtaposition, and I'm sure he did as well.

Alas, there was no secret hidden in the folds of my life. I was not a spy working for the CIA, or a Syrian refugee hiding my identity, or any of the other things people suspected. At some point, I realized that most people will simply believe what they want to believe, and there was no value in offering lengthy explanations.

Through the laughs, and sometimes the violence, the one constant in my life was change. If I was anything, I was a simple time traveller.

Acknowledgments

The idea of writing a book did not hit me like a bolt of lightning. It was only after years of friends, colleagues, and family saying, "you should write a book," that I decided to collect all the stories and notes I wrote over the years and review them to see if there was really a book in there or if people were simply being polite. During the covid pandemic I decided it was now or never, so I sat down and wrote *The Couscous Chronicles*.

I want to thank some of the people who encouraged or outright badgered me to write down the various stories that I've enjoyed telling over the years:

Jason Bell, the executive vice president at IFAW, The International Fund for Animal Welfare, and Kelvin Alie, senior vice president, strategy, delivery and field partnerships at Conservation International, are like brothers to me. Either they were faking all the laughs they had listening to my stories or they were genuine in their encouragement.

After encouraging me to write a book for years, Vivek Menon, founder and executive director of the Wildlife Trust of India, bluntly asked me why I hadn't done it. I didn't have a good answer, so I want to thank him for saying, "Good God, man, just sit down and bang it out." He also told me he had the best set of eyes to look at a first draft: his wife, Karthika V.K., publisher at Westland Books. Karthika gave me wonderful advice and very specific suggestions about how to weave the stories together. She told me that she did, in fact, laugh out loud, but she also pointed out that she knows me personally and could imagine the stories in my voice, whilst a new reader would only hear my voice through the written word. That advice was invaluable.

I want to thank my dear friend, Jane Goodall, for writing the fore-word and for giving me hope that the book could be published. Jane was very clear that she was not going to write the foreword until she read a near-final draft, so I kept her updated on my progress. When she said that she had truly enjoyed the book and was ready to write the foreword, I was greatly encouraged and humbled.

I want to thank Kris Pauls, my publisher at Disruption Books, for having faith in me and for publishing my first book.

Last, and most important, I want to thank my lovely wife Nadia, also known as the girl from Tangiers, my son Aziz, my daughter Amira, and my son Charif, all of whom appear in the book. Without them, I would not be the person I am today.

About the Author

Azzedine Downes is the President and CEO of the International Fund for Animal Welfare (IFAW). Before joining IFAW, he served as the Chief of Party for the U.S. Agency for International Development in Jerusalem and Morocco, as well as the Acting Regional Director for the U.S. Peace Corps in Eurasia and the Middle East. Fast Company has named Downes one of the 100 Most Creative People in Business. He is a member of the Global Tiger Forum Advisory Council and the Jane Goodall Legacy Foundation's Council of Hope, and currently sits on the U.S. Trade and Environmental Policy Advisory Committee. He lives in Providence, Rhode Island. *The Couscous Chronicles* is his first book.